domino
THE BOOK of DECORATING

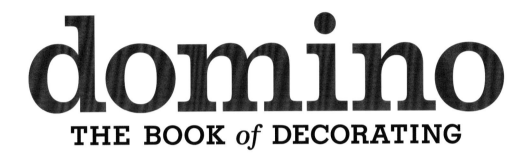

domino

THE BOOK *of* DECORATING

a room-by-room guide to creating a home that makes you happy

Deborah Needleman
Sara Ruffin Costello & Dara Caponigro

Produced by

 MELCHER MEDIA

Published by

SIMON & SCHUSTER

New York   London   Toronto   Sydney

Published by
Simon & Schuster, Inc.
1230 Avenue of the Americas New York, NY 10020

First Simon & Schuster hardcover edition October 2008

SIMON & SCHUSTER and colophon are registered
trademarks of Simon & Schuster, Inc.

For information regarding special discounts for bulk purchases, please contact Simon & Schuster Special Sales
at 1-800-456-6798 or business@simonandschuster.com

Produced by
MELCHER MEDIA, 124 West 13th Street, New York, NY 10011,
www.melcher.com

Printed in China
10

Library of Congress Cataloging-in-Publication Data
Needleman, Deborah.
Domino : the book of decorating : a room-by-room guide to creating a home that makes you happy /
Deborah Needleman, Sara Ruffin Costello, Dara Caponigro.
p. cm.
1. Interior decoration--Handbooks, manuals, etc. I. Ruffin Costello, Sara. II. Caponigro, Dara. III.
Domino (Condé Nast Publications) IV. Title. V. Title: Book of decorating.
NK2115.N34 2008
747—dc22   2008015072

ISBN—13: 978-1-4165-7546-7
ISBN—10: 1-4165-7546-4

Cover art: de Gournay wallpaper pattern "Portobello" on dyed silk.
www.degournay.com

for the lovely and talented staff of *domino*

table of contents

introduction

When we started *domino* in 2005, my fellow editors and I began with a straightforward and somewhat naïve goal: to demystify and democratize decorating.

In my fleeting attempts to decorate the places in which my family lived—a series of Manhattan apartments and a ramshackle weekend house in the Hudson Valley—I'd encountered the obstacles familiar to many of our readers. Simply choosing which sofa to buy was complicated enough, and getting wallpaper nearly impossible. I couldn't even gain entrance to the arcane temples known as design showrooms, which were open only "to the trade." The familiar shelter magazines, including the one where I'd worked for several years, were filled with "aspirational" homes: strikingly beautiful fantasies, with little relation to the way I lived or anything resembling a budget I could afford. I wanted my home to make me happy. But the route there seemed designed to frustrate me.

We were convinced that decorating didn't have to be a mystery, a burden or an additional source of anxiety in our busy lives. As I say, we were a bit naïve. We thought all we had to do was explain the decorating process, share secrets from the professionals we most admired and bust a few antiquated cartels. What we discovered along the way was that we had to do something more than gain direct access to the wallpaper supply. We had to create an alternative route for our readers, who faced the same decorating quandaries we did: How can you decorate without making unnecessary, costly and time-consuming mistakes? How can you produce a result that reflects who you are, how you live—and perhaps even the image you want to convey?

This book reflects everything my co-authors and I have learned about answering those questions. Connoisseurs say that looking, looking and more looking is the key to learning about anything visual, whether it's great rooms, gardens, art or architecture. But over the years, I've found that I can understand a subject more readily and appreciate it more deeply when I have some context—a base of knowledge—on which to ground my thoughts while I look. So that's how we organized the book.

We decode pictures of spaces we love in order to show how to "read" a room (*Great Rooms and Why They Work*). We break rooms down into their components to illustrate how they can be "layered" piece by piece (*Building a Room*) and also arm you with the need-to-know facts we wish someone had given us. We share the insights we've garnered from the homes we've been lucky enough to visit (*Ideas to Steal*). And finally we reveal the stories behind how our own rooms came into being (*The Domino Effect*)—because, of course, real life is messier and less linear than any manual.

Just three years after we started, decorating is a lot more democratic than it used to be. If you consult the back of this book, you'll find that "civilians" have more access to resources and insider tricks than ever before. I'd like to think that our magazine has played a role in that transformation. But more than that, I hope this book reflects the spirit that has guided us—the joy of finding your own style and creating a home that is about the way you choose to live.

Happy decorating!

Deborah

Deborah Needleman

getting started

1. find inspiration

CAST A WIDE NET in looking for ideas. Magazines and books—decorating and otherwise—are natural starting points, but movies, art, fashion, nature and travel are also rich resources. Don't think about it too much—just grab what you love: Tear out or copy pages, save images from the Internet, gather photos and postcards (being sure to mark the specific attributes you love for future reference). Be literal—collect paint chips from the hardware store—and be populist: A matchbook in the right color can be every bit as useful as a photo of Jackie O's boudoir. Don't be shy about including fantasies: You might not get to replicate that palace ballroom, but a picture of it could supply a solution or help shape your aesthetic.

START A FILE of these favorite things. Depending on how you like to organize, you can use a basket, an accordion folder, a bulletin board or a binder, or you can save in an online file (like "My Deco File" on dominomag .com). It can be as high- or low-tech as you like: The best system is the one you'll actually use.

LOOK FOR THEMES in the images you've compiled. After you've spent some time amassing, take stock. Have you picked several things that feature the same yellow? Lots of gilding? African-esque patterns? Are you drawn to rooms filled with stuff or ones that are more spartan? Get a little ruthless now with your images and ask yourself: "Do I really love this? Does this merit keeping?"

Facet
Classic

Facet

Classic

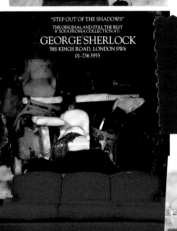

THE WELL-LIVED LIFE
YVES AND MICHELLE HALARD
CAPTURED ON FILM BY THEIR SON, FRANÇOIS HALARD,
TWO OF FRANCE'S GREAT DECORATORS ENJOY THE
RESULTS OF A LIFETIME OF COLLECTING IN THEIR
DISTINCTIVE HOUSE IN THE SOUTH OF FRANCE

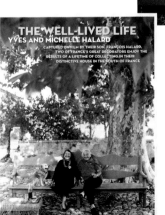

13

2. determine your style

Gather all the threads you've identified, and try to attach words to them. Don't worry about settling on one term; people tend to have a style that's mostly this with a little bit of that: kind of bohemian plus a dash of classic, mostly Dorothy Draper with a dollop of Sid Vicious. It might seem like a parlor game, but naming your style really helps you focus and filter out the things that don't fit and pinpoint those that do. It makes it easier to answer the question "Is this me?" as you flip through a catalog or face down a chair in a store. You see the trendy chair and think, "It's cute but I'm going to get tired of it because I'm more into tailored classics," and then you walk away—money saved and mistake averted.

bohemian *feminine*
elegant *vibrant*
masculine **clean**
tailored organic
classic **traditional**
modern
exuberant **bold**
unconventional
sentimental *witty*
comfortable **punk**
ladylike edgy cozy
zen romantic **noir**
dramatic pop

classic and neutral
but also a little bohemian

theatrical, unconventional
yet spare and modern

laid-back, glamorous and
traditional, but with a twist

15

3. consider how you'll use the room

THINK ABOUT YOUR LIFESTYLE and decorate accordingly. Being honest about how you live is essential to creating great spaces. Practical needs, not just style aspirations, should guide your plans. You may fantasize about a formal living room where you can hold fancy parties, but if a) you don't entertain all that much, and b) you end up with a setup that doesn't accommodate the things you or your family enjoy, like watching movies, then someone's going to be unhappy. Bear in mind that a room that looks like a showroom also feels like one, and nobody will want to set foot in it (and there's nothing sadder than an unused room).

OBSERVE WHAT DOESN'T WORK in your current scheme, and strategize about possible fixes. Do you never listen to music because your speakers are in the wrong room? Do you resent the too-small coffee table when guests come over? Addressing the failures and hassles allows you to create a room that benefits you, as opposed to one that dictates how you live.

How many people do you need to seat?
Will the room be for entertaining, for family or both?
Do you have children? Pets? Is it more of a daytime or nighttime space?
Will it function as a formal parlor or more like a den? Do you want to be able to put your feet up on the coffee table?
What activities will happen here? Work? Art projects? TV watching? Do you want to hide your TV?

4. assess your stuff

PHOTOGRAPH everything (yes, everything!) in your home—furniture, rugs, lamps, art—and lay out the images. Seeing each piece in isolation gives you distance and makes it easier to decide whether it passes your style filter. (Photos also make it simpler to envision new schemes because you can "move" things from room to room.)

SORT your pictures into four groups: keep, change (paint, reupholster), give away and sell. Take a good hard look at each item you've photographed and ask yourself, "Do I love this? Do I need this? Does it fit with what I'm trying to create? Is it my style?" Be tough in determining what works in your life. If you've hung onto Grandpa's desk for 10 years but could never stand the sight of it, you're not going to start loving it tomorrow. So let it go. Unless something is beyond repair, donate it or give it away on freecycle.org rather than putting it in the trash.

MEASURE all the things you're keeping so you'll know exactly what can work where when you're devising floor plans.

Empty cabinet; paint it red and move to the kitchen.

Love these—find a spot for them!

Reupholster with brighter fabric.

Time to bite the bullet and buy a flat-screen.

Coffee table too big for sofa—find replacement.

Donate!

5. draw up a floor plan

LOOK AT THE BONES OF THE ROOM and decide what to highlight (e.g., a fireplace) and what to hide (radiators). Also, think about how the room will appear when you walk in. For example, some people don't like seeing the back of a sofa.

SELECT TOOLS to simplify the job. You can use graph paper and pencils, make life-size paper templates of furniture to move around in the actual space or find tools online (icovia.com has a handy drag-and-drop program). Whichever method you choose, bear in mind that all guides are rough and that furniture in two dimensions always feels smaller than it looks in three.

MAP OUT OPTIONS rather than trying to find one perfect solution. Every plan involves compromise, but if you spend some time considering a few arrangements, you'll find one that's best for you. Remember the importance of function and that composition and style go hand in hand. If your look is formal, you'll be happier with a traditional sofa plus a pair of armchairs rather than a more offbeat layout.

one room, three ways

fireplace as focal point

Comfortable and built to foster conversation, this closed, symmetrical layout has a more buttoned-up feel, though it's made up of modern pieces. A so-so view of the TV makes it clear this is definitely a living room, not a den.

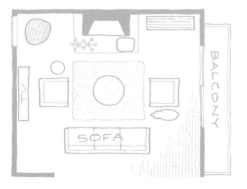

all eyes on the TV

With the sofa positioned to face the screen and big pillows scattered on the floor, this casual layout is good for movie nights (or marathon TV sessions) and is especially cozy for children (or adults who don't mind sprawling on the floor).

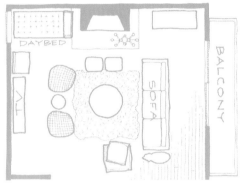

ideal for entertaining

Turning the sofa to face the view and positioning a low daybed opposite keep the sight lines to the window clear and set the stage for mingling: Traffic easily flows to and from the balcony; the daybed makes a perfect group perch.

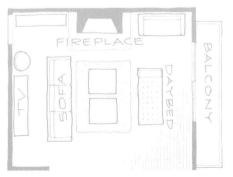

6. set a budget

FIGURE OUT WHAT YOU HAVE TO SPEND and be realistic about how much things cost. Many people will drop $300 on a pair of shoes but balk at the same price for a side table guaranteed to last much longer. If you're renovating, remember that it almost always costs more than you think it will and can easily consume your entire renovating and decorating budget. It pays to be conservative and factor in a buffer, so you'll have enough money left for decorating afterward.

CHOOSE AN APPROACH that meshes with your personality. Impatient types might want to do the entire space at once, even if that means using less expensive pieces. More tortoise-like characters are happy collecting slowly over time. And some people like to splurge on one major element that eats most of their funds, leaving them to just keep what they have or go totally cheap on new additions.

MAKE A SHOPPING LIST that allocates the money you've got among the stuff you need. Use this list to track what you should spend versus what you actually do spend, so you can stay on budget.

LIVING ROOM BUDGET

	ESTIMATED	ACTUAL
sofa	1,500	
side chair	600	
console	400	
coffee table	700	
curtain fabric	1,500	
rug	400	
pair of lamps	700	
floor lamp	500	
TOTAL BUDGET	6,500	

do the whole space at once

If you're up for devising a master plan and carrying it out, figure out the cost of the big-ticket item (for instance, the draperies here) and then divide the rest of your budget among what's left to buy.

collect slowly over time

Locating the pieces of your dreams can take a while, but sometimes doing without for a stretch is preferable to settling for second best. If you spent a mint on dining chairs, it's okay to eat in the kitchen until you can afford that just-right table.

splurge on one major piece

A single showstopper, like this statement-making wallpaper, can completely transform a room.

7. research, research, research

Once you have an idea of what you are looking for, investigate what's out there in your price range. It pays to educate yourself and shop around. Pound the pavement, check out design blogs and post questions on their forums, talk to friends about their favorite sources and buy a bunch of magazines to familiarize yourself with resources. Begin to gather your finds—paint and fabric swatches, catalog clippings, printouts of online items—in a file or box.

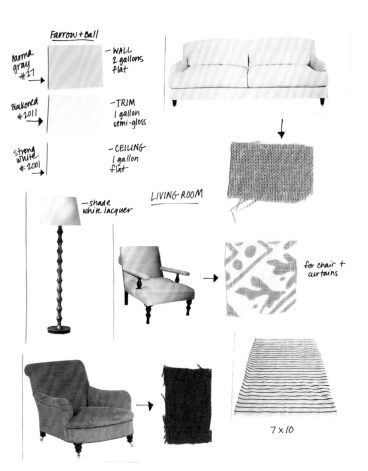

Farrow + Ball

parma gray #27 — WALL 2 gallons flat

Blackened #2011 — TRIM 1 gallon semi-gloss

strong white #2001 — CEILING 1 gallon flat

— shade white lacquer

LIVING ROOM

for chair + curtains

7 x 10

8. create a design scheme

This transitional step between planning and doing is all about narrowing down your options and seeing how everything looks together. It's hard—both to make decisions and to factor in practical considerations—but like doing a puzzle, it's also fun and creative.

CONSOLIDATE the information you've amassed. Pull together your floor plan, your list of things you need, pieces you're keeping and/or changing, images of favorite items, fabrics and paints, and the size of your budget. Factor in limitations (e.g., this rug is available only in these three colors).

SEE HOW YOUR CHOICES STACK UP TOGETHER. If you're set on a neutral sofa, those beige paint chips might go out the window and the blues you selected might become keepers. If it turns out all your chairs are really leggy, your best sofa bet might be the one with the skirt, which offers a little balance.

9. make a decorating schedule

Even if you're not a to-do-list person, you'll want to take this final step because it saves so much time and cuts way down on confusion. Draw up a list of everything that needs to be done and be specific: Order this sofa, order this fabric for throw pillows, buy two gallons of this paint, hire a painter, send this chair to the upholsterer. Breaking a project down into steps reminds you that you don't have to do it all at once, makes very clear what needs to be done and keeps the process from feeling overwhelming—all of which will help you carry it through to completion.

- Order paint. (Confirm with painter when he will be coming.)

- Order sofa in pale natural linen. Make sure to specify <u>with</u> skirt.

- Order 2 club chairs in navy solid.

- Order occasional chair. Send them fabric.

- Make appt. with local decorating shop to discuss making curtains. (Take my domino book with me!)

- Call antique shop and see if I can take floor lamp out on approval.

- Order 7 x 10 striped rug.

23

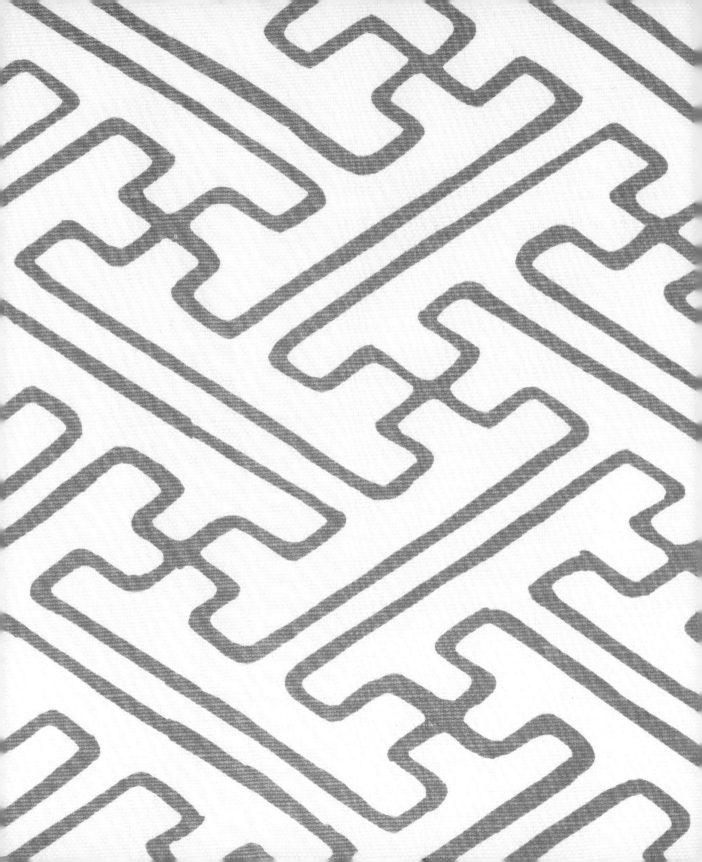

CHAPTER TWO

the entryway

the style:
happy graphic

VIVID POPS OF COLOR White walls and an ebony floor create a flexible backdrop for Crayola-bright accents—an orange side table and primary-colored accessories that give the area its peppy personality (but could easily be switched out for a whole different palette and mood).

DIVIDED BUT CONNECTED A see-through folding screen creates an entry where there isn't actually one, while also allowing sunlight to filter in. The half-in, half-out zebra-printed cowhide rug links the entry to the rest of the apartment.

LIGHT AND AIRY Uncluttered open shelves and the simple fretwork of the screen ensure the space has ample room to breathe. Even the giant mirror contributes to the sense of expansiveness with its delicate, peacock-y detailing.

FRIENDLY FORMS The furniture plan is very casual—no serious pieces, no imposing symmetry. All the elements are pleasantly askew, except for the centered mirror, which creates a sight line and holds everything together.

Fashion designer
Liz Lange's
entryway, decorated
by Jonathan Adler

the style:
brave bohemian

GUTSY SPECTRUM The teal entry hall (with red pendant lamp—
nearly its opposite on the color wheel) and the bold hues leading off from it
work together because they are all equally rich. White trim offers a breather
between them.

COLOR AS A MASK The nook may be unremarkable architecturally,
but it feels confident and considered, thanks to the daring paint application,
which graciously hides the flaws. Painting over mismatched molding and
unappealing pipes allows them to recede from view, while the red pendant
draws attention up and away from the drab floor.

OFFBEAT SENSIBILITY There is a flea-market magic to the
combination of a Venetian mirror, an industrial-looking lamp and a
chinoiserie chest against a saturated backdrop. Leaning the mirror, as opposed
to mounting it on the wall, enhances the vignette's casualness, as does the tiny
picture hung off-center.

Entryway of
James Leland Day,
stylist

the style:
cool collector

WHITE LINING Epoxy floors and stark walls create a gallery-like setting for art, sculptural chairs and a mahogany chest, allowing the individual pieces to stand out. As full as the room is, there is a certain lightness accentuated by chrome, gilding, Plexiglas and the reflective floor finish.

UNEXPECTED FURNITURE Instead of a console or bench, a classic dresser anchors the space. It feels sober and historic, balancing the more playful elements like the mix of colors in the art and the 18th-century grotto chairs. The black picture frames and lamp shade pick up on the dark wood chest to tie things together.

DEVIL-MAY-CARE ATTITUDE A column of art hung behind the door from ceiling to floor feels informal and proclaims its unconventionality. Strings of beads draped loosely atop the lamp shade, the messy stack of books on the chair and even the missing knob from a drawer signal a laid-back demeanor. On the chest, little toys mingled with a fancy gilded frame are a final stroke of bad-boy behavior.

Entryway of Johnson Hartig,
fashion designer

the big piece: consoles, chests and benches

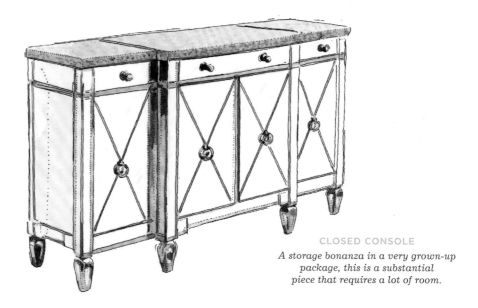

CLOSED CONSOLE

A storage bonanza in a very grown-up package, this is a substantial piece that requires a lot of room.

DECORATIVE CONSOLE

Immediately announces your sense of style. This is a pure statement piece. (Storage? Who needs storage?)

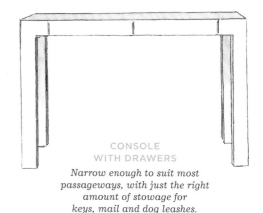

CONSOLE WITH DRAWERS

Narrow enough to suit most passageways, with just the right amount of stowage for keys, mail and dog leashes.

BENCH

*Used as a drop zone for bags or a perch
for taking off or putting on shoes, this can
be accessorized with hooks installed
overhead and baskets underneath if closet
space is lacking.*

CHEST

*Not for cramped quarters (be mindful of
its depth), this looks very homey topped with
a pair of lamps. Readily holds both current
needs and out-of-season gear.*

OPEN SHELVES

*A slender profile that won't bulk up a small
space. Slip baskets onto the
shelves to create additional storage.*

DEMILUNE TABLE

*Semicircular with delicate legs, this graceful
option has a formal, old-fashioned feel.
It offers minimal storage, but
an easy-to-navigate shape (no corners
to bang into!) makes it perfect for tight spots.*

CENTER

*Classic, graceful. Tends to be more formal.
If you have a big enough entryway, this is often
the best solution, floating or centered in the
space. Can double as a dining table in a pinch.*

INSTANT EXPERT:
buying an entry table

SIZE The length of consoles varies, but the height (30" to 32" is standard) and depth (about 14") are fairly consistent.

PLACEMENT Position the piece so it's a focal point as you walk into your home—whether that means it's front and center or off to one side (ideally not behind the door). Clearance is important: There should be enough space not just for the door to open but for a person to enter comfortably.

how to mix and match

gilded bamboo

'80s decadence

earthy fibers

parisian glamour

ornately eastern

scaled-up kasbah

storied refinement

minimalist mirror

flashy floral

feather-capped diva

golden bowl

Bold, blingy and decorative, this rich collection trumpets **Park Avenue fabulousness**. Gold accents unite high-end pieces, including a very traditional candlestick lamp with an eccentric pheasant-feather shade. A simple natural-fiber rug keeps the glitz in check, and a gilded shell bowl bridges the showy and the organic.

translucent pyramid

glossy tray

This **modern Moroccan** group marries exotic embellishment—a fanciful mother-of-pearl mirror and a graphic rug—with contemporary materials such as the translucent lamp and the laminated tray. A mirrored finish relates the 1930s cabinet to the shiny elements on the mirror and lamp.

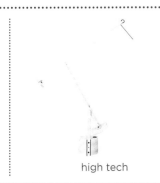

high tech

'70s mod

An unusual blend of the past and the modern age, this **futuristic neoclassical** mix is united by a crisp palette and an elegance of form. The rug—a blown-up riff on a standard floral—connects the intricate table with the streamlined tray, lamp and mirror.

very important tips

function & style

A TWO-TIMING SPACE Your entry is a way station, but it's also the mood-setter for your home, so practical and design concerns need equal attention.

SET THE SCENE Fresh flowers, neat tabletop compositions and dimmers on your light sources (or low-wattage bulbs) help create a pleasant atmosphere. Because the entry is where first impressions are made, it's an ideal place for a scent, whether you prefer a candle, incense or a diffuser.

MAKE IT WORK FOR YOU Establishing designated spots for the things you deposit or pick up as you go in or out cuts down on chaos. Use a tray to corral essentials like keys, cell phones, wallets and sunglasses; add a bowl for coins; hang hooks or get a coatrack to keep scarves, coats, hats and bags at the ready (and off the floor or table). An umbrella stand can also hold sports gear, and a wastepaper basket lets you toss junk mail as soon as it arrives: Once it fills, just transfer to the recycling bin.

lighting & mirrors

TABLE LAMPS If you have the space, a lamp or two on a console bestows a welcoming glow. No room for lamps? Go for sconces.

OVERHEAD FIXTURES A pendant lamp or chandelier in the entry offers major impact. Hang it at least 7' from the floor (so nobody gets hit on the head) and clear of the door.

DIMMERS Putting light sources on a dimmer lets you control the brightness depending on the situation (bright for reading mail, low for parties).

MIRRORS When in doubt, go big: A grand mirror makes a dramatic focal point. Match the frame to your table for a pulled-together look, or mix things up. If you find a mirror you like but aren't sure about it, ask to take it home on approval, a request many dealers are happy to accommodate. If nothing in the stores seems right, consider custom. At a good frame shop, you can choose the exact size, frame and type of glass (antiqued, tony-looking beveled, plain). This option is not necessarily cheap but yields exactly what you want and is a great way to copy an unaffordable antique.

storage

COAT CLOSET Little additions will help you make the most of the space. A basket for each family member enables everyone to find his or her stuff in a hurry. Low hooks on the back of the door allow children to hang their own coats. Matching wooden hangers are the easiest way to keep bulky coats in order; those with a thin profile save room but are still sturdier than plastic. If possible, shift off-season outerwear to another spot in your house, so the hall closet isn't jammed. It makes hosting (and even hanging your own coat) a much more gracious experience.

NO COAT CLOSET Opt for a piece of furniture with ample storage, such as a chest or a closed console. Choose hooks or a standing rack that works with the main piece. If you use individual hooks, mount them far enough apart so coats drape nicely (and consider installing them in a slightly out-of-sight spot, like behind the front door). Turn the major piece of furniture into a de facto closet by giving every area of it a purpose—fit it with drawer organizers (ideally in the top drawer) for smaller items, as well as dividers (in the lower ones), either giving each family member a space or grouping items by type.

floors

RUG SIZE Furniture is typically set off the rug in an entryway—but beyond that, there aren't many rules for floor coverings. A rug that takes up most of the floor space helps the area feel more like a room, a runner is good for a narrow corridor and a border (see above) adds definition, but it's also perfectly acceptable to go rugless.

RUG DURABILITY For this high-traffic zone, choose something flat (so the door can open over it) that can handle a lot of traffic. Sea grass isn't particularly durable, but it's inexpensive and works in any setting. Well-made antique rugs can usually take quite a beating (and likely already have).

PAINT INSTEAD Painted floors are an easy, low-maintenance option (you can sweep or mop them). If you're inspired, stencil a pattern or stripes (be sure to seal the surface after it's thoroughly dry). Since the entry is a contained area, it's a good spot to try something fun.

decorating tricks

CEILING-MOUNTED CURTAINS flanking a doorway add drama to the act of entering the house and also keep out drafts.

A TUNNEL OF EXUBERANT WALLPAPER is an exciting lead-in to a serene living room.

ONE BOLD WALL framed with grosgrain ribbon is a bright way to say "Come in."

FAKE A STAIR RUNNER—and the decorative border—with glossy paint.

A CHEERFUL STENCILED FLOOR is a playful alternative to an entry rug.

more decorating tricks

CREATE ARCHITECTURE
by introducing molding to walls
and doors.

INTENSELY PATTERNED WALLPAPER can be a surprisingly unifying backdrop for disparate pieces of art.

ONE GIANT PHOTO anchors a sea of smaller ones and makes an event out of a blank space.

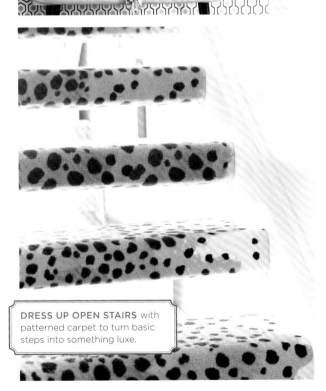

DRESS UP OPEN STAIRS with patterned carpet to turn basic steps into something luxe.

ONE REPEATED MOTIF lining a hallway is intriguing and original.

small-space solutions

A NONSPACE MAXED OUT
with standout pendants,
over-the-top wallpaper and
vividly painted doors becomes
an attention-getting entry.

ESTABLISH AN ENTRYWAY
with a chest and a chair placed near the door.

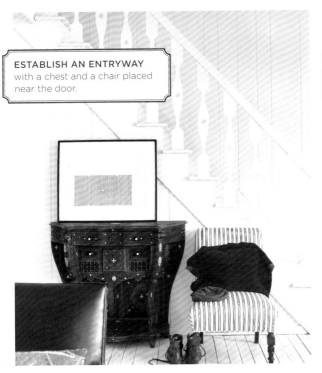

RIG UP A VESTIBULE that eases the transition from outside to inside.

CARVE OUT A "COAT CLOSET"
with wall-to-wall hooks and baskets for hats and gloves.

SCONCES FREE UP SURFACE AREA in a petite foyer, leaving room for favorite objects.

finishing touches

DECKING OUT AN ENTRY
with a punchy umbrella stand, a
pretty tray for keys and a basket
for newspapers makes staying
organized more pleasurable.

HUNG TIGHTLY, an assemblage of art and mementos feels full and leads the eye up the stairs.

A BASIC POTTED PLANT is a low-maintenance but equally lovely alternative to flowers.

DRAWER DIVIDERS in this desk allow it to function like a clutter-free command center: leash, envelopes, stamps—check!

COMPOSING A TABLEAU with beautiful objects makes it even nicer to come home.

the domino effect

the starting point

"The tiny entry hall in my equally tiny one-bedroom is a space I wanted to give some importance to."

RITA KONIG
domino *contributing editor*

"An entrance should smell good because scent is the first thing you respond to when you walk in a house."

"I don't usually like overheads, but this metal light on a long chain makes my lofty ceiling feel more intimate."

dark elements

my inspiration

"I brought my mother [decorator Nina Campbell] to Odorantes, and she was so taken with the birds and the black of the shop that she designed this wallpaper. It was perfect for my entry."

"To highlight the wallpaper, I painted the door and everything around it black— even the doorbell."

"This is Odorantes, a little flower shop in Paris. They prop the place with a rotating collection of taxidermy— woodland animals, butterflies, birds. The walls are dark, and all the colors of the flowers just pop against them. I went there for a *domino* story, and I couldn't stop thinking about it."

"The hats are here because they take up a lot of space in the closet, and they fit nicely here."

"I don't smoke, but this ashtray has stayed with me through every apartment I've had. I just adore the color. I saw it in an antiques shop with my mother, and she bought it for me as a gift."

"I love a lamp illuminating something like a vase of flowers, giving it some weird prominence, as if it's on a stage."

finishing touches

"I wasn't sure about this, but I brought it home to try and it worked beautifully."

"I like small pictures propped against the wall—it's so easy to switch up the art."

"When I added the table and lamp, suddenly my sliver of a hall became a room."

major pieces

my entryway

"The lovely thing about wallpaper in an entry is that it gives the feeling that the space goes on and on—continuing beyond what you can see—whereas with paint your eye stops at the edges." —RITA KONIG

CHAPTER THREE

the living room

the style:
edgy classic

HISTORIC HUES WITH A TWIST A Colonial robin's-egg blue is rendered in a brighter shade, pulling it out of its old-fashioned shell. The pea-green fabric on the curtains and daybed complement the blue, while acid-yellow pillows—a riff on formal Georgian yellow—are a punchy grace note. The painted ceiling creates a sense of being wrapped in color.

WALLS/CEILING

CURTAINS/DAYBED

PILLOWS

MODERN MOMENTS The room is dotted with bygone accents—a brass library lamp, the crystal chandelier—but the central element is a clean-lined daybed, which bridges casual and formal. The bare floor, uncommon in a traditional living room, enhances the unfussy feel.

PROPORTION PLAY The mingling of grand and small pieces infuses the space with a lively rhythm. The curtains, the tall mirror and the bust on the stand add height to the low seating.

OFF-KILTER SYMMETRY A pair of chairs placed at a diagonal help tie the room's two seating areas together. Asymmetry pops up around the mantel, where frames are staggered rather than perfectly aligned. Even the tilted hat on the bust shakes things up—it says the room doesn't take itself too seriously. Like the overall mix, it's a relaxed take on classicism.

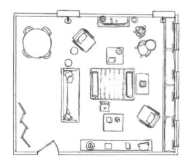

floor plan

This layout is all about maximizing seating. A double-wide daybed divides the large space into separate areas—one oriented toward the fireplace for entertaining, the other side for TV-viewing. A banquette offers yet more places to sit.

Living room of Sara Ruffin
Costello, *domino creative director*

the style:
earthy modern

TEXTURED NEUTRALS This is not cold-lined modernism. The all-white backdrop is a stage for warm hues represented by diverse materials—cowhide, wood, leather, wool and cashmere. Silver accents bring some sparkle to the brown-and-white scheme.

WALLS   SOFA   SOFA   RUG

LOW FURNITURE The whole room happens below the windows, creating a lounge-y atmosphere. Short bookcases draw the eye horizontally and feel just right in relation to the close-to-the-ground coffee table, which signals casual, on-the-floor hanging out.

SCULPTURAL LIGHTING In lieu of standard table lamps, moonlike lanterns and an arced floor lamp add to the sense that the room is all abstract forms.

GEOMETRIC ASSEMBLAGES While the sofas aren't the same height, they work back-to-back, thanks to side tables that balance the composition. The TV is a focal point of the room, but surrounded by similar rectangular shapes (the art around it and the open shelves beneath), its central position is minimized.

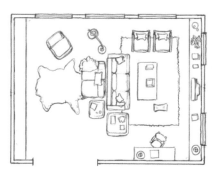

floor plan
Sofas divide this big space into two sitting areas—an open one that faces a wall of floor-to-ceiling bookcases and another centered around the TV. Nonmatching rugs help define each area.

Living room of Derek and
Michelle Sanders, *architect
and fashion director*

the style:
mid-century elegant

GLAMMED-UP BEIGE The secret here: neutrals played up by sumptuous fabrics and hits of icy blue, which add polish to the camel tones. A push-pull dynamic between cool (blue pillows, pewter curtains) and warm (gilt mirror and coffee table) makes the space both serene and inviting.

ICONIC PIECES Classic designs, both modern and traditional, appear in a mélange of textures: the thin paper of the Noguchi lamp, the smooth leather of the Arne Jacobsen chair, the wood of the Richard Schultz side table and the plush velvet of the Billy Baldwin sofa.

LADYLIKE DETAILS Shiny silk curtains, satiny pillows and floral fabrics contribute a subtle layer of femininity.

TOUCH OF ANTIQUE A gracefully time-worn mirror and round coffee table (an excellent foil to a boxy seating area) introduce some history and patina to the modern mix. The photographic seascape is a cheeky stand-in for a formal oil painting, its placement charmingly unexpected.

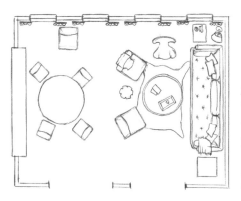

floor plan
A rug defines the sitting area in this loftlike all-purpose room, which is open to the dining area and a wall of bookcases. The furniture arrangement is easy and comfortable for socializing—an intimate spin on a formal setup.

Living room of model
Haylynn Cohen, decorated
by David Lawrence

the style:
cultured irreverence

STRANGE BEDFELLOWS Contrast drives the room's punk-patrician effect. A gilt Louis XV sofa mingles with a '70s Bond-like chrome chair and crystal candleholders—wildly different styles, but they feel harmonious because they are all glamorous, decadent and a little rock and roll. The large see-through coffee table also helps unify—it's simple, so the other pieces can be outrageous.

POP COLORS Glossy floors and stark walls (offset by a rustic wood ceiling) provide a calming backdrop for a cornucopia of art in vivid hues.

CONTROLLED CHAOS The salon-style art assemblage could feel unwieldy, but strict framing and hanging (pictures line up precisely around a dominant central work) yield a sense of happy order.

EXAGGERATED PROPORTIONS In Lucite, the massive table doesn't overwhelm. Its scale is cleverly mirrored by the giant Damien Hirst spin-art painting.

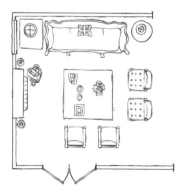
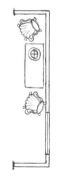

floor plan
Situated to the right of the front door, the living room functions as an entry hall (a chest and two chairs make up the actual entry). The formality and symmetrical arrangement of the furniture signal that this is not a comfy den but a salon.

Living room of Johnson
Hartig, *fashion designer*

the big piece: sofas

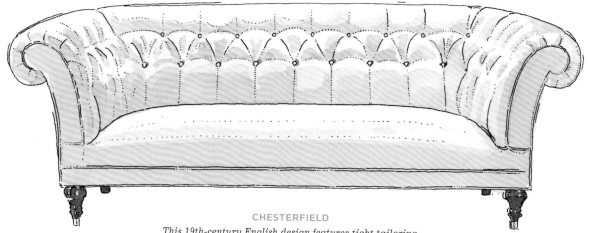

CHESTERFIELD

*This 19th-century English design features tight tailoring,
a high back, rolled arms and tufting. In leather, it's clubby and
masculine. Done in a bright wool, it's neo-traditional.
In linen, it's elegant and refined. (Whichever material
you choose, make it a solid.)*

CAMELBACK

*Dating back to 18th-century British designer
Thomas Chippendale, this piece has an
old-world sophistication but also looks surprisingly
modern in a solid linen. Hand-me-downs
can be updated with a tailored slipcover.*

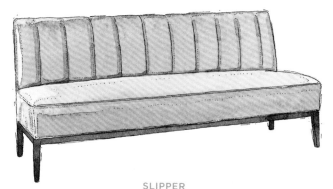

SLIPPER

*Streamlined and unfussy, like an elongated
slipper chair, this option is made more for
entertaining than lounging. Usually lean and
open, it does well in small spaces.*

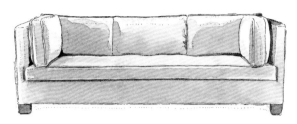

TUXEDO

A signature of society decorator Billy Baldwin, this sofa is luxurious yet decidedly no-frills. A straight profile (the arms and back are the same height) give it a more masculine feel. Works in any room, modern or traditional.

FRENCH SETTEE

Often seen in a Louis XIV style, this regal option is delicate, formal and architectural. The exposed carved-wood frame provides a structured contrast in a room of heavily upholstered pieces.

ENGLISH THREE-SEATER

Rumpled yet aristocratic, this British country-house staple has soft, deep cushions and low arms that make it ideal for TV watching.

SECTIONAL

Casual, with a '70s louginess. Good for establishing a sitting area in a loft. Minimizes need for other seating. A version with legs cuts the bulkiness.

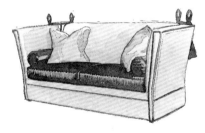

KNOLE

Named after a grand house of King Henry VIII. Super-classic and formal but very cozy and sheltering. Hinged sides untie and drop flat, so you can lie down.

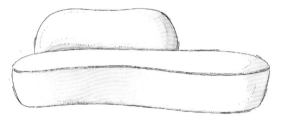

MODERN

More sculpture than sofa (this one is a mid-century design by Vladimir Kagan). Can float in the middle of a room.

INSTANT EXPERT: buying a sofa

WELL-STUFFED Knead the edges of the arms to see if a sofa is amply padded. It shouldn't be easy to detect the wood under the stuffing.

COMFORTABLE Test the seat depth (too deep can be awkward unless you like to sit with your legs curled up), the angle of the sofa back and the height of the arms.

FLAWLESS STITCHING Make sure the seams are straight and create a smooth, continuous line, without obvious zigzags, lumps or gaps.

STRONG FRAME Wood blocks in the bottom corners of the frame reinforce a sofa by dispersing weight. Feel underneath to check—not all sofas have them.

how to mix & match

streamlined modern

colorful kilim

classic gourd

properly skirted

floral indulgence

nature undercover

danish angularity

op art

animal magnetism

sculptural cube

rugged butterfly

There's nothing formal about this comfy, inviting setup built of browns and gray with a touch of red. A distressed-leather chair, a raw wood table and a handwoven rug paired with a slick sectional and a glossy lamp add up to a look that's **earthy yet urbane**.

lacquered curves

dazzling color

Ladylike tailoring and playful touches run throughout a mostly white lineup that's feminine but not at all princess-y. The cushy sofa and demure pillow are typical girl props, but the gold-lined lamp shade, mid-century-esque stool and grape-colored armchair take the decor a step beyond dutiful daughter.

pale minimalism

updated slipper

Rich textures—a ribbed rug, smooth black leather and cool marble—bring a sensual element to an **elegant, neutral collection** of largely modern shapes. The organic warmth of a pendant lamp made of antlers interrupts the strict geometry.

very important tips

coffee tables

SIZE The standard height is 17" to 19". Lower feels more modern. Length depends on the size of your space, but a good rule of thumb is to pick a table one-half to two-thirds the length of your sofa, so it's accessible from the entire sofa. Place the table about 18" away—within easy reach, yet leaving enough room for legs.

THE RIGHT SHAPE A square or rectangular design offers an orderly backdrop for decorative items, particularly books and trays. A shelf beneath can stash newspapers or remotes while keeping the top clean. Circular always looks neat because it's never crooked and is a good way to balance out hard-lined furniture. For a laid-back option, try an ottoman (a tray on top will make it functional), which can also double as seating.

SOLID OR TRANSPARENT A see-through table (glass or acrylic) can make a small room seem more spacious. A solid that matches the rug or floor (above) tends to disappear.

rugs

DIMENSIONS Standard rugs measure 6' x 9', 8' x 10' and 9' x 12'. Whether you go the standard or custom route, get one that leaves 4" to 8" of bare floor on all sides, so it looks intentional, rather than like imprecise wall-to-wall. Rugs with borders tend to be more traditional and are a nice way to lend polish to a room.

RULE-BREAKERS Conventional wisdom says all four legs of the sofa should be on or off the rug, but if you're buying a standard-size rug and the math just doesn't work out, don't panic—having two legs on is also okay.

COLOR & PATTERN A rug that brings in all the colors of the room can pull a space together; a patterned rug is often used to offset a scheme full of solids (above). But don't feel compelled to introduce a pattern—sometimes a textured solid rug can add all the interest you need.

LAYERING Throwing a smaller rug over a larger one (particularly of sisal or sea grass) helps define an area, like the spot where the coffee table sits.

window treatments

SHADES OR CURTAINS Curtains add drama and soften a stark space. Shades (like the roman ones above), are tailored and neat, and especially good for smaller spaces. You can match the style and fabric of your curtains to your room to play up what's already there or use them as a counterpoint. Sheers bring a fancy room down a notch, while formal drapes dress up understated furniture.

CURTAIN STYLES Lined curtains are weighty and rich, and feel formal. Unlined are breezier.

BEYOND ROLLER BLINDS If you want some glamour without a lot of bulk, try a lush hybrid like a roman shade or a swankier London shade (has a swag of fabric at the bottom). If you stick with a basic roller, you can elevate it with a border or trim, like pom-poms or tassels.

MOUNTING An inside mount (above) gives a crisp look and is especially nice with attractive woodwork. An outside mount for shades can make the window appear bigger. With curtains, hanging the rod higher and wider than the frame has the same effect.

lighting

LAMPS The easiest way to pull together a living room is to place a pair of matching lamps symmetrically on end tables or behind the sofa. For a looser but still unified feel, split a pair—one on an end table and one on a desk.

HANGING FIXTURES A chandelier in the living room is a nice surprise, adding elegance and dimension. You need a minimum ceiling height of 9', and hanging the chandelier over the coffee table ensures people won't bump their heads.

MIXED SOURCES A combination of table and floor lamps allows you to distribute light more evenly around a room (a matched set plus one floor lamp is a good starting point). Ditch the overheads if you can—they cast a harsh light.

WHERE TO PUT LIGHTS Make sure there are good lamps by reading chairs. Use smaller lamps to create a glow in unlikely places, such as on a mantel or a bookshelf.

decorating tricks

A BLAST OF COLOR in an elegant black-and-white scheme makes a potentially intimidating space friendly.

POUFS DO EVERYTHING— they're extra seating, footstools and even coffee-table stand-ins.

GRANNY UPHOLSTERY feels fresh on a sofa with modern lines.

ONE SPECTACULAR PIECE with scale and drama is like an exclamation point in a room.

USE YOUR RUG AS INSPIRATION for your overall palette—just borrow the colors for paint, furniture and accessories.

more **decorating tricks**

A TABLE THAT HOVERS just off the floor invites guests to sit on the rug and hang out.

HIDE AN UGLY SOFA with a piece of linen or another weighty fabric that pools a bit on the floor.

FRAMED WALLPAPER is an affordable way to bring in an expensive pattern.

A BAR TRAY conveys old-fashioned hospitality. You don't need a special piece of furniture—any tiny table will work.

GIANT HOUSEPLANTS lend regal symmetry and drama to a neutral space.

more decorating tricks

LAYER FLATWEAVE RUGS that share the same basic palette for a kasbah effect.

A SINGLE UPHOLSTERED WALL in a warm print softens stark furniture and stands in for art.

TWO COFFEE TABLES, instead of one, shake up the monotony of the living-room suite.

DIFFERENT-COLORED CURTAINS add theatricality to a space with high ceilings.

PAINT A BORDER to give character and depth to a room that has no molding.

small-space solutions

A HEADBOARD BECOMES A MINI WALL between living room and sleeping area in a studio apartment.

CLEVERLY PLACED ART can distract from messy storage.

SKIPPING THE COFFEE TABLE can make an undersize living room feel airier.

LET THE BED BE THE CENTER OF ATTENTION—no need to apologize for living in a studio!

CREATE A ROOM DIVIDER out of a backless bookshelf, giving privacy to the bed without blocking light to the interior.

hanging artwork

A **HUGE PIECE, CENTRALLY LOCATED** on the wall, anchors any arrangement. No matter how randomly you lay out the smaller ones, it looks considered.

DIFFERENT COLOR FRAMES prevent a geometric grouping of like pieces from feeling static.

OVERSIZE AND HUNG LOW, simple images can become the focal point of a room.

ONE VERTICAL, ONE HORIZONTAL—in a pair of intriguing graphic frames, it almost doesn't matter what's inside them.

AN ARTFUL GRID turns personal photos into poetry.

arranging a mantel

IN A MONOCHROMATIC STILL LIFE, varying materials and textures keeps things interesting.

A JUMBLE OF FAMILY PHOTOS lightens up an orchestrated mantel.

TUCKING A SMALLER ELEMENT behind a major mirror adds a layer of intrigue.

UNIFIED TONE PLUS ONE COLOR—a basic strategy that always works.

BRIGHT VASES AND UNUSUAL FLOWERS invigorate the symmetrical mantel recipe.

the domino effect

the starting point

"I wanted the living room in our loft to do two things I hoped weren't contradictory: function as an elegant, grown-up space for entertaining and be welcoming for my children."

DEBORAH NEEDLEMAN
domino *editor in chief*

major anxiety: my sofa

"I was completely paralyzed: What if I bought one and hated it? I decided a classic Billy Baldwin sofa was safe: It could add a little glamour if I wanted to go modern or clean lines to a more antique-y room."

my inspirations

"I'm always drawn to faded, subtle colors over bright, clear primaries. I prefer creams and ivories to whites, and I love chalky grays."

"Filled with a spot-on mix of styles, *domino* Editor at Large Tom Delavan's house is spare, sexy and comfortable. There's not a lot of color, but it's enveloping and warm and full of interest."

"This Brooklyn town house—which was kind of grand but totally cozy in that charming English-aristo way—had this rich, medieval-looking velvet I totally fell for."

stuff I ditched

"I've never been comfortable with anything too of-the-moment. So goodbye to my trendy missteps—a flokati rug, a Philippe Starck chair and Mercer Hotel-inspired dark bookshelves (which got a shiny coat of white paint)."

stuff I kept

"Everything I held on to felt a little timeless, handmade and collected: things I found in Stockholm with my husband, a modern Indian table I'd obsessed about for weeks, a French ticking pillow given to me by Dara Caponigro."

friend-erator to the rescue

"I couldn't quite pull it all together until I enlisted help. Tom Delavan chose furniture and fabric (like painted chairs and mousy-gray velvet) that would only look better as they got a little beat up."

"Tom also balanced my fussier pieces with more sculptural shapes and introduced modern elements, like giant paper lanterns and a Lucite coffee table."

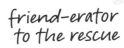

my living room

"Coming home to a calm space makes me so happy and lets me take total pleasure in the wildness of my children. If the place felt or looked chaotic, I don't think I could love all the chaos it contains quite as much." —DEBORAH NEEDLEMAN

CHAPTER FOUR

the dining room

the style:
urbane organic

SOPHISTICATED NEUTRALS This basic brown-and-white palette is earthy but polished. Pickled-wood floors and pale Venetian-plaster walls add texture and make furniture seem to float.

CHAIRS SEAT

BACKS OF CHAIRS

WALLS

THOUGHTFUL PROPORTIONS Key sculptural elements anchor the room. The Noguchi paper lantern is large enough to serve as a focal point for the whole space, but it's also delicate, so it doesn't overpower the dining table. Similarly, the massive table feels light, thanks to its arched base.

ROUGH WITH REFINED Wicker storage baskets, industrial metal shelves and a raw wood ball play against the elegant mid-century dining table by T. H. Robsjohn-Gibbings and linen-upholstered Louis XVI chairs.

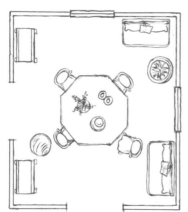

floor plan
The room has a lot going on—it's both TV den and dining room—but basic geometry keeps it from feeling busy. A pair of sectional sofas is split up into two corners and balanced by a pair of bookshelves, all of which surround the central table.

Dining room of
Dara Caponigro,
domino *style director*

the style:
ladylike luxe

FEMININE PALETTE All the colors in the scheme come from the wallpaper's pale blue, brown, silver and white. Contrast provided by the dark chairs and patterned pillows grounds the soft tones.

WALLPAPER   CHAIRS   SETTEE   PILLOWS   BENCH

FANCY AND FRIENDLY The seating is all aristocratic in style (Chippendale-style bench, Regency settee, Directoire chairs) but mismatched, for a cumulative effect that is offbeat and inviting. The sea-grass rug is casual (unlike a formal oriental), underscoring the idea that this is not an off-limits environment.

POSH ELEMENTS This room does not shy from sumptuousness. Cascades of silk taffeta pool on the floor; velvet upholstery (a thread that ties together the stylistically disparate seating) brings richness. Silver objects, a mirrored cabinet and a glass chandelier lend sparkle.

ALWAYS WELL-DRESSED With the good silver on display (and in use), the room looks perfectly accessorized all the time. Having something on the table keeps the mood welcoming.

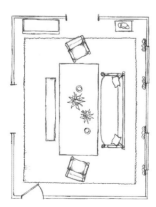

floor plan
In this funky layout, a traditional centered-table configuration is shaken up by unusual seating— a bench, a settee and armchairs that stand in for conventional dining chairs.

Dining room of
Windsor Smith,
interior designer

the style:
enchanted mod

SNOW-WHITE COLORS The juxtaposition of hues from nature (forest-y green, deep ocean blue) with icy walls and upholstery has a charming vividness.

CURTAINS   CHAIRS   CHAIRS   WALLS

DELICATE LINES From the Saarinen-esque table and leggy chairs to the wall-mounted bookshelf, everything seems weightless (even the curtains hover slightly above the ground). There's plenty of air around the furniture, which helps give the room its ethereal, otherworldly quality.

FAIRY-TALE SCALE Small furniture heightens the grandeur of the big, high-ceilinged space. Superlong curtains and a tall bookshelf further elevate the drama.

A DASH OF PIXIE DUST The starlike acrylic chandelier stunningly combines mid-century lines and magical ornament.

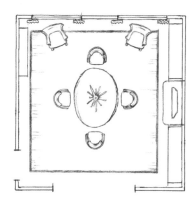

floor plan
Symmetry is the perfect nod to formal architecture—it makes sense to follow rather than fight the bones of a room. A classic arrangement here makes the modern pieces feel at home among grand proportions.

Dining room of
Fawn Galli,
interior decorator

the big piece: tables

TRADITIONAL

Refined, prim and likely the most-handed-down table of the bunch. Usually made from mahogany or cherry and featuring leaves. Paired with unmatched chairs, it feels less formal and suite-y.

TRADITIONAL PEDESTAL

Dates to the Roman Empire and repopularized in 18th-century England. A round table is easy to sit at— no legs to navigate. Can come with leaves, which expand its surface into an oval.

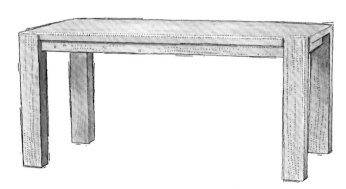

RUSTIC MODERN

In a rough-hewn material, this is earthy, spare and substantial. Warms up a minimalist room, and its simple shape guarantees it goes with any chair.

MODERN PEDESTAL

Elegant, versatile mid-century classic designed by Eero Saarinen for Knoll. Takes any chair and complements any style room.

FARMHOUSE

Common in the 18th century, especially as a kitchen worktable. Rustic, with a laid-back country quality, this works well with modern chairs.

SWEDISH

Based on an 18th-century design inspired by French neoclassicism, this style is typically light and often casual in feel. Painted finishes give the look an unpretentious quality.

TRESTLE

Generally fabricated of a coarse wood that improves with wear, this form dates to the Middle Ages. Sitting at the ends can be a challenge.

INSTANT EXPERT: buying a table

SHAPE & MOOD
Round tables are great for group conversation. A more interesting alternative to one large rectangle is to try two smaller squares—use one for dinner with a smaller group, and push both together when you have a crowd.

STANDARD HEIGHT
Most tables are 29" to 30" high. If you find something lower that you like, be sure to pair it with similarly proportioned chairs so sitting and eating aren't uncomfortable.

HOW MANY PEOPLE FIT?
A 48"-diameter table seats four and can squeeze in six. A 54" table accommodates six comfortably; a 60" seats eight to ten. Standard size for a traditional rectangle for eight people is 36" x 72".

THE RIGHT SURFACE
Think about how you live and what you can tolerate: If stains and rings make you crazy, pick a piece that gets better with age—like a farmhouse table rather than an unsealed marble-topped one.

how to mix & match

tailored simplicity

glossy chippendale

opalescent brilliance

functional sculpture

parisian couture

modern art

sleek icon

playfully exotic

theatrical flourish

streamlined federal

greek key

Formal with subtle twists, this collection of **unstuffy classics** features traditional designs in unexpected materials or finishes— a chandelier strung with oyster shells instead of crystal, a chair in bright white rather than dark, polished wood—and a dramatic contrasting mix of dark and light.

urbane swagger

beige border

An elegant **1930s French** spirit infuses these compact elements just right for smaller spaces. Varied in texture, they bring together the warmth of camel (seen in the chair, table and plate) offset with white.

fiery statement

ethnic texture

A medley of patterns and multiple reds lends this group of youthful and **happy chinoiserie** pieces a distinctly modern bent. A clean white Saarinen table and ikat-embellished plates keep the look from veering off into a Chinatown theme park.

very important tips

chairs

HEIGHT Standard seat height is 18" (a table is 29" or 30"). Generally, you want your chair backs to be higher than the table. If you're going for a super-modern, low-back chair, make sure the back is at least table height.

COMFORT If the store allows, bring home a chair to test with your table before committing to a whole set. Have everyone in your household try it out. Upholstered chairs are usually more comfortable than hard ones, but there are other factors to consider—the shape and size of the seat and the angle of the back and material.

UPHOLSTERY OPTIONS If stains on upholstery are going to drive you crazy, get unupholstered chairs. Leather works well in the dining room because it's easy enough to clean and gets better with age. Patterned fabrics help hide spills, and outdoor or specially treated fabrics can make stains less of a big deal (downside: Stain-resistant chemicals are not so great for the environment).

buffet tables

PURPOSE These are multitasking pieces—a cache for linens and dishes, and a sideboard for dinner parties.

HEIGHT A buffet is typically taller than a dining table. Standard height is 36"; width and depth vary.

MATERIALS & STYLE Consider the buffet an opportunity to round out the room—it can visually balance the table and chairs, in form and finish.

OPEN OR CLOSED Most buffets are closed, but the open shelves in the picture above provide an airy counterpoint to a covered table and solid chairs. And think about whether you want your dishes and glasses on display. If you have pretty tableware, you might opt for open. In that case, neatness counts.

curtains

SOFTENING A ROOM Between all the "hard" furniture it contains—like table, chairs and buffet—and the legginess of the table, the dining room is a natural spot for fabrics. Even if you don't have them in other rooms, it might make sense to put up curtains here.

FABRICS & PATTERNS A foolproof way to pull together a room is to match curtains to the chair upholstery or, as in the room above, to a tablecloth. It's old-fashioned and straightforward, but it's cute and it works. In terms of volume, curtains should be full, not skimpy. A no-fail fabric formula for generous coverage is to order at least one and a half to two times the width of the window.

MOUNTS It is customary to hang a rod 4" above the window frame and 6" to 8" past the frame on each side. Hanging higher can make the ceiling seem taller, while mounting wider can make your window appear bigger. Only mount curtains inside the frame if your window is very large.

lighting

CHANDELIER SIZE & HEIGHT Choosing a fixture one-third the length of the table is a good rule of thumb. The bottom of the fixture should hang 30" to 34" above the table. Have extra links on hand when hanging, and be there when the job is done: The only way to really tell if the height is right is to have someone stand on a ladder and hold the light above the table.

BULBS Round candelabra bulbs are good in modern fixtures. Use a simple torpedo-shaped bulb or a more ornate flame-shaped one in traditional chandeliers. To decide between frosted and clear varieties, buy and try both to see what looks better.

TABLE LAMPS & SCONCES Lighting at different levels—on the walls, on the buffet—makes the space warmer. Use dimmers everywhere for total mood mastery. And don't forget about the option of shutting off lights and using candles.

decorating tricks

FRAMING WALLPAPER makes it feel like a grand piece of art.

TRANSLUCENT CHAIRS keep a tight space from looking cluttered and lighten the mood of a heavy table.

ONE ODD STOOL tones down the formality of a coordinated dining set.

PALE BLUE ON THE CEILING adds soothing color to a neutral room.

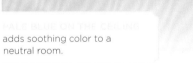

SEATING A BIG CROWD can be affordable—forgo traditional dining chairs and invest in stackable stools.

more decorating tricks

A CUSTOM TABLE SKIRT
transforms any old piece
into an elegant buffet table and
provides hidden storage.

ROSA ALBA (*Flore pleno*)   ROSIER BLANC ORDINAIRE

PAINTING THE CHAIRS of a traditional matching dining set updates the look.

CUSHIONS ARE AN EASY PLACE TO GO BOLD—try solids in different colors or a mix of related patterns, like these tartans.

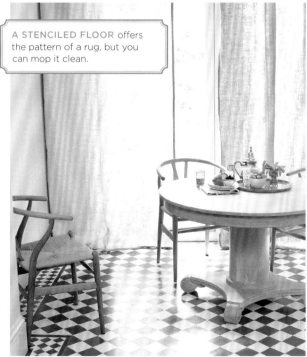

A STENCILED FLOOR offers the pattern of a rug, but you can mop it clean.

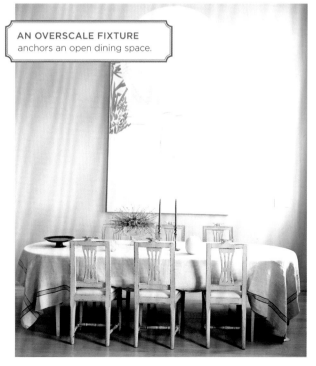

AN OVERSCALE FIXTURE anchors an open dining space.

small-space solutions

A BANQUETTE TRANSFORMS a nook into a dining area and can offer built-in storage.

AGAINST A WINDOW, a table takes up about 3' less floor space (and can be pulled out for dinner parties).

A MIRRORED WALL gives the sensation of being in a much grander venue.

WITH A SCALED-DOWN TABLE, you can have all the elements of a proper dining room in tiny quarters.

EMBRACE THE SMALLNESS— lining an already tight room with bookcases enhances its coziness.

finishing touches

BETWEEN DINNER PARTIES, STYLE UP THE TABLE with stacks of books and objects.

MULTIPLE SHORT BOUQUETS are very conversation-friendly (no neck-craning necessary).

A GRAPHIC RUNNER is a lighter, more modern alternative to a full-on tablecloth.

LAYERED TABLECLOTHS, such as a patterned square over a plain solid, prove that two is more fun than one.

SUCCULENTS are an easy-care and long-lasting centerpiece.

the domino effect

the starting point

"I live in a loft in a super-industrial neighborhood, but I wanted my dining area to feel nostalgic and garden-y—I'm a cozy girl at heart."

LILI DIALLO
domino *contributing stylist*

"To keep with the table, I wanted a couple of things that were very traditional and architectural."

classical elements

an existing table

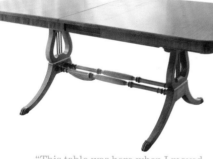

"This table was here when I moved in. It wouldn't have been my choice, but I figured it was kind of nice to have an antique-y thing—and it was too heavy to get rid of."

a bit of pop

"I needed something bold and sculptural with the table—it was hard to find dining chairs with a high enough back."

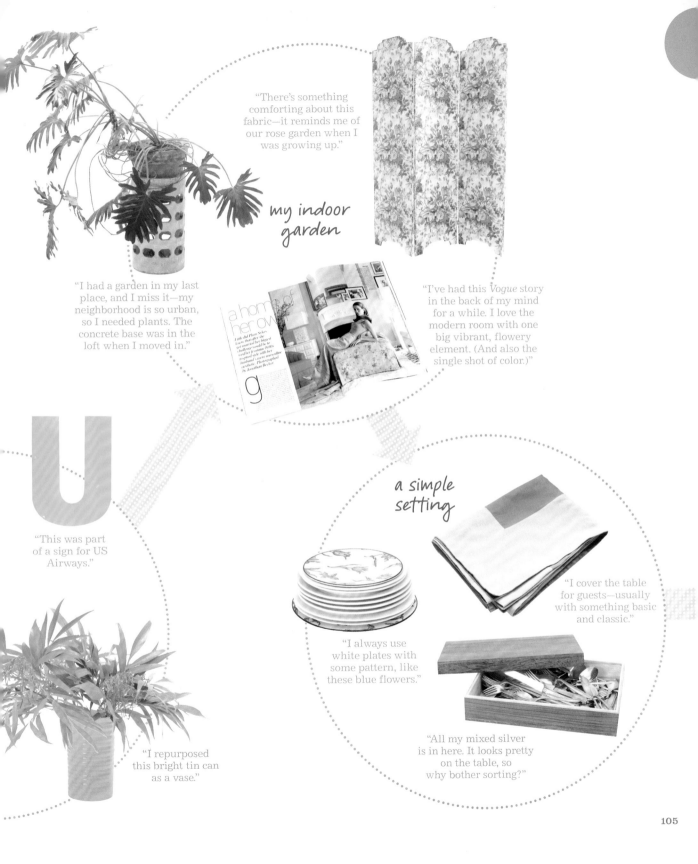

"There's something comforting about this fabric—it reminds me of our rose garden when I was growing up."

my indoor garden

"I had a garden in my last place, and I miss it—my neighborhood is so urban, so I needed plants. The concrete base was in the loft when I moved in."

"I've had this *Vogue* story in the back of my mind for a while. I love the modern room with one big vibrant, flowery element. (And also the single shot of color.)"

"This was part of a sign for US Airways."

"I repurposed this bright tin can as a vase."

a simple setting

"I cover the table for guests—usually with something basic and classic."

"I always use white plates with some pattern, like these blue flowers."

"All my mixed silver is in here. It looks pretty on the table, so why bother sorting?"

my dining room

"This is my little Proust 'madeleine moment.' The floral screen brings me back to my childhood. Some people have outdoor gardens—I have my chintz dining area." —LILI DIALLO

CHAPTER FIVE

the kitchen

the style:
vintage modern

WHITE ON WHITE ON WHITE Subtle variations in hue and outspoken differences in styles and materials animate the one-color scheme. Shiny walls, two types of marble (one glossy and one matte, on the countertop and table, respectively), plus utilitarian ceramic sconces and an ornate porcelain chandelier provide a world of interest.

INDUSTRIAL COMPONENTS The kitchen is outfitted with restaurant-quality appliances, including a pot-scrubber faucet, an old-school scale and a massive stainless-steel stove and hood.

COLD AND WARM MATERIALS The time-worn look of Belgian baked-oak floorboards (waxed rather than stained for extra depth) and curvy, unfinished dining chairs balance the cool of the floor-to-ceiling tiles.

CONTEMPORARY LIFE Built-in nooks on either side of the stove accommodate a collection of cake stands, a pop '60s plastic calendar and a bright graphic letter. Personality permeates the space, and chairs clustered at the counter and a casual dining area make clear it is designed for family living.

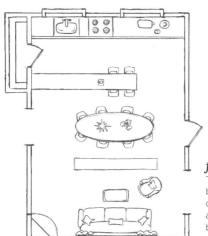

floor plan
The room has multiple zones, but all feel connected. The dining area is bordered by a long island and an open bookcase, which allows you to see through to a sitting nook.

Kitchen designed
by Ilse Crawford

the style:
refined
pastoral

OLD HOUSE, NEW SPACE The room lives in the present with stainless appliances, steel-legged tables and early-modern Thonet chairs but nods to the house's 19th-century past with countrified valances, subway tiling, historic paint colors and farmhouse-y storage baskets.

PRACTICAL SIMPLICITY Under- rather than overdecorated, the room is filled with casual, spontaneous solutions: A steel table stands in for cabinets, a metal bar-turned-pot rack hangs smack across a window and a plain narrow shelf sits atop the microwave. Weathered pans and a *tagine* are prominently on view, along with oils, spices and a crock of cooking utensils, all of which are easy to access.

BASIC, SOPHISTICATED HUES A subdued palette highlights the accessories on display, which are mostly black and white, keeping the scheme calm and soothing. The doors, trim and valances are also a quiet neutral, and the light-blue penny-tile floor is similarly unfussy.

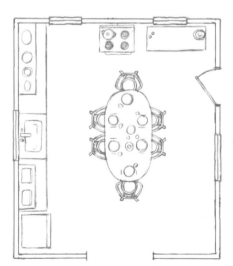

floor plan
Storage and prep areas are kept to a minimum, leaving ample space for a generously sized table ready to accommodate dinner parties, after-school snacking or homework projects. Having no upper cabinets makes this feel like more of a room than just a functional kitchen.

Kitchen of Sharon Simonaire,
interior designer

the style:
industrial glamour

SHINY SURFACES The mirrored backsplash and glossy white epoxy floor are essential elements in this polished, high-end mix. Gleaming stainless appliances and semiopaque glass cabinet faces also help amplify the available light.

LUXE CABINETRY Built with complicated profiles and finished with substantial, handsome hardware, the custom cabinets dress up the laboratory-like features.

MODERN ELEMENTS The stainless-steel table/island, professional stove, seamless floor and recessed counter lighting bring a muscular, utilitarian energy into an otherwise traditional space.

EFFICIENT & AIRY What feels like a large kitchen is actually quite compact. The built-in storage runs all the way to the ceiling and makes use of corners and wall space over doors, while the glass fronts and mirrors lighten the arrangement.

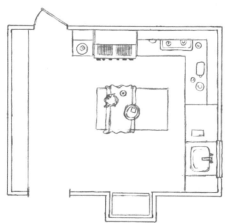

floor plan
Storage is maximized with a solid wall of floor-to-ceiling cabinets (far left) plus two short walls of upper and lower cabinets. The fridge tucks into a nook opposite the stove, freeing up space for the small prep table.

Kitchen designed
by Thomas O'Brien

the big piece: cabinets

UPPER CABINETS

Above-the-counter styles date to the early 20th century. Doors can be solid or have inset panels made of clear, frosted or wavy Restoration Glass (new glass fabricated to look old).

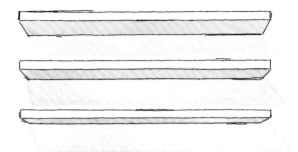

OPEN SHELVES

Light and airy—the lack of upper cabinets makes a kitchen feel more like a room. Great for displaying objects and keeping high-use pieces handy.

STAINLESS STEEL

Industrial appearance can be toned down by a warm countertop like wood. Shows fingerprints and can accumulate scratches over time; a powder-coated paint job can add color and keep fingerprints at bay.

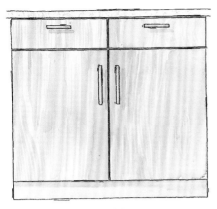

WOOD

Organic and cozy. Best finishes:
a very pale, bleached effect or
a very dark, almost black stain.

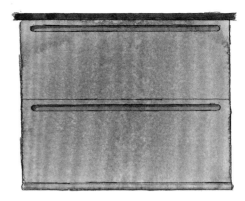

CUSTOMIZABLE MODERN SYSTEM

Sleek and built to function (think Boffi,
Poggenpohl, Alno). The ultimate in organization,
with the feel of a European race car.

LAMINATE

Neat-looking and subtle, which helps play
up hardware, counters and other elements.
Simple enough to look good in a color.

PANELED

Modern simplicity meets old-world
craftsmanship. Best when painted.

INSTANT EXPERT: buying cabinets

STANDARD SIZES
Base cabinets are usually 34½" tall and 24" deep. The width increases in 3" increments. Upper cabinets range in height but are generally 12" deep. Upper cabinets are usually hung 16" to 18" above countertops.

STOCK VS. CUSTOM
In terms of both styles and sizes, off-the-shelf options are limited, but prices are lower and delivery times shorter. Semicustom cabinets offer additional styles, colors and storage features but, like stock, come only in standard-size increments, so you might end up installing filler panels to close gaps between the cabinet and wall. Go custom and you'll have total control over aesthetics, functionality and fit. You can play with counter height, colors, flourishes and profiles and perfectly maximize your kitchen's layout.

CABINETS VS. DRAWERS
Instead of lower cabinets, many people prefer drawers, which provide ready access without digging.

how to mix & match

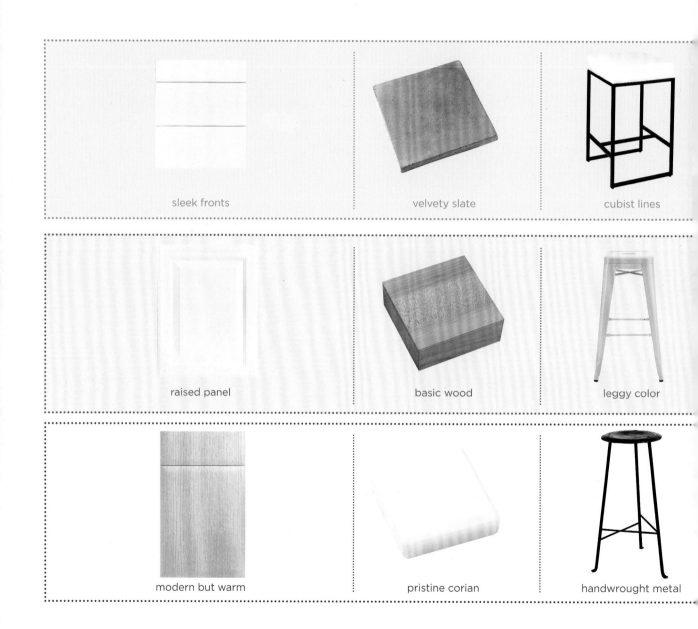

sleek fronts

velvety slate

cubist lines

raised panel

basic wood

leggy color

modern but warm

pristine corian

handwrought metal

utilitarian chic

streamlined stainless

Uniformly minimalist and functional, this setup makes a clear statement of **industrial Euro cool**. Everything is absolutely smooth to the touch, stripped-down and unapologetically high-design.

no-fuss shine

easy-bake cheer

You don't need the whole box of crayons to build a space that's **cute, bright and happy**. A canary-yellow stool and stove have all the electricity required to light up a neutral, can't-go-wrong assemblage of pendant lamps, wood countertops and classic cabinets.

playful baroque

haute-tech oven

Pickled-wood cabinets, spare white countertops and appliances, and a rough-hewn stool set the tone of this **sophisticated Swedish** look. A curvy white-resin chandelier is the un-kitchen-y wild card that keeps it from being too stark.

very important tips

counter/backsplash

WHERE TO START Cabinets set the kitchen's tone, but counters and backsplashes allow you to make the space your own. Be creative but also realistic: Pick a material that suits your life-style. You might love butcher block, but do you have time to keep up the necessary maintenance? Or love marble but will freak out over the inevitable marks?

CLASSIC COUNTER CHOICES The standard is a large slab counter and a backsplash of small tiles. Butcher block is inviting, stainless steel is sleek and marble can swing old-world or modern. Eco-friendly quartz composites, engineered to mimic natural stone, work in a variety of settings.

ONE MATERIAL OR TWO Juxtaposing two materials is more common, but using the same on both surfaces creates a seamless effect. Large, single slabs look cleaner than multiple tiles but are more expensive.

ALTERNATIVE BACKSPLASHES Because backsplashes aren't subject to the same use as countertops, you have some freedom with the materials. Think about installing a sheet of Plexiglas over a favorite wallpaper or using pressed-tin ceiling tiles or mirror.

sinks/faucets

MOUNTING Sinks may be dropped into a countertop (leaving the sink's rim visible) or undermounted (slipped below the counter). Generally, undermount sinks have a sharper look and are easier to keep clean than drop-ins.

STAINLESS VS. PORCELAIN SINK This depends on personal taste, maintenance compulsions (porcelain stains, stainless spots) and a kitchen's style. Stainless feels modern or industrial, while porcelain can read as elegant or country.

SELECTING A FAUCET A modern kitchen calls for a modern faucet (a traditional design would look out of place). In a traditional kitchen, however, you don't have to go fussy Victorian. A more streamlined tap can fit right in. Whatever you choose should be functional and comfortable to handle.

lighting/hardware

LIGHT PLACEMENT Think about how you use the room: You'll probably want more focused illumination for the spaces where you cook, more ambience for dining areas. It's common in kitchens to repeat a light, so go ahead and double or triple up if it suits your purpose.

UNCONVENTIONAL OPTIONS Lights normally found in living or dining rooms can add a lot of character: Consider a chandelier rather than a standard kitchen light. A small table lamp tucked in a corner instantly makes the space more homey.

SIMPLE HARDWARE Handsome pulls and hinges can make a moderately priced kitchen look a lot richer. Avoid gimmicks: Knobs shaped like corn on the cob might seem like a good idea, but these details should complement the kitchen as a whole, rather than call attention to themselves.

FUNCTION Before you buy a piece, hold it: The right hardware is as much about feel as it is about looks. Pulls versus knobs is a matter of personal preference, but for heavily used doors or drawers, pulls are usually the way to go.

floors

INDUSTRIAL Glossy epoxy yields an unbroken surface that can make small spaces seem bigger. Factory-chic concrete is great for those who want something edgier underfoot. Done in bright colors, rubber can be fun and highly functional: cushion-y for the cook, slip-free for the kids.

WARM If you want a softer look, or spend a lot of time on your feet cooking or washing up, think about wood, engineered wood or bamboo. For even more resiliency, try cork. Eco-friendly linoleum now comes in sophisticated colors and is as inexpensive as ever. Graphic patterns like a two-color stripe, a plaid or a dramatic field of all-black are very modern.

decorating tricks

A CONTINUOUS PATTERN across counter and backsplash is graphic and unexpected.

ACRYLIC SHELVING preserves the purity of a colorful wall.

A BUILT-IN DESK in the kitchen is a small indulgence that makes a multitasker's life easier.

BRIGHT, WIDE STRIPES draw attention away from less-than-stellar cabinets and countertops.

APPLIANCES NEED NOT BE ALL STAINLESS—white or colored ones can add a bit of joy to a basic kitchen.

more decorating tricks

COLORFUL, MODERN **CABINETS** are a happy alternative to sleek white designer systems.

VINYL WALLPAPER as backsplash is glamorous, practical and economical too.

A WHOLE WALL OF TILE reads like wallpaper (but it's simpler to clean).

LIVING-ROOM FURNITURE IN THE KITCHEN makes a utilitarian space feel decorated.

HORIZONTAL STRIPES fool the eye—a narrow galley kitchen suddenly looks wider.

small-space solutions

DITCHING THE UPPERS in favor of open shelving lightens the look but still holds everything that a cabinet can.

A WALL-MOUNTED ORGANIZER lets a petite kitchen multitask as office.

MINI APPLIANCES, including a two-burner stove, and a tiny sink make it possible to squeeze a "full" kitchen into a compact corner.

CARVE A BREAKFAST NOOK out of the tightest space using a scaled-down table and stools that tuck underneath.

A READY-MADE, ALL-IN-ONE UNIT—with stovetop, fridge, sink and storage—is ideal for cramped apartments.

tricks for renters

DARK WALLS and a door painted a contrasting color quickly transform even the humblest rental.

SET UP A FULL-TIME BAR in the kitchen if your life-style is more about cocktail hour than dinner parties.

A PLATE RACK is extra kitchen storage you can take with you when you move.

A PRETTY LACE VALANCE gussies up a style-challenged rental kitchen.

TURN A PLAIN-JANE FRIDGE into a garden of flowers with wallpaper (maybe check with your landlord first).

the domino effect

the starting point

"I have a kitchen that doubles as a living room and a dining room. It had to be practical enough for kids, pretty enough for entertaining grown-ups."

SARA RUFFIN COSTELLO
domino *creative director*

my reality: kids

"Even though we're city dwellers, I definitely had the urge to go back to my suburban roots and create a hangout kitchen—one that could meet my kids' needs—homework and projects."

my fantasy: an english conservatory

"I love the whole idea of Cecil Beaton's garden room—a little proper, a little eccentric, with a lot of greenery."

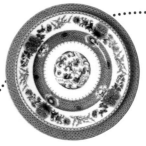

"My blue-and-white wedding china reminded me of Cecil's garden stool and felt like a step in the right direction."

posh bits

"Café au lait paint—elegant as a whippet."

"Without a real dining room, these inherited candlesticks lived in a cabinet. But I pictured them one day as part of a mise-en-scène between plants."

"Since the island is the center of the room, the faucet there needed to be more than just functional. This one has height and elegance."

practical considerations

"Giant drawers with equally substantial hardware give this kitchen lots of storage plus a little drama."

"Upholstery's almost never used on kitchen stools for a good reason. So I was happy to find this Moroccan oilcloth—chic and spillproof."

"I've had this classic table in every one of my apartments. It's small enough to fit in the kitchen, but you can squeeze in six people."

simple shapes

"I wanted houseplants that have great forms, and an oversize topiary was the obvious place to begin."

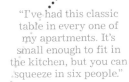

"This burlap-covered Louis settee was a major score—perfectly diminutive and actually comfortable."

my kitchen

"It's actually a high-functioning studio apartment—everything from taxes to massively messy art projects to dinner parties happens here."

—SARA RUFFIN COSTELLO

CHAPTER SIX

the bedroom

the style:
romantic modernist

SPARKLY NEUTRAL PALETTE Soft "greige" walls, a milky canopy and shiny metallic accessories create a peaceful space that's cool and refined. Silver and cream go together like pieces in a formal place setting.

PAINT   BED CURTAINS   SHEETS   BLANKET

SLEEK COCOON The long drapes, which break gently on the floor and stretch all the way to the ceiling, feel structural and columnlike. The bed is warm and inviting, yet sparely made with Euro shams, standard pillows and a tucked-in quilt—nothing frilly.

SIMPLE SHAPES, SUPPLE TEXTURES The bedside tables, lamps and frames share a clean-lined aesthetic that's tempered by sensuous materials (wood, glass, silver). The same idea is at play on the bed, where sateen sheets balance out the heavy-duty linen bed skirt and drapes. A small chintz pillow offers the room's single moment of pattern.

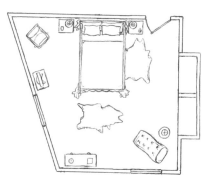

floor plan
The queen bed flanked by bedside tables is oriented to have prime views of the windows. A nearby chair makes the most of a tight angle. In the opposite corner, a chaise and a floor lamp form a reading nook.

Bedroom of Dara
Caponigro, domino
style director

the style:
sweet
asceticism

SIMPLEST PINK, OTHERWISE WHITE This super-minimal scheme plays the sugariness of pale pink off the coolness of white to create an oasis of calm. The white also functions as a border, emphasizing the geometry of the space.

WALLS   WALLS   COVER

SPARENESS BEGETS SERENITY The furnishings are spartan and the walls bare, which encourages an instant melting away of mental clutter. Unembellished bed linens, angular table lamps and white wood blinds are clean and streamlined, and the glossy painted floors reflect light.

FLOATING FURNITURE With a raised platform bed and leggy side tables, everything is off the ground and airy-feeling.

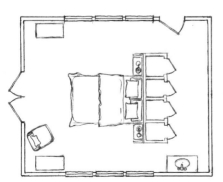

floor plan
The bed tucks into a freestanding alcove wall, which serves as a headboard and separates the sleeping area from the bathroom—a sink plus four closets (that house a toilet, a shower, clothes and linens).

Bedroom of Camilla and
Benjamin Trigano, *marketing
director and gallery owner*

the style:
sophisticated froufrou

RICH FABRICS With its cranberry-red flowers and black branches, the curtain print is a spunky take on regal chinoiserie. Pea-soup-green velvet makes the formal, tufted headboard feel even more luxurious.

CURTAINS HEADBOARD BEDDING

BLACK TONES DOWN THE GIRLINESS A dark ceiling delivers high drama and guarantees that even with all the ruffles and flowers, the room isn't stereotypically feminine.

SERIOUS WITH FLIRTY DETAILS The classic, tidy bedmaking is tempered by an unexpected mix of styles—tailored hotel borders with scalloped matelassé. Abundant wraparound curtains and a valance are fairly proper, but funny flea-market lamps and mismatched bedside tables lighten the mood and keep the look young.

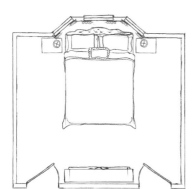

floor plan
Bay windows can be a challenge, but here they're used to great advantage as a framing device, cradling the bed. A large armoire, fit snugly between the doors, offers ample storage.

Bedroom of Chloe Warner,
interior decorator

the style:
masculine bohemian

STRONG COLORS AND PATTERNS Confident dark stripes appear in varied scales—from the broad-banded area rug to the narrow-striped duvet—and ground the room's theatricality with a bit of New England prep. Rich-brown walls provide a warm, enveloping backdrop.

RUG   CHAIRS   CHAIR   WALLS

NEW MIXED WITH OLD A mélange of antique pieces—a grisaille screen, unique bedside tables and lamps, and a knobby chair—soften a very modern steel bed. Coordinated lamp shades and simple curtains keep a lid on the eccentricity.

UNUSUAL ACCESSORIES There aren't a lot of accent pieces here, but all of them are out of the ordinary, including the ornate and shell-encrusted lamps, the screen and the uplit figure of St. John the Baptist.

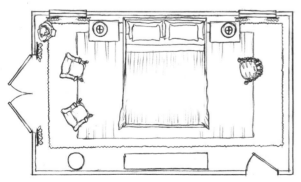

floor plan
This bedroom is an inviting hangout spot, thanks to three occasional chairs oriented around the bed as if it were a sofa. Layered rugs enhance the cocoon-y feel of the large four-poster bed.

Bedroom of Johnson Hartig,
fashion designer

the big piece: beds

MODERN PLATFORM
*Low, minimalist, masculine.
Substantial but works well in small
spaces because it has no footboard.*

IRON CANOPY
*Style dates back to 18th-century France. Feminine,
grand. Floats nicely in the middle of a room.
With a canopy of fabric, it's even more romantic;
bare, it's architectural.*

FOUR-POSTER
*This form dates to the 15th century, but there
are very modern options. Tall and commanding,
it can make ceilings seem higher.*

UPHOLSTERED

Glamorous and luxurious, yet handsome. The padded back is comfortable for reading in bed. Nail-head trim and piping can be used to accentuate the shape.

BAROQUE

Style dates back to 17th-century Europe. Intricately carved wood headboard. Opulent and majestic. Consider keeping other furnishings spare and modern.

SLEIGH

Wood versions hail back to the Roman Empire. Contemporary upholstered ones are more comfortable.

COUNTRY SWEDISH

Delicate but unpretentious. Straight or curved high head- and footboards, with panels sometimes upholstered or caned.

INSTANT EXPERT: buying a mattress

STUFFING Traditional innerspring mattresses are made of steel coils topped by padding (usually foam, felt and polyester or cotton fibers) and wrapped in a fabric cover. Eco-friendly options include those made of untreated, organic cotton; chemical-free wool; or natural latex (as opposed to the synthetic variety).

COMFORT TESTING Spend plenty of time reclining on the models you like. That blissful first impression can be deceiving. Pillow tops, aka the final layer of padding, come in many thicknesses, and stores' floor models tend to sport the thickest version. If you prefer something firmer, ask to test other options.

CHECK THE COIL COUNT This refers to the number of springs inside—the higher, the better. But a coil count tops out at about 400 for a queen—beyond that, you'll unlikely feel a difference. **BTW:** This is a moot point for latex mattresses, which are coil-free.

BOX SPRING You may not need one. A bed frame that has a base to support a mattress (slats, for instance) can usually do without. But if you like to climb into bed, literally, a box spring can give you that extra height.

how to mix & match

tufted elegance

carved stand

crisp bedding

tropical four-poster

featherweight polish

cheery coverlet

solid foundation

boxy accents

ethnic texture

why these pieces work together

timeless anchor

blue dazzle

Classics get a modern jolt from an azure chandelier. The dark Biedermeier chest adds gravitas to all the neat white elements.

weathered warmth

ruggedly nautical

United by a light and airy aesthetic, everything from the rope-wrapped lamp to the cotton batik coverlet has a **casual, by-the-sea feel**. A whitewash finish ties the dresser to the rest of the group.

linear statement

clean orb

A Native American–inspired blanket brings fresh color and a handcrafted quality to a **quiet, handsome and angular** collection of textured woods and shell-topped tables. The round chrome pendant breaks up the geometry.

very important tips

bedside tables

DIMENSIONS As a general rule, the table should be about the same height as the mattress. Deep tables (anything beyond 24") make it difficult to get in and out of bed.

COMPOSITION The simplest thing is to top matching tables with matching lamps. But tables and lamps certainly don't have to be in matching pairs. If you vary one of the tables, for instance, use two of the same lamp or vice versa.

STORAGE Most people like to have drawers or shelves, but minimalist types can use any beautiful table. If you fall in love with a table that doesn't have a drawer, tuck a smaller table or stool underneath as a place to stow books or a phone.

LIGHTING Install a dimmer switch if you can. If your lamp has two bulbs and no dimmer switch, using two different-wattage bulbs lets you control the mood: 40 watts for ambience and 60 to 75 watts for reading. Non-opaque shades are ideal for reading. If space is at a premium, consider installing sconces.

window treatments

INFORMAL VS. FORMAL Generally speaking, shades are casual and curtains formal, but both options can swing either way: You can dress up a shade by using a more formal fabric (above) or dress down a drape with a casual one. Because they require less fabric, shades are usually cheaper.

PATTERN AND COLOR Bedrooms tend to be more matchy and romantic than other rooms, so you can go as far as you want in coordinating your window treatments with other components in the room. Coordinate them with your wallpaper, chairs and/or bed skirt—the more pieces you include, the more "done" the room will appear. As an alternative, you can simply pick up on the room's colors, as in the photo above.

BLACKOUT Both shades and curtains can be lined with blackout fabric to block light. Hang blackout shades behind curtains for maximum darkness.

MOUNTS For shades, inside mounts (above) fit inside the window frame; outside mounts run from outside edge to outside edge of the frame (see photos to the left and right) and can make the window look bigger. Curtains, however, are almost always mounted outside the window frame.

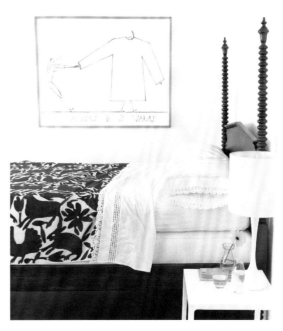

rugs

AREA RUGS A large rug can unify a room, but in order to maximize its impact, it needs to be big enough not to disappear when topped by a bed. In an ideal world, the bed is either entirely off or on the rug, but as long as about three-quarters of the rug is under the bed, it's okay.

THROW RUGS Helpful in dividing the room into zones, a small rug and a bench at the foot of the bed can demarcate a seating area. Placed on each side of the bed, a throw rug in a soft material makes a luxurious landing pad (above). To add more texture, layer smaller rugs over larger area rugs.

WALL-TO-WALL Because it's the place you're most likely to be barefoot and least likely to spill food, the bedroom is ideal for allover carpeting. Natural fibers like wool are always a good bet.

bedding

SHEETS Natural materials like cotton and linen feel best and, if of high quality, age beautifully. How to choose? Feel before you buy. Thread counts are not the be-all and end-all. Some manufacturers count the thin strands that make up a thread, which can triple or even quadruple the final score.

MIXING AND MATCHING SHEETS The easiest way to combine different patterns is to make sure they share the same background color (such as white or ivory).

BEYOND STANDARD PILLOWS Built for looks rather than sleeping, square Euro shams (24") are also fine props for reading; a petite boudoir pillow is a sweet finishing touch. If you have a king-size bed, be sure to use king-size pillows to fill the bed's whole width.

BED SKIRTS Ready-mades usually come in three styles: kick pleat, box pleat and ruffle. When buying, make sure to get the correct length by measuring from the top of the box spring to the floor—a too-long skirt looks sloppy and too short looks silly. A custom version can pull together a room when the bed skirt is done in a fabric used elsewhere in the room. Lining makes it look more substantial, and prewashing the fabric before it's sewn prevents future shrinkage.

decorating tricks

UPHOLSTERED WALLS
imbue a bedroom with warmth
and coziness.

A DIY CANOPY is a low-cost and easy alternative to a proper four-poster.

ONE COLORFUL CHANDELIER can carry a neutral room.

A DESK CAN DOUBLE AS A BEDSIDE TABLE—it's often the same height as the average bed.

A SOLID CANVAS ABOVE THE BED is a graphic substitute for a headboard.

more decorating tricks

GRIDDED FAMILY PHOTOS make a striking installation. The frames are duct-taped together at the back and hung as a unit.

FRAMED WALLPAPER takes up little space and is far less expensive than a full-fledged headboard.

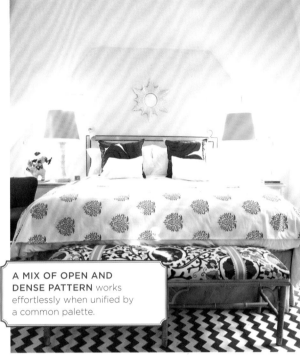

A MIX OF OPEN AND DENSE PATTERN works effortlessly when unified by a common palette.

BRIGHT COLOR can transform a featureless room into something exciting.

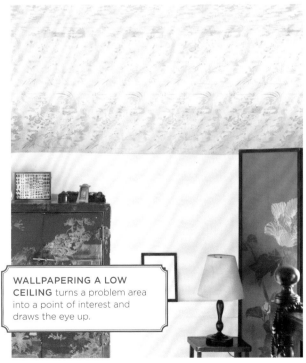

WALLPAPERING A LOW CEILING turns a problem area into a point of interest and draws the eye up.

small-space solutions

CREATE TWO ZONES in one room, with a love seat as the bridge.

BOLD CURTAINS are a space-saving alternative to bi-fold closet doors.

FLOAT A SHELF above the bed if there's no room for a proper bedside table.

A SHADE AND CURTAINS CONCEAL STORAGE and form a sweet nook for sleeping.

EXUBERANT COLORS in high-gloss convert a big closet into a bedroom.

making the bed

A BEAUTIFUL TEXTILE AS COVERLET is charming and bohemian—just pull it up to the headboard and add a few pillows in different patterns that share a hue (here, red).

COORDINATING THE COVERLET AND SHAMS is a no-fuss formula. A vivid blanket and throw pillow keep it from being boring.

THIS SUPER-FANCY ARRANGEMENT featuring eight flanged pillows and matching sheets requires a hot iron and a lot of starch. To balance the pillow madness: a matching duvet neatly folded at the foot.

FOR THIS NO-MAINTENANCE MOD setup, fluff the duvet (you don't even need a top sheet—that's how the Europeans do it), crown with two bright throw pillows and go.

THE RECIPE FOR A WELL-MADE (AND REALISTIC) BED: sheets, pillowcases, tucked-in coverlet, folded blanket and one throw pillow. Nothing more, nothing less.

the domino effect

the starting point

"I had to decorate my bedroom from scratch on a seriously tight budget and didn't want to waste money buying lots of cheap things."

KIRSTEN HILGENDORF
domino *graphic designer*

"A shag rug channels that mod thing and is cozy with the low bed."

"I like the lounge-y feel of a mattress on the floor—and the money I didn't spend on a bed frame went to other things."

the main elements

"Bright paint is such an inexpensive way to transform a room. This shade has some drama, but it's also pop-y and cheerful."

my inspiration

"I'm a '60s modern girl, in fashion and decor. I've always been a fan of Rudi Gernreich's bold, minimalist designs, especially on model and muse Peggy Moffitt."

graphic notes

"I wanted artwork that would really stand out against the yellow walls."

"The chandelier silk screen is a leftover from a college art class."

"Instead of buying expensive throw pillows, I decided to make one!"

finishing details

"I try to keep my bedside tables very organized, and these bowls help. The teacup was only $1 because it was chipped."

"A pair of vintage '70s side tables cost me $20. I love how they're just simple white boxes—and the perfect height for my low bed."

"A Jonathan Adler lamp I liked was way out of my price range—I found this one at West Elm."

big-ticket items

"I've always coveted these mid-century classics. I bought them used on eBay."

"I splurged on the white TV—we featured it in *domino*, and everyone on staff wanted one."

my bedroom

"This room is totally easygoing. It's about kicking back, listening to records and waking up to sunshine (even on a cloudy day)."
—KIRSTEN HILGENDORF

CHAPTER SEVEN

the bathroom

the style:
rustic zen

MOODY PALETTE Deep, sumptuous blacks (on the walls, window shade and tub exterior) give this bathroom its edge. In contrast, the porcelain tub interior has an almost celestial brilliance.

WARM TEXTURES Brass fittings, an earthy plaster wall and an amber glass pendant add depth and sheen to the somber elements. The herringbone wood floor has a worn, imperfect quality that imbues the space with a certain European character.

SCULPTURAL ELEMENTS The components are minimal—only a claw-foot tub, an exposed shower pipe, a pendant and a towel rack—but set in isolation, each feels architectural and luxurious.

OPEN LAYOUT The bathroom flows into the bedroom, evoking a seductive antechamber. A rich oriental rug hovering at the threshold adds to the roomlike atmosphere. With the toilet separate and hidden behind doors, this is a true retreat.

Bathroom of Jenna Lyons
Mazeau and Vincent Mazeau,
creative director and artist

the style:
girly drama

CONFECTIONERY FLOURISHES This scheme defies
the unremarkable bones of the space by establishing a visual identity
with color and pattern. The pink is unabashedly feminine, but using
it in two very different scales—wide painted stripes and a small zigzag
shower curtain—lends it sophistication.

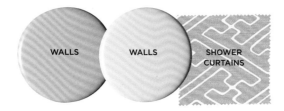

WALLS · WALLS · SHOWER CURTAINS

A BIT OF THEATER Bold stripes converge on the ceiling,
forming a trompe l'oeil circus tent. The shower curtains, treated like
fancy drapes (complete with tiebacks), heighten the ta-da effect; the
tub becomes a stage. A vintage chandelier introduces a curlicue shape
to counter all the strong lines.

DRESSY DETAILS Clever little touches—from whimsical
drawer pulls that revitalize basic white cabinets to a pretty blue tray
for perfumes—complete the transformation from blah and boring
to glamorous.

Bathroom of Krista Ewart,
interior decorator

the style:
hotel luxe

CLEAN, OPULENT SURFACES Marble, marble everywhere—on the floor, surrounding the tub, even traveling up the wall—conjures a posh English estate. Mirrors inset into the molding create the illusion of an even grander space. Classic fittings like the nickel-and-porcelain, telephone-style bath fixture enhance the old-world feel.

REAL FURNITURE An antique bureau, a stately lamp and a suede-and-brass stool (no white laminate here) are lavish yet bring warmth and character to the room.

SPA HERE, STUFF THERE One side of the room remains hotel-like and pristine, with the marble-framed tub, simple white towels and uncluttered planes. Personal tchotchkes and toiletries stay on the bureau side.

Bathroom of Allison Sarofim,
domino contributing editor

the big piece: sinks

WASHSTAND

*Old-world styling is graceful
and light. A large flat top
(typically marble) holds
essentials, and a crossbar hangs
towels. Visible plumbing. Legs
come in glass, acrylic or metal.*

PEDESTAL

*Comes in traditional, modern and
Art Deco versions. Simple base
hides plumbing and takes up little
floor space. Top can be flat, which
will hold a few items.*

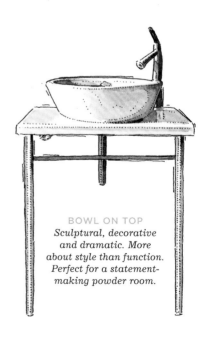

BOWL ON TOP

*Sculptural, decorative
and dramatic. More
about style than function.
Perfect for a statement-
making powder room.*

WALL MOUNT

This legless option keeps the floor clear.
Available in various styles and shapes, including
corner options great for tiny spaces.

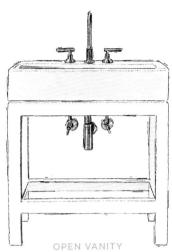

OPEN VANITY

Has a lighter appearance than a
closed unit. A single shelf offers a
place to stack towels or hold
a basket. The large basin is part
of the piece's architecture.

VANITY

Ample storage below and on top. Works
well in two-sink versions.
With legs, feels more like a piece of furniture.

CONSOLE

Made entirely of porcelain,
from legs to backsplash, this
romantic piece feels right for an
old house. A nice option in the
double-sink version.

INSTANT EXPERT: buying a faucet

STICK WITH ONE LOOK
Pick a faucet that's in keeping with the style of your sink. This is not a place to experiment (e.g., putting a modern tap on a vintage-style sink).

MATERIALS
Good for modern baths, chrome is the cheapest option; nickel is warmer and pricier and works in modern or traditional settings. Unlacquered brass, especially "dirty brass," has an appealing patina.

FINISHES
You can't go wrong with bright and sparkly polished hardware on a modern sink. A brushed finish hides water stains but is more expensive.

ONE PIECE OR THREE
A "single-hole" faucet is all one piece—with handles and spout connected. "Center-set" faucets unite handles and spout on a 4" base. A "widespread" is three components—spout plus two handles. Check your sink's spread (the distance from center to center of the outer holes) before you buy.

how to mix & match

chunky silhouette

fanciful floral

basic profile

old-school washstand

luxe marble

lavishly plated

minimal chic

ethnic drama

barely there mirror

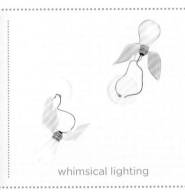

whimsical lighting

subtle stripes

Cheery and European in feel, this **playfully modern** group uses a straightforward, substantial sink and mirror to balance out look-at-me tiles and sconces. The Turkish fringed towel lends sophistication to the spirited theme.

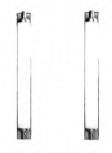

deco forms

four-star plushness

Elevated versions of standard-issue bathroom furnishings, these picks have a **classic 1930s handsomeness**. The medicine chest and lights are sheathed in polished nickel, and the subway tile isn't the usual suspect—it's high-end Carrara marble. Edged in charcoal, the towels are simple and tailored.

ladylike contours

statement pattern

In this casual, **Moorish-goes-mod** setup, the spareness of the vanity and mirror doesn't compete with the headliners: Moroccan tiles, a shower curtain with an exotic motif and a pair of elegant sconces. As clean-lined as the mirror they flank, tall lamp shades warm up the room.

very important tips

fixtures & fittings

CHOOSING TUBS Depending on how much space you have, the layout of your bathroom and your style preferences, you can get a drop-in model (usually sunk into a platform), a corner unit that attaches to the wall or a freestanding one (these come in an array of styles besides claw foot, including many very modern ones, like the one above). Regardless of the model's shape or style, look for a tub that goes with your sink and toilet. A practical note: Freestanding tubs are romantic, but this old-fashioned design has old-fashioned limitations—namely, no supereasy way to include a shower (think wraparound curtain sticking to your legs).

TOILETS This is a good place to go the classic route. Toilets should also coordinate with your tub and sink. Seek out low-flow options that conserve water.

TOWEL BARS AND SHOWER RODS Typically bought as a suite, these fittings function best as a cohesive unit. Don't forget about hooks, which are useful, friendly and great for any and all towels.

lighting & mirrors

LIGHTING A combination of sources affords the most flexibility. Using a chandelier or sconces typically found in a dining room, or a table lamp that could be at home in a living room, is a great way to bring style to the bathroom and connect it to the rest of the house. Try a dimmer switch to tone down the glare during evening soaks in the tub.

SCONCES Sconces placed on either side of the mirror tend to cast flattering light, but one sconce over the mirror provides more focused illumination. To be safe, match finishes to the rest of your bathroom hardware.

MIRRORS AND MEDICINE CHESTS In a small bathroom, medicine chests are often a storage necessity. There are recessed and nonrecessed versions; the former is usually preferable because it's less intrusive, but it's more complicated to install. If you don't need the storage, a framed mirror adds a nice decorating note and feels less utilitarian than a medicine chest; in a powder room, a mirror is the natural choice.

floors & walls

MIXING MATERIALS Using one material from floor to ceiling (as above) creates a continuous, sleek skin that's more modern. Having two materials draws attention to the room's planes. Note that if you combine different types of tile, it's best to vary the scale.

FLOORING OPTIONS Matte tiles are less slippery than shiny ones. A wood floor is common in old houses and can look very handsome but does best when sealed. Marble can be luxurious—the bigger the slab, the fancier the effect and the more expensive. Bamboo is au courant and eco-friendly.

WALLPAPER This is an excellent way to usher in personality and color. It does well in powder rooms or guest bathrooms, where it won't be subject to a lot of moisture.

accessories

SHOWER CURTAINS The bathroom's major style statement can, of course, be bought ready-made, but if you don't find one to your liking or your tub doesn't accommodate a standard length (72" x 72"), go custom. Select an outdoor fabric and you can forgo a liner. Rings shouldn't be an afterthought—the right set is a nice finishing touch.

FURNITURE Whether you use it to hold a stack of towels, help you through your beauty routine or provide seating for someone to chat with during a bath, a small chair or stool is inviting (especially with terry-cloth upholstery).

decorating tricks

AN **ORNATE MIRROR** injects personality into a super-modern interior.

A PAINTED FAUX TENT turns a boxy bathroom into a graphic alternate reality.

SHIMMERING ELEMENTS like pearlescent tile reflect so much sun, you can leave off the lights.

LIVING-ROOM-STYLE CURTAINS in the shower are an elegant surprise. A curtain track (instead of a rod) heightens the effect.

A HAND-PAINTED MOTIF can have the drama of patterned wallpaper (without the risk of mold and peeling).

more decorating tricks

OUTFIT YOUR BATH WITH REAL FURNITURE (if you have the space)—think beyond terry cloth and chrome legs.

LINING A WHOLE ROOM WITH SMALL TILES makes surfaces seem almost reptilian.

A FREESTANDING TUB gives even the most modern bathroom a romantic edge.

A GLASS WALL, instead of a shower curtain, allows the room to feel as airy as possible.

WILD WALLPAPER in a powder room is a trippy surprise.

finishing touches

SIDE TABLES—like these water-resistant cork ones—can be both functional and beautiful under a sink or beside a tub.

CASUAL SNAPSHOTS AND POSTCARDS make a fun substitute for wallpaper.

MATCHING BASKETS that fit your shelves perfectly keep things artfully tidy.

A POTTED FERN thrives in the bathroom (it loves moisture!) and softens a stark space.

DRESS UP YOUR BATHROOM with the good stuff, like a collection of blue-and-white porcelain.

the domino effect

the starting point

"My house came with a small, ugly bathroom that was crying out for a gut renovation. I wanted to keep it low-cost and DIY."

CHASE BOOTH
domino *set producer*

"Finding this was a wonderful surprise. It let the outside in, and I just followed that lead, going organic and green wherever possible."

bringing in nature

"Like the ground outside, only richer."

"The fern is so happy in here because of the steam."

before the renovation

"This bathroom was a disaster, so I began by tearing everything out. I was a novice but knew I wanted simple materials—nothing ostentatious. When I tore down the vinyl-covered walls, I uncovered my real decorating inspiration—a huge hidden double window."

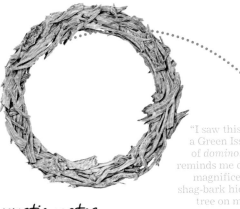

rustic notes

"I saw this in a Green Issue of *domino*. It reminds me of this magnificent shag-bark hickory tree on my property."

"A hand-carved teak stool where I put my glass of wine, my candle and my book—comfort central."

classic elements

"The sink was rescued from a Fifth Avenue renovation—it would have been trashed."

"Subway and penny tile—clean, neutral and timeless."

"I'm not a big fan of curtain rods. With a track on the ceiling, the hardware just disappears. I made a linen curtain that goes all the way to the floor, and the result is really dramatic."

finishing touches

"A beautiful contrast with the brown on the walls—fresh and kind of delightful."

"An Edison bulb on this industrial fixture throws off the most flattering, warm yellow light."

my bathroom

"It's like being in a serene grotto, with the earthy walls, the gentle breeze and the fern overhead."

—CHASE BOOTH

CHAPTER EIGHT

the office

the style:
rich & handsome

WARM TEXTURES All of the surfaces are covered, from the sea-grass walls to the dark trellis-chain-link rug, providing a luxurious, tactile enclosure for layers of books, furnishings and objets.

WALLS · RUG · SHADES · CHAIR · CHAIR

UNIFIED PALETTE A disciplined color scheme dominated by browns can support a few contrasting patterns without looking off-kilter. The prints on the rug, chair and window shades offer graphic drama that accentuates the sumptuous beauty.

STORAGE AS DISPLAY Reproductions of Anglo-Indian bookshelves hold a well-considered collection of books and small-scale art. The careful placement of stacks alongside portraits and ephemera creates an intriguing yet ordered tableau.

UNCONVENTIONAL FURNITURE A shapely chair upholstered in suede and another wearing a tiger print provide major impact not usually seen in an office.

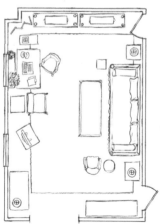

floor plan
Formerly a spare bedroom, this large study has an open, hospitable feeling, thanks to a living-room-like seating area. Freestanding bookcases on both ends of the room are a low-commitment alternative to built-ins in this rental apartment.

Office of Markham Roberts,
interior decorator

the style:
functional chic

RECASTING A PLAIN SPACE This room started life as a garage (a shed or attic would fit the bill too) and was reinvented with a wash of white, on everything from the floors to the shelves. Floor-to-ceiling doors let in plenty of light and foster an indoor-outdoor ease.

OPEN ORGANIZATION Though the all-white scheme communicates a crisp vision, the room also has a no-nonsense utility. The glossy file cabinet is in full view, and one wall is completely given over to shelving. Inexpensive uniform storage boxes impart a tidy look to the shelves, despite being chockful of supplies.

CHROMATIC UNITY The envelope of bright white creates a fresh, motivating background, underscored by the super-polished and painted cement floor. Pops of red—in storage boxes and throw pillows—bring contrast into the one-color space.

SOFT TOUCHES A large, slightly wild plant in one corner adds a natural element to a room that could otherwise feel cold. Likewise, the antique desk, painted white with a cut-to-fit glass top, infuses a personal and pretty aura. The simple sofa and glass coffee table make for an inviting seating area, while the pillows and throw help soften a highly utilitarian space.

floor plan
This is a seriously high-function layout, ideal for someone who likes to move around while working. The desk nestles in one corner, while the sofa and coffee table on the opposite side provide a place to relax— or just get a new perspective. The room-width open shelving is super-accessible.

Office of Kelly
Rutherford, actor

the style:
hollywood glamour

PASTELS WITH DRAMA Pale blue on one wall and the floor seems more Tiffany than baby-boy here because of the luxe furnishings. White tones it down, accentuates the architecture and brightens the room. Black frames cut the palette's sweetness.

FEMININE FURNITURE There's nothing high-tech or work-y in here. A Chippendale desk chair and a pair of velvet club chairs read more like something from the living room. A glass-top desk with no drawers could be a dining-room table. Pagoda shades on the lamps are romantic and bedroom-y, as is the silk rug.

MAXIMALISM REINED IN WITH SYMMETRY Even though the desk is packed with fancy objects and the walls with pictures and swatches, the room feels calm, thanks to the placement of the lamps and the club chairs. A bit of structure gives license to go a little wild in the details.

ART THAT SIGNALS ELEGANCE A wall of iconic imagery— mostly pages torn from books—makes a graphic composition. The floral mural behind gives the nook a subtle depth.

floor plan
The large desk, with chair facing outward into the room, dominates the space—and makes clear who's boss. Two large upholstered chairs echo the lamps and balance the slighter desk chair. The file cabinet is tucked discreetly into a small nook opposite the sofa.

Office of Mary McDonald,
Interior designer

the big piece: desks

CAMPAIGN

First used by British army officers in need of portable pieces. Has a sturdy, masculine appeal and a large work surface.

CUBBY

Streamlined version of a conventional model with drawers. George Nelson's mid-century classic is shown here, but more traditional styles are available. Lean and airy.

SECRETARY

Tall cabinet with fold-down desktop dates to the early 18th century. Its verticality makes it practical for a small room.

CLASSIC WITH DRAWERS

*Symmetrical kneehole style dates back to the
reign of Louis XIV. Serious workhorse
with lots of storage, but can be decorative.*

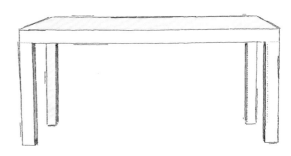

PARSONS

*Versatile 1930s icon—width of
the legs equals thickness of the top.
Crisp, clean, modern.*

TRADITIONAL

*Reminiscent of an 18th-century English
sideboard. Leggy and feminine with a rounded
opening. Pretty enough for any room.*

DINING TABLE

*Unconventional yet still functional.
Can float in the room.*

FILE CABINETS + TOP

*No frills and totally utilitarian.
Cute-ify with colorful
cabinets and a nice surface.*

INSTANT EXPERT:
buying a desk

THE RIGHT PIECE Your desk might live in
a dedicated office space, or it might have
to double as your dining table. Consider the
room it will be in when choosing a style. If it
will go in your bedroom, a guest room or the
living room, select a piece that is suited to
those rooms, doesn't seem too office-y and
will look good when not in use.

how to mix & match

prim and leggy

luxe neutral

artful refinement

sleek metal

kelly green

a fancy foil

simple lines

schoolhouse chic

industrial strength

delicate brass

lighthearted monogram

These subtly feminine and formal elements look like they belong to an **uptown lady decorator**. The antique-y wood desk sets the tone, while a circle-back seat in a lighter finish and a sculptural lamp soften the stateliness. The neutral palette keeps the genteel style quietly understated.

crisp piping

traditional stamp

The contrasting palette of white, green and black unifies designs inspired by different eras, with an overall **clean and preppy** effect. The modern desk and utilitarian Eames chair make the elaborate repro French *bouillote* lamp an elegant surprise.

delicate rusticity

organic pattern

The mid-century Jean Prouvé chair epitomizes the **warm yet cool** look created by a French workshop lamp, woven storage baskets and floral stationery, with a sharp white secretary as backdrop.

very important tips

chairs

FORM + FUNCTION If you use your home office full-time, find a chair that provides support and style. A modern ergonomic chair can be chic in a traditionally furnished space—think antique desk paired with Aeron chair. The opposite can be true too.

SMOOTH SITTING Casters on office chairs are great, but make sure they're given an even plane to roll across.

lighting

FORM + FUNCTION No need to stress about matching eras with the rest of the room. A modern task lamp looks surprisingly good in a traditional setting. Decorative lamps may be lovely, but they generally don't offer enough focused light to be the sole source for this utilitarian environment.

BULBS Good lighting is key here. CFLs (compact fluorescent lights), though a great energy-saving alternative to incandescents, may not be intense enough for your work space. LEDs (light-emitting diodes) are a better fit for the office. These energy-efficient bulbs are extremely bright and long-lasting.

storage/tech support

FILE CABINETS They don't have to be ugly! In a vibrant color (like the green above) or metallic (far left), cabinets can be a happy decor element. Lateral cabinets are generally more stable than vertical ones (check that the unit is counterweighted so it doesn't topple when open and full), and they supply an extra work surface. If you prefer your files out of sight, hide them in a closet or under a skirted table.

WIRE MANAGEMENT Until the day tech goes completely wireless, the best we can do is keep cords as orderly as possible. A cord organizer will help avoid the big tangle. Also, if you use a desktop computer, position the desk against the wall to hide wires. A laptop offers the freedom to float the desk elsewhere in the room.

accessories

KITTING IT OUT WITH PANACHE To put the finishing touches on your office, be thoughtful down to the last accessory. Beauty counts. Go for some form of unity by limiting your choices to a basic palette and/or style—all pop color, say, or all earthy modern.

THE CHECKLIST A place for everything allows everything to return to its place. And having supplies you need at hand ensures no scrambling around searching for tape or a pen.

☐ storage baskets/ boxes

☐ organizing trays

☐ wastepaper basket

☐ pens, pencils & cup

☐ clock

☐ stapler, tape dispenser & scissors

☐ paper clips & holder

☐ mouse pad

☐ bulletin board & pushpins

decorating tricks

FRAMING A DESK with a whimsical canopy and curtains makes finances a little more fun.

A DESK PLACED IN FRONT OF A BOOKCASE can work when wall space isn't available.

DISGUISING A FILE CABINET with "chinoiserie" (really just vintage fabric enlarged on a photocopier) is a quirky reinvention of a decorator favorite.

AN EMBELLISHED CLOTH SKIRT attached with Velcro provides easy access to high (but hidden) tech.

RIG UP A DESK with filing cabinets and a laminate top—the all-white scheme keeps it from looking like a DIY project.

OFFICE IDEAS TO STEAL

more decorating tricks

SCULPTURAL STOOLS AND
BENCHES are attractive mini
workstations.

A LUSH WALLPAPER is an antidote to an antiseptic office.

FROUFROU CHAIRS are a surprising pairing with an industrial table.

AN EXTRA-LONG DESK mounted on the wall accommodates more than one person in slim confines.

BACK-TO-BACK TABLES make an impromptu partners desk in a space that needs to fit two.

small-space solutions

NO ROOM FOR AN OFFICE?
Try a table behind the sofa or somewhere in the living room.

FOR LIKE EVER

USE NEGLECTED AREAS—a secretary and a shelf carve out a work nook under the stairs.

FLOOR SPACE IS OVERRATED! A desk, a chair, bookshelves and a daybed all fit in this tiny room, which can double as guest quarters.

A SECRETARY DESK easily hides its official duties (just flip up the "Murphy" tabletop) and reads as pretty furniture.

TURN A CLOSET INTO A SECRET WORK ZONE with a makeshift desk plus a shelf for storage. Close the doors after 5 P.M.

finishing touches

ART BELONGS IN THE
OFFICE TOO—layer it and hang
it for an energetic composition.

A PERSONAL ASSORTMENT of accessories adds a little joy to paying bills.

COLOR-CODED BINDERS lend cohesiveness to storage space.

GLAMOUR IS IN THE DETAILS—uniformly polished desk accessories telegraph "I've got it together."

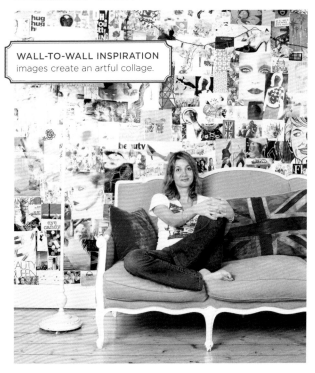

WALL-TO-WALL INSPIRATION images create an artful collage.

the domino effect

the starting point

"We had a spare room in our new apartment—finally. I wanted to make it into a personal haven that felt like another realm from the sunny apartment I share with my husband and kids."

DARA CAPONIGRO
domino *style director*

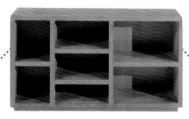

existing furniture

"When we moved in, I had six of these bookcases. I decided to stack them as a group, so the room would feel more like a library than an office. To fill the wall, I ordered three more. This desk had been my bedside table, but now that I had extra space, it became my desk."

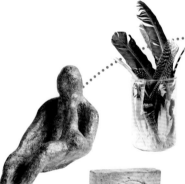

"The objects I love most have some kind of meaning to me—either a friend designed them or they came from a trip and have a memory attached. I collected these feathers when I was little."

"A sculpture made by my mother."

sentimental pieces

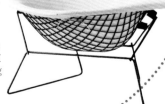

"This was our living-room chair from the '60s. Having grown up in a modernist house, I always need something modern in a room."

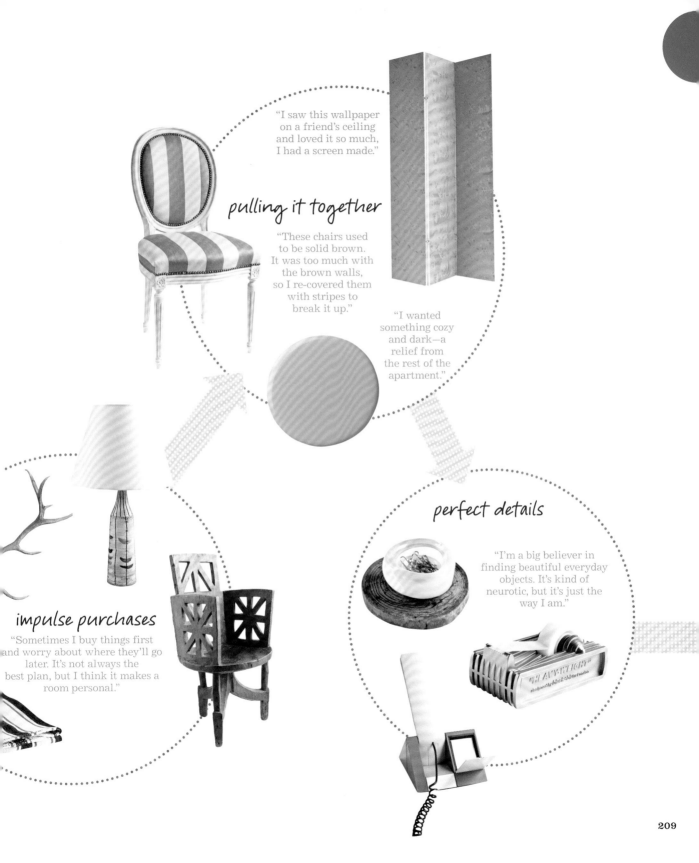

"I saw this wallpaper on a friend's ceiling and loved it so much, I had a screen made."

pulling it together

"These chairs used to be solid brown. It was too much with the brown walls, so I re-covered them with stripes to break it up."

"I wanted something cozy and dark—a relief from the rest of the apartment."

perfect details

"I'm a big believer in finding beautiful everyday objects. It's kind of neurotic, but it's just the way I am."

impulse purchases

"Sometimes I buy things first and worry about where they'll go later. It's not always the best plan, but I think it makes a room personal."

my office

"I wanted my office to look lived-in—even a little messy—because I grew up in a very neat house."

—DARA CAPONIGRO

CHAPTER NINE

the kids' room

the style:
urbane cowboy

SLEEPY PALETTE WITH A SHOCK OF RED Dusty-green walls and vintage-inspired curtains set a soft, subdued tone. The nightstand and box-spring covers pick up on the crimson in the curtains, providing a jolt of energy. A dark hardwood floor fits in with the rustic, home-on-the range vibe.

WALLS CURTAINS RUGS COVERLETS

A HODGEPODGE OF PATTERN An adventurer's spirit runs throughout the similarly scaled mix of fabrics. The Navajo-style rugs tie into the Old West theme of the curtains, while a swanky zebra print on the headboards offers an element of surprise.

COMPLEMENTARY SHAPES A subtle wave design in the coverlets accentuates the beds' feminine silhouettes; the curvy bed frames balance out the boyishness.

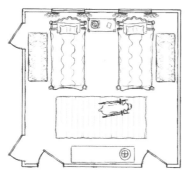

floor plan
Twin beds in a single occupant's space are tailor-made for sleepovers. Placing the beds side by side against the windows establishes a pleasing symmetry.

Kid's room of Vesta
Fort, decorator

the style:
mod baby

HIGH CONTRAST A single black wall stands in stark relief to white walls and the yellow-and-white striped ceiling. The *noir* dresser blends into the backdrop, creating a chic yet theatrical visual effect.

WALL   CEILING   WALLS   BEDDING

MODERN AMUSEMENT Circus-y stripes painted on the ceiling give the room a flipped-upside-down curiosity. The graphic lines assist a simple mobile in keeping a baby's eyes busy before bedtime.

TIMELESS CLASSICS A crib that is both aesthetically pleasing and functional is a wise investment that will last generations. Likewise, a tall, solid dresser with beautiful gold detail and interesting pulls can reside in the room even after the child goes to college.

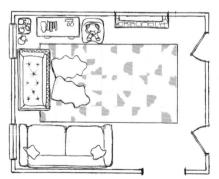

floor plan
Placed between two windows, the crib is shielded from direct sun but still benefits from natural light. The center of the room remains open and airy to accommodate play, while a sofa gives adults a comfortable place to sit.

Kid's room of Jenna Lyons and Vincent Mazeau, *creative director and artist*

the style:
plush & pretty

ENCAPSULATING COLOR Pairing lavender walls with cornflower-blue curtains and headboard gives the quaint room an all-encompassing elegance. White bedding and accents exert a crispness on what might otherwise feel overly fussy.

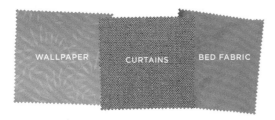

WALLPAPER　　CURTAINS　　BED FABRIC

LAYERED SOPHISTICATION The faint floral of the wallpaper adds interest without overwhelming. Cotton-velvet upholstery and voluptuous floor-length Indian silk curtains (the rods are longer than the width of the frame, feigning larger windows) create an air of luxury in a tight space.

POSH BUT PRACTICAL LIGHTING A simple swing-arm wall sconce frees up surface area on the bedside table. Also, to temper the frippery, an undulated modern orb hangs overhead.

LAVISH COMFORT This enormous tufted sleigh bed forges an ultra-cozy setting that makes other furniture seem unnecessary. It has an architectural, room-within-a-room allure.

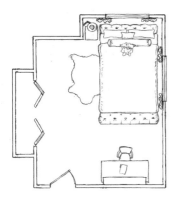

floor plan
The big bed is the dominant element in this small room, transforming the space into a giant spot for lounging. A wide closet and wall-mounted shelving above the desk provide ample storage.

Kid's room of Sharon
Simonaire, *interior designer*

the big piece: kids' beds

PLATFORM

*Supermodern and unfussy.
Doesn't scream "kid,"
so it can easily grow with
your child.*

BUNK BED

*Space-saving and always a hit. Comes in
modern and traditional styles.*

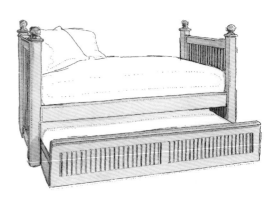

TRUNDLE

*Dates back to when mistresses and their maids
slept in the same room. Great for sleepovers.*

CANOPY

Grown-up yet girly. Creates a little haven, with or without a fabric canopy. This one piece makes a room feel decorated.

UPHOLSTERED

Luxurious and grown-up. Makes for a cozy bedtime story.

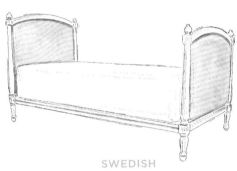

SWEDISH

Casually refined, with a wood frame and inset upholstery. For a small space, look for one without a footboard.

IRON

Classic and romantic. Often available painted.

COTTAGE

Charming and unpretentious. Cute in a pair.

SPOOL

A 19th-century, turned-wood design. Painted, it's sweet in a girl's room; a natural wood finish is great for boys. Nice in a guest room later.

how to mix & match

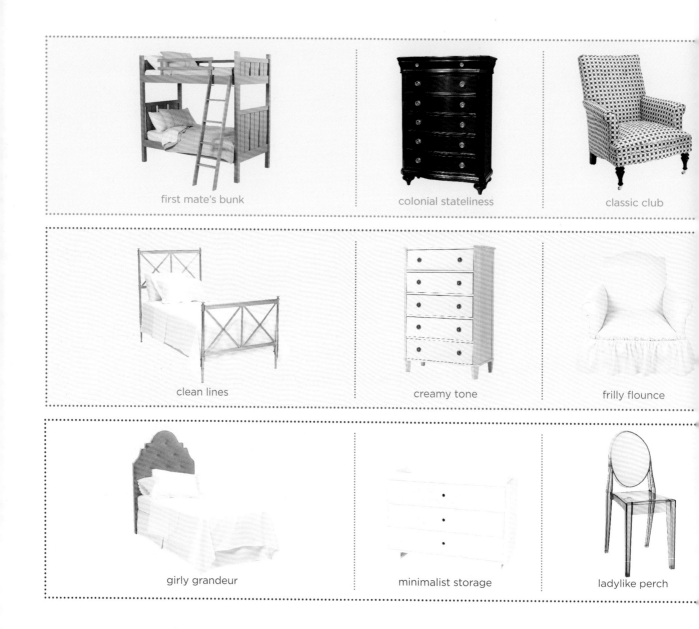

first mate's bunk

colonial stateliness

classic club

clean lines

creamy tone

frilly flounce

girly grandeur

minimalist storage

ladylike perch

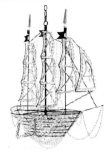

seafaring chandelier

rugged rope

Tailored, traditional elements combine with upscale maritime accents to impart a **preppy nautical** mood. The youthful pop of pattern on a grown-up chair links to the green bunk.

organic lace

baroque touch

Silver, cream and straw hues connect the more boxy, straightforward shapes to a cozy ruffled chair and a scalloped chandelier for a **tidy, neutral and feminine** feel. Crocheted detailing and a hint of print add texture.

fun & funky

earthy texture

A tufted headboard, a witty take on a Louis XV chair and a Chinese paper lantern are fanciful accoutrements for a **modern-day princess**. The sleek bureau and nubby basket keep the look from going over the top.

very important tips

paint/fabric

SELECTING A COLOR Don't be afraid of a sophisticated palette—try a hue you'd want in your own room. If you do subscribe to the prescribed pink-for-girls-blue-for-boys approach, consider variations. A vibrant fuchsia or blue-gray are refreshing alternatives to powdery pastels. The key—particularly for older kids—is to select color combinations that have longevity and suit a range of styles.

BEDDING AS DECOR Graphic sheet sets and duvets are a great affordable way to liven up a basic room. They help set the tone: Dainty florals have a sweet vibe while a geometric pattern feels punchy and modern. More interchangeable than furniture or window treatments, bed linens can also better accommodate evolving tastes.

DURABLE MATERIALS When outfitting a child's room, pick fabrics that can withstand wear and tear. If something is white, make sure it's machine-washable. Cotton duck, twill and canvas are all low-maintenance and built to last.

furniture

PIECES TO GROW WITH Unless you plan on constantly redecorating, choose heirloom-worthy pieces that children will come to appreciate. A beautiful armoire is practical for housing everything from toys to clothing. And if a basic rocking chair cramps your style, there are more sophisticated options, like the Eames rocker (above). Furniture likely to adapt over time—a crib that converts into a bed, a bureau repurposed as a changing table—is more cost-effective. Think about what's normally found in other parts of the house that could function in a child's room; a large modern coffee table, for instance, makes a versatile post for art projects and tea parties.

ALL-IMPORTANT LIGHTING Children should have access to an abundance of light: bright overheads, task lamps for desks, reading lamps for bedside tables and even night-lights, so toes aren't stubbed on the way to the bathroom.

GROUND EFFECTS A rug provides insulation for hardwood floors, extra padding for busy knees and another blast of color or pattern.

storage

THE BIG IDEAS Children have tons of stuff—now figure out where it's all going. Space permitting, plot out where to use organizational pieces: a tall chest of drawers, a bookshelf, shelving, cabinets, etc. Take advantage of the room's architecture. If there's a recess or indentation in the wall, install shelving (as above). But keep the height of the child in mind. Toys, books and puzzles should be within arm's reach, so he or she can pull items out and put them away. Other, more decorative bits can live higher up.

MIDDLE GROUND While labeled boxes, bins and baskets may seem semi-neurotic, they actually preserve sanity. Everything from superheroes and dinosaurs to model modes of transportation can have its own designated spot. This will encourage organization and make for easy after-play cleanup that kids can be involved in.

THINK SMALL Take advantage of all usable space. Stow off-season clothes and out-of-favor playthings under the bed. Put up a bulletin board for loose papers and memorabilia. Hang peg hooks (low!) inside a closet door for jerseys, hats and belts. Same goes for behind the bedroom door.

baby room

HEALTHY CHOICES A lot of children's furniture is, unfortunately, made with toxins like formaldehyde. Scrutinize material information and, when possible, go for natural alternatives, like wood, sea grass, sisal, hemp or jute. Many paint companies offer water-based, low- and non-VOC (Volatile Organic Compounds) products, which won't release harmful gases into the air. And an ever-growing variety of eco bed linens and fabric (bamboo, organic cotton, hemp, etc.) for curtains and upholstery is ripe for the picking. Even mattresses come stuffed with all-organic filling and wool casings.

A NOTE ON THEMES Keep in mind that overly juvenile, cartoon-y motifs aren't necessarily going to make children happy. A well-decorated space sans theme, which leaves room for the imagination, will appeal to everyone in the family.

decorating tricks

CARPET TILES can be pieced together into a pattern (and readily replaced if need be).

PINK DOESN'T HAVE TO BE GIRLY when it's offset with a black rug.

WHIMSICAL WALLPAPER on the ceiling gives kids something fun to look at when they're lying in bed.

REINVENT A BEAUTIFUL CHEST into a changing table by topping it with a snug cushion.

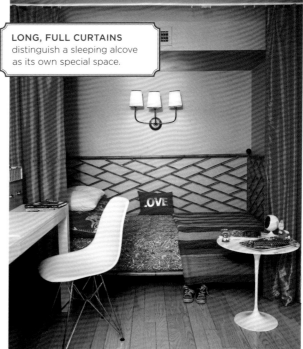

LONG, FULL CURTAINS distinguish a sleeping alcove as its own special space.

more decorating tricks

GRASS-CLOTH WALLS lend warm sophistication to a child's room and serve as a massive bulletin board for artwork.

SET OFF A TRADITIONAL PINK with bright orange to take a girl's room from toddler to tween.

SIMPLE HOOKS keep jackets and bags off the ground.

CHALKBOARD PAINT is lower-commitment than a real board, but just as fun.

A COOL STENCIL in a bright color becomes abstract art for the modern kid.

small-space solutions

A SLEEPING LOFT has indoor treehouse appeal and frees up valuable real estate below.

IF ALL THE KIDS BUNK IN ONE ROOM, another bedroom can be dedicated to play.

ONE GIANT GUEST ROOM with lots of beds doesn't limit your invitations.

REAPPROPRIATE A HALL CLOSET if there's no proper storage in the nursery.

CREATE INSTANT PRIVACY with curtains on a track.

finishing touches

CURATE A COLLAGE of framed and taped-up photos, postcards and souvenirs that highlight a passion or hobby.

SPELLING OUT A CHILD'S NAME in bold, mismatched letters will make him feel like a rock star.

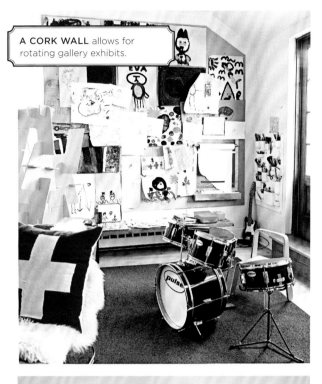

A CORK WALL allows for rotating gallery exhibits.

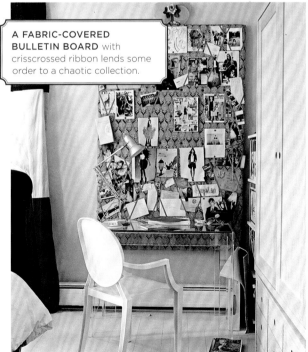

A FABRIC-COVERED BULLETIN BOARD with crisscrossed ribbon lends some order to a chaotic collection.

LET ONE BIG IMAGE be the room's focal point. A giant map of the world is perfect—colorful and educational!

the domino effect

the starting point

"I wanted the nursery for our daughter, Eloise, to be very girly but also simple and uncluttered—just a place to lie on the floor and play around. Easy for her and easy for me."

RUTHIE SOMMERS
domino *contributing editor*

the room's inspiration

"This chandelier was here when we moved in. It gives me this magical, weird feeling that the woman who sold us the place, Helen, is keeping an eye on us."

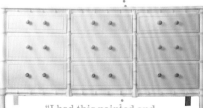

'70s country-club palette

"I wanted an AstroTurf look for the floor—darker than the green on the chandelier, so it wouldn't be too preppy with pink walls."

"I had this painted and lacquered—and then I realized the room is for Eloise and not me, so I bought knobs with little elephants and kittens on them."

"I copied the pagoda idea from a magazine. The mural, which was painted by a friend, ties in with it—just something for Eloise to look at from her crib."

decorator touches

elements of whimsy

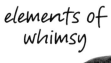

"I found this in Palm Beach."

"These were in my store for two years, and they never sold. They came home on sabbatical. Eloise loves to pat the kitty, so they're here to stay."

"An old French miniature commode—the right size for this room."

tiny but proper furniture

"All of these scaled-down pieces pick up the colors in the chandelier. The seat cushion of this pink chair lifts for storage."

my kid's room

"When I'm in here, I always feel so appreciative. My daughter is what I see most in this room, not loads of toys, photos and accoutrements— just her. Pink for healthy, pink for girly." —RUTHIE SOMMERS

the decorators' handbook

a guide to window treatments and upholstery

windows: curtains

CURTAIN STYLES

DOUBLE PANEL
The most popular style, a pair of panels bracketing a window establishes symmetry and order.

good to know: If your room—or your window—is small, double panels can overwhelm. Pick a lightweight fabric that's not too voluminous, or opt for a single panel.

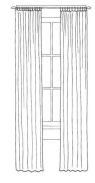

SINGLE PANEL
A single panel works well in snug spaces or when windows are closely set. A dynamic sweep of fabric caught to one side with a tieback is romantic, while a simple straight-hung panel in front of the window is casual.

good to know: Can look prim tied to one side, but done in a sheer fabric, it's elegant.

PANELS WITH VALANCE
A soft fabric valance gives plain panels a more romantic quality. Taut or shirred, it can run straight across at the bottom, or can undulate.

good to know: Unpretentious solids, like linen and cotton can foil the potential fussiness. A valance alone (without panels) can add softness to an uncovered window.

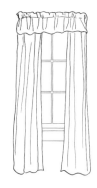

PANELS WITH PELMET
Enclosing the top of the curtain in a structured frame, a pelmet lends a well-mannered air.

good to know: Not for windows that open inward. Pelmets themselves are often adorned to highlight their shape.

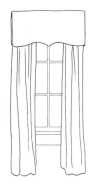

STACKED CURTAINS
The epitome of boutique-hotel chic, a voluminous cascade of floor-to-ceiling fabric gives a sumptuously clean look that's surprisingly minimalist when rendered in gauzy fabrics. This enveloping style fosters the illusion of bigger windows and mellows the lines of a stark room.

good to know: This is a lot of fabric, so keep it light.

CAFÉ CURTAINS
Hung at a window's midpoint or above, café curtains add a hint of color and flounce where full-blown coverage isn't needed.

good to know: Although not the best for tempering sunlight, café curtains effectively screen views when hung at just the right spot.

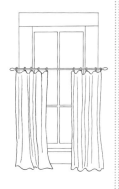

FABRICS

COTTON
pros: Incredibly versatile and easy to clean.

cons: Some stiffer cottons don't have enough give for graceful draping styles.

LINEN
pros: The open weave provides texture and refinement. Looks substantial lined but can also be left as is to play light off the fabric's openness.

cons: Some linen is dry-clean only, so not well suited for rooms or windows that get lots of dirt and dust.

SILK
pros: Refined yet light, silk catches a breeze and billows beautifully.

cons: Often too sheer to screen light and views very well, unless it's lined.

SHEERS
pros: Cut glare while still filtering light, thus great for where you need a bit of privacy but don't want the hassle of opening and shutting curtains all the time.

cons: The translucent weave won't block light, so pair with a heavier curtain in a bedroom. (See p. 245.)

VELVET
pros: Velvet's richness feels luxurious. Its plush weight also offers privacy and good insulation from drafts and sunlight.

cons: Can be expensive and formal—and a little heavy for warm climates.

WOOL
pros: Wool drapes beautifully and is strong enough to support heavy embellishments like fringe and tassels.

cons: While summer-weight wool is all-seasonal, its moisture absorbency makes it ill-suited to beach environments. Wool is dry-clean only.

CURTAIN HEADINGS

POLE POCKET
A straightforward option in which the curtain rod slips through a channel in the top of the panel, creating a gathered effect without the use of pleats or rings.

good to know: It can be hard to move the fabric back and forth, so this is best for stationary curtains.

PENCIL PLEAT
Bestowing instant posh, these tight, even pleats create a nicely refined shirring. Great for stacked curtains.

good to know: The look leans pretty debonair, so restrict it to fairly upscale confines.

FLOPPY
A fold of fabric at the top, which forms a composed ruffle and draws the eye up, brings a little frill without going overboard.

good to know: This pretty treatment is somewhat lighthearted, so best in cottons and linens.

GROMMET
The rod threads through grommets, making rings unnecessary. These circular metal perforations read as fun and modern.

good to know: If you're prone to casually pushing curtains open and shut, grommets may prove a bit challenging.

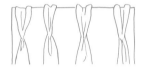

PINCH PLEAT
A succession of gathered pleats at the top of the curtain unfurls in a graceful cascade, creating a sense of movement. Double pleats (above) are more tailored, while triples yield extra volume.

good to know: Also called French pleats, this tailoring works well with heavy or light fabrics, telegraphing folds from top to bottom.

SOFT INVERTED PLEAT
These elegant pleats are made by folding the fabric back, rather than forward.

good to know: Crisper fabrics will highlight the tailoring.

TIE-TOP
Tied directly onto rings or a rod, these charming panels are girly fastened in bows. In knots, they're less feminine.

good to know: These tops let you adjust how closely the curtain hangs to the rod—leave a bit loose for a lived-in boho look.

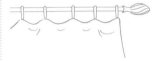

PLAIN HEADING
One of the most common options, these understated panels hang flat and require the least fabric.

good to know: With no ties or tabs to attach the panels to a curtain rod, these usually affix with clip-on rings, which should be evenly spaced to avoid looking messy.

TINY SOFT PINCH PLEAT
Achieved by pinching together the very top of the fabric panel, these delicate pleats are looser than pinch pleats and more bohemian.

good to know: These require less yardage than the more structured pinch pleat.

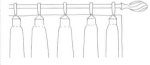

BOX PLEAT
These big, flat folds convey a custom quality that's equal parts Dorothy Draper and old-school Hollywood glam.

good to know: This classic style veers a bit traditional. Also, because the pleats fold the fabric under itself, wild patterns might not work.

HIDDEN CURTAIN DETAILS

LINING
An extra layer of fabric backing gives curtains body and makes them substantial. While many fabrics—like cotton or silk—drape better when lined, your choice is also a matter of aesthetics. You can use unlined linen to make a fancy living room less formal or opt for lined velvet panels to step up a laid-back bedroom.

INTERLINING
Interlining is a hidden panel sewn between the lining and the fabric you actually see in the room. It ensures that the curtain is opaque and adds weight, so that the curtain falls nicely.

WEIGHTS
Stitched into the hem, weights help fabrics hang with more heft and keep curtains in place so you don't have to futz with them.

windows: curtains, cont'd

CURTAIN LENGTH

BRUSHING THE FLOOR
Imparts a crisp and tailored look, like a well-cut suit. Curtain panels that just touch the floor offer a perfect canvas for edging or borders. This structured style is best with heavier fabrics like velvet and lined cotton. It will, however, call attention to crooked floors (which can be disguised by a bit more length).

BREAKING THE FLOOR
A little softer than curtains that just brush the floor, those that break onto the floor by an inch or two are relaxed and voluptuous. Going a bit longer also allows some room for imperfect measuring.

POOLING AT THE FLOOR
More than two inches of extra curtain tracing the floor imbues a lush, romantic sensibility. Any trim along the bottom will be less visible since the curtains will scrunch up a bit.

A NOTE ABOUT SHORT CURTAINS
Short curtains are tricky to pull off, unless they're café-style. They can work when their bottoms are hitting something, like a radiator cover or a bookcase, but can seem out-of-date if they're just dangling in the air. For a window that can't take full-length curtains, a shade is often the perfect solution.

PELMETS

A pelmet is a wood box cut to shape, sometimes padded and usually covered with fabric. Curvy profiles are more traditional. Pelmets can also be made entirely of finished wood, which can help counteract a room with fabric overload.

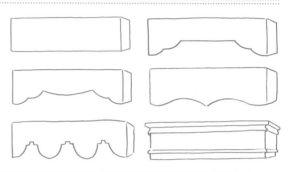

BORDERS & TRIMS

CURTAIN BORDERS
Contrasting fabric or tape defining the bottom, sides and/or top of the panel breaks up an expanse of material—and can tie colors in to the rest of the room. Often only the inside edge and bottom have borders.
good to know: An inset border a few inches from the edge is less graphic and more refined.

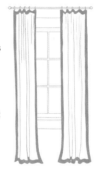

CURTAIN TRIMS
Fringe, pom-poms ruffles or other embellishments (known collectively to pros as passementerie) along the edge of a curtain bring a polished quality that's more delicate than a bold border. A great way to customize off-the-shelf panels.
good to know: Trims can go on the inside edge only, along the bottom only or all around a panel.

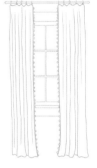

TIEBACKS

FABRIC
A strip of cloth that hooks to the wall confers a finished quality. Mount low for a dramatic swoop of fabric or high to rein in panels tightly.

ROPE
While loosely draped curtains are always stylish, a rope tieback, attached to the wall by a hook, offers a sophisticated, European look.

METAL BRACKET
Hardware in brass, iron or bronze is the easiest way to pull back curtains—especially those you're constantly opening and closing.

ROSETTE
Rosettes can be unfussy or ornate and come in a variety of materials (brass, bronze, even mercury glass). Curtains simply drape over them.

HANGING OPTIONS

HOW HIGH?
Curtains often look best mounted a few inches above the top of the molding. Hang even higher to downplay crooked windows or create the illusion of higher ceilings. Keep rod placement in mind when buying curtains. Measure from rod to floor, accounting for length of rings and how much you want curtains to break. When in doubt, overestimate. You can hem them later.

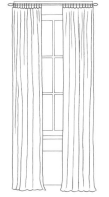

HOW WIDE?
Rods work well when they continue at least a few inches beyond the window molding. Just how far depends on your desired look and how much daylight you want. To maximize light, extend the rod at least 10″ beyond the frame on each side. Hanging extra-wide also makes small windows seem bigger.

CUSTOM VS. READY-MADE

Like a bespoke suit, custom drapes just fit better. Consider this, especially if you're particular about your curtains or if your windows don't conform to standard sizes. Custom allows for more variation. Ready-mades might lack that tailored appeal, but they're less expensive, don't require long lead times—and if what you receive isn't what you had in mind, you can return them. If you're getting curtains made, have the fabric laundered first—and remember that gathering, pleats and elongated styles all mean more yardage.

CURTAIN-ROD STYLES

ROD WITH FINIAL
These come in a variety of materials, most commonly wood and metal. Different metals have different moods—brass is traditional, iron is understated. Wood rods add warmth. Paint them to highlight a color in the room.

RETURN ROD
These U-shaped rods curve into the wall, obviating the need for finials. Ideal for rooms that demand complete darkness, since the fabric wraps around the side of the windows to seal out light. They're streamlined and less fussy than other choices.

CABLE ROD
Cables are simple to install, anchoring right into the wall with screws. You can adjust the tension so the cable hangs tightly or a little slack for a more relaxed look.

CEILING TRACK
Somewhat tricky to install—it's best to enlist a professional, especially if you want it flush-mounted (flat to the ceiling)—a ceiling track generally entails custom-designed curtains, which clip on with hooks. But once in place, a track is effortless to use and takes full advantage of ceiling height.

SIDE-WALL MOUNT
Although curtain rods are usually mounted on the same wall as the window, you can instead anchor them to perpendicular side walls for a dramatic sweep of uninterrupted curtain.

TENSION ROD
The easiest and least expensive option (also the least finished-looking), these can be picked up for just a few dollars at the hardware store and slipped inside the window frame. They're best with pole-pocket curtains and won't hold heavy drapes.

CURTAIN-ROD ACCESSORIES

RING WITH EYE
Most curtains attach to rings via curtain hooks. The curtain hook threads through the eye of the ring.

RING WITHOUT EYE
The poshest curtains are stitched directly onto eyeless rings, making professional cleaning a must. These rings also work for tie-tops.

RING WITH CLIP
These affix to curtains like clip-on earrings, and can convert any piece of fabric into a curtain.

FINIALS
Adorning the ends of rods like jewelry, finials are an effortless way to add style.

BRACKET
These support the rod and are typically mounted near its ends. Sometimes a center bracket is needed to help hold an extralong rod.

windows: shades

SHADE & BLIND STYLES

ROLLER
These simple shades roll up via a spring-load mechanism or chain. Roller shades come in a variety of styles and perform expertly in snug confines where cascades of fabric or weighty curtain rods would overwhelm. You can upgrade off-the-shelf versions with trim or decorative pulls.

MATCHSTICK
The natural material adds a warm quality. These blinds temper strong daylight without totally obliterating it. Hung solo, they're casual. Paired with a fancier curtain, they become almost dressy.

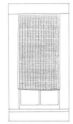

WOOD VENETIAN
Made of stacked slats, these blinds tilt to any angle to reduce the light while letting in views (or vice versa). You can often customize the color of the "ladder tape" that runs top to bottom. Unlike paper or fabric blinds, which are easy to vacuum, these can be challenging to clean.

FLAT ROMAN
Roman shades are formed from fabric folds that stack neatly as they're opened. Streamlined and architectural, they lend themselves well to having borders.

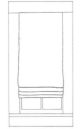

RELAXED ROMAN
These operate the same way as the classic flat-fold version, rising via a pulley mechanism. Softer than a flat roman, they feature a subtle, voluminous drape and a design that can show off patterned fabric.

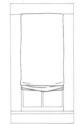

PLEATED ROMAN
Similar to a standard roman shade, this style is distinguished by horizontal pleats, which highlight detailing even when lowered.

LONDON
These hang with a dashing swag of fabric at the bottom. A great ornamental style for windows that don't need shades to be opened and shut frequently.

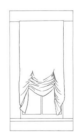

BALLOON
These literally "balloon" out in little puffs of fabric, bestowing a sweetness that can lean a bit saccharine. Keep it pared-back by choosing a plain fabric or a subtle print.

FABRICS

SHEER VS. OPAQUE
The sheerer a fabric, the lighter the look and the more daylight it will admit, whereas heavier fabrics help diminish street noise or drafts but can darken a room.

good to know: If you need to screen views but want ample light, pick an opaque weave in a pale color, like white or cream.

PATTERN VS. SOLID
Just like with upholstery, a patterned shade is livelier than a solid. Patterns work best on styles without pleats. Also consider how light shining through may make the pattern more diffuse. Using a lining can keep it visible.

good to know: Fancy styles like balloon shades and london shades can be played down with solid fabrics—they have plenty of embellishment on their own.

PLACEMENT OF THE PATTERN
Whether you're planning to sew your own curtains or have them custom-made, center the pattern.

good to know: If your chosen fabric features an oversize motif or large repeat (see p. 246), account for extra yardage so the pattern can align correctly on the shade.

BLACKOUT
In rooms where you want complete darkness, there are a few ways to go. Many off-the-shelf roller blinds are available as blackout shades. If you're ordering custom, you can request blackout lining.

MOUNTING OPTIONS

INSIDE MOUNT
The most common mounting method, this works well with any style shade and nets the cleanest look.

good to know: Hang shades so they skim the inside of the window moldings—close enough to block out light, but with enough space to raise and lower without catching. Can make small windows seem even smaller.

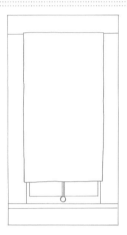

OUTSIDE MOUNT
A good option for when you want to create the illusion of wider windows, cover unattractive frames or seal out daylight completely.

good to know: To make your ceiling appear higher, hang outside-mounted shades several inches above the window frame (remember to measure from where you plan to hang to the top of your sill). When you raise a high-mounted shade, just remember not to roll it up past the top of the window.

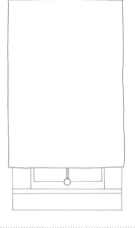

CONSIDER LEAVING WINDOWS BARE:
• When you want to accentuate a drop-dead view in a public room, like the living or dining room.

• When you want to highlight elaborately carved moldings or window frames.

• When you have a pared-down room that begs for windows that are free of frippery.

LAYERING

CURTAIN + ANOTHER CURTAIN
when to go for it: When one style can't perform all the functions you need, pick two curtains of different weights, hanging one in front of the other. This allows you to adjust for sheer coverage or total opacity.

how to make it work: Get a double rod that's designed just for this purpose.

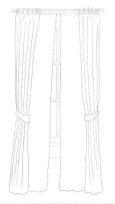

CURTAIN + VALANCE/PELMET
when to go for it: When you want to draw attention to a window or create a sense of drama.

how to make it work: It's foolproof if you use the same fabric for both curtain and valance (or pelmet).

CURTAIN + SHADE
when to go for it: In spaces like bedrooms, where you need a functional treatment but also want some decorative flair. They're less bulky than a double layer of curtains and simpler to pull off.

how to make it work: Coordinating shade and curtain fabric will be too matchy here, so choose contrasting hues or materials that still have a shared sensibility. The shade should always be inside-mounted.

upholstery: sofas & chairs

UPHOLSTERY STYLES

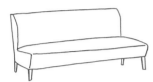

TIGHT BACK, TIGHT SEAT
Streamlined and without cushions, it's pleasingly tidy and formal.

good to know: With no cushions to flip, stains can't be hidden.

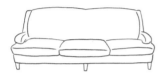

TIGHT BACK, LOOSE SEAT
Has a neat profile but is still enveloping.

good to know: The back can be a bit stiff, so consider adding throw pillows.

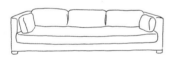

LOOSE BACK, LOOSE SEAT
Loose cushions confer a worldly but lived-in vibe and are usually more comfortable.

good to know: Make sure the cushions have enough firmness to hold their shape over time. If not, they can start to look sloppy.

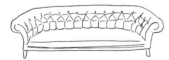

TUFTED
Button tufting spruces up a broad stretch of sofa with a quilt-like succession of stitches. Elegant and European.

good to know: You can tuft the seat, the back or both. Solids and large-scale patterns work best. Small patterns can get lost in the tufting.

SEAT CUSHIONS

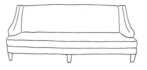

SINGLE CUSHION
pros: This streamlined look is clean and formal. It can squeeze in more people comfortably—no one has to sit on a crack between cushions—and is great for napping.

cons: In the event of stains or wear, you have only one chance to turn over the cushion.

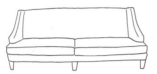

MULTI-CUSHION
pros: Generally a bit cozier. You can move cushions around frequently, so they wear more evenly, and flip them if they become stained.

cons: Less crisp than a single cushion and can veer a bit sloppy.

CUSHION TYPES

BOX
An upholstered cushion or pillow shaped like a box, with flat sides. Welting (see next page) accentuates the squared-off form, while elaborate trims, which slip into the seams, have a tempering effect on otherwise crisp linearity.

BULLNOSE
The most common style, upholstered cushions sewn together with a single, circumnavigating seam have a slight curve to the edges. The shape is softer and a bit puffier than flat-sided box cushions, but can likewise be dressed up with welting, cords or fringe.

BUTTON
A grid of buttons can smarten up a plain box-cushion design or lend texture to a large-scale piece. Covered in the same fabric as the cushion, buttons look quite clean. Pick a contrasting color or material for a livelier effect.

THINGS TO THINK ABOUT

FILLER
There are three types of stuffing for your cushions: foam, down or a combination of the two. Foam springs back into shape after you stand up. Down filler stays squished and requires constant fluffing. The best of both worlds—and quite common—are cushions with a foam core surrounded by down.

FABRIC
Your fabric choice should suit both your frame style and your life. Account for pragmatic considerations such as how much wear the piece will be subject to—children, pets or strong sunlight should influence your choice.

PATTERN
Always consider orientation of the pattern: Most fabrics that are directional (like stripes) are upholstered vertically. Patterns are generally centered, which means buying additional yardage if your print is oversize.

REPEAT AND SIZE
The "repeat" is the interval at which a pattern recurs. Large repeats require more yardage. You'll need enough to continue the patterns over seams and to achieve symmetry across a broad expanse.

SOFA & CHAIR SKIRTS

STANDARD TREATMENT
A standard skirt—i.e., the panel of fabric that covers the leg—starts below the apron (the section between the cushion and the base) of the sofa or chair.

WATERFALL TREATMENT
A skirt that starts just below the seat cushion creates a more elongated, graceful look.

KICK-PLEAT DETAILING
Simple pleats at each corner are a classic treatment that works in both modern and traditional settings. For a nice surprise, pick a contrasting fabric for the inside.

SHIRRING DETAILING
A skirt that falls in delicately ruffled shirring is ultra-feminine and brings a dose of shabby chic, but exaggerated ruffles can look too froufrou.

BOX-PLEAT DETAILING
A neat series of box pleats brings well-appointed elegance without being overly feminine. Not for patterned fabrics.

NO SKIRT
Skip the skirt for a cleaner look. Also, pass if your piece is already squat, the legs kick outward past the frame or there are a lot of other skirted pieces in the room.

WELT OPTIONS

WELT VS. NO WELT
Welting (aka piping) is a fabric-covered cord tracing every seam. It imparts a more finished, resolved look. Having no welt is a simpler choice that works in modern settings and in traditional rooms that need toning down.

SELF-WELT VS. CONTRASTING WELT
Welting that matches the upholstery fabric—called self-welt—is the more standard way to go. For graphic pop, choose welting in a different color (contrasting welt) instead.

NAIL HEADS
Tracing the outline of an upholstered piece, nail heads can highlight a shapely frame. Casting a reflective shine like jewelry, the tacks come in various sizes and finishes, from burnished bronze to brazen nickel. Depending on what fabric the tacks are paired with, the result can feel quaintly old-school or a little punk rock.

SLIPCOVERS

Like a dress for your sofa, these fit right over the existing frame (with separate covers for cushions) and can be removed and cleaned, or changed seasonally. One way to liven up a careworn antique, a slipcover hides a multitude of sins: stains, bad upholstery or an overwrought, carved-wood frame. A custom slipcover sized exactly to your piece offers the most elegant tailoring. Use light fabric like cotton or linen, and prewash it (if you have multiple pieces to be covered in the same fabric, wash the fabric together so it fades evenly.)

C.O.M.

An acronym for "customer's own material." When ordering an upholstered piece from a manufacturer, some companies allow you to supply your own fabric (purchased elsewhere), instead of using one of the fabrics that the manufacturer provides. Sometimes there's a small charge for this service. Most upscale brands offer C.O.M., but so do some big retail stores. It's an easy way to customize a standard sofa or chair.

LEG STYLES

TURNED
Articulated turned-wood legs suggest antique pedigree.

BUN FEET
Choose one with carved detail rather than a plain round ball, to add sophistication.

STRAIGHT
The most modern look, tapered wood legs with strong lines have universal appeal.

beds

UPHOLSTERED HEADBOARDS

Headboard shapes range from a simple rectangle to an intricately curved silhouette. While there are many retail upholstered-headboard options, an upholsterer can create almost any shape. Leave the headboard as is, or add definition with welting or nail-head trim. Welting can be the same color as the headboard or a different one. Welting or nail heads can run either right along the edge of the headboard or a few inches in, forming a border. Nail heads tend to make a headboard more masculine.

BED HANGINGS

CURTAINS
Straight-hung panels are a nice way to adorn a classic four-poster. Curtains with tie headings are the easiest to hang.

UNSTRUCTURED CANOPY
A draping canopy over the top of a four-poster bed (tied to the corners) gives delicate coverage without bulk.

PELMET WITH CURTAINS
A space-saving decorative pelmet or valance projecting just over the pillow defines a small sheltering nook within a larger room.

CANOPY WITH CURTAINS
Cascading curtains at every corner plus a decorative canopy with pelmet establishes an enclosed aura of intimacy.

BED SKIRTS

KICK PLEAT
Dressing up the four corners (and sometimes the middle of the long sides), this standard treatment produces a clean, unfussy line.

SHIRRED/RUFFLED
An uninterrupted shirred skirt is romantic and feminine.

BOX
Disciplined box pleats wrap around the base of a bed with classical elegance.

PRACTICAL FABRIC CHOICES

HEADBOARDS & BED SKIRTS
For headboards, heavy materials like leather, velvet, wool and canvas in medium to dark colors will stay new-looking longest. With bed skirts, washable fabrics are best—cotton or linen. If going custom (to match the bed skirt with other fabrics in the room), have your fabric prewashed, to ensure that the final product won't shrink when it's laundered later.

throw pillows & trim

THROW-PILLOW SHAPES

SQUARE
Versatile squares are the most popular variety. Mix up a few sizes.

RECTANGLE
The elongated proportions of a rectangular pillow are elegant at a sofa's midpoint, flanked by groupings of square pillows.

BOX
Depth and dimension give a standard square throw pillow more structure.

ROUND
A circular pillow tends to feel retro and plays well against a squared-off seat and back.

ROUND BOX
A round pillow with a few inches of thickness also has retro charm.

BOLSTER
Use these accents on your bed or on both ends of the couch—like armrests.

ANATOMY OF A PILLOW
filler Pillows can have a synthetic filling, be filled with down (the lightest, fluffiest, most expensive feathers), or contain a blend of regular feathers and down. Down is softest but tends to lose its shape, while synthetics hold their form but are stiff. A feather-down blend is moderately priced and holds its shape while still being soft.

closures Both zippers and envelope-style closures allow you to remove the pillow cover for cleaning. Zippers are usually hidden near the seam. Envelope closures are on the back of the pillow and are more casual and less expensive.

TRIMS FOR PILLOWS, CURTAINS & UPHOLSTERY

GIMP
Ribbonlike fabric tape—often ornamented with a braided detail—that smooths over the gap where fabric meets the frame of a chair or sofa.

TAPE
Plain as it is, tape still bestows a couture polish when tracing the edge of a pelmet or sofa.

ROPE
Use rope to add texture and color to the edge of a throw pillow or to make a staid seat cushion more interesting.

RIBBON
Artful, judicious use of ribbon can accentuate the bones of a piece without getting fussy.

POM-POMS
Dangling pom-poms are a sweet touch on demure sofas and chairs. They also fall nicely along the inside edge of curtains.

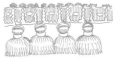

TASSELS
They bring a sense of movement to furniture and curtains but should be avoided on streamlined pieces because they're so elaborate.

FRINGE
Fringe comes in a multitude of styles. Some, like loop fringe (above), are perfect complements to a well-made curtain in a highly decorated room.

BULLION FRINGE
A cascade of long, weighty, twisted cords works best along the bottom of a heavy curtain or skirted sofa.

THROW-PILLOW DETAILS

WELT: SELF VS. CONTRASTING
On a throw pillow, a welt (or piping) feels finished. Self-welt (in the same fabric as the rest of the pillow) provides the most minimal styling. Or choose an accent fabric/color for definition.

NO WELT/KNIFE EDGE
A knife-edge pillow is one without welting (just a straight seam) and lets patterns wrap around the sides continuously.

FLANGE
A flat-panel border (usually in a solid) encircling a pillow is a way to embellish while still keeping things simple.

RUFFLE
A voluptuous, ruffled edge is as girly as it gets—even more so in colorful chintz or a bold floral.

TIES
Pillowcases that close with little ties instead of a zipper are quite charming, especially when the outside sleeve contrasts with the fabric inside.

the big black book

a guide to the best decorating resources

resources by category

$ = AFFORDABLE $$ = MID-RANGE $$$ = HIGH-END   X = **NO E-COMMERCE** (BUT PRODUCTS CAN BE VIEWED

Don't forget to check out **domino.com** for home decor finds that will help you bring *domino* style and inspiration into your home. Shop fresh ideas, current trends and editor favorites.

ART

ART STAR $$
(888) 488-757; artstar.com
This genius site serves as your very own e-curator by custom printing, framing and authenticating works by emerging contemporary artists that are then delivered right to your doorstep.

CLIC $$$
(212) 966-2766; clic.com
With locations in New York, St. Barth and the Hamptons, Clic carries a chic selection of contemporary photography, travel and fashion books, as well as small home goods, to match its nomadic roots.

PICTURE ROOM $$–$$$
(212) 219-2789;
goodsforthestudy.mcnallyjackson-store.com
Around the corner from New York City's McNally Jackson Books, this smartly organized space sells "goods to enrich your study practice"—whether that be a handsome brass paperweight or sleek ballpoint.

TAPPAN $$–$$$
(213) 226-6452;
tappancollective.com
The place "where today's best emerging artists meet their collectors," Tappan takes pride in carefully selecting each work—without charging you the steep gallery markup. We especially love Claire Oswalt's abstract watercolor collages in soft blues and grays.

BEDDING

AREA $$
(212) 924-7084; areahome.com
This design studio specializes in cleanly graphic modern bedding that's slightly playful but always sophisticated.

CALVIN KLEIN HOME $$–$$$
(866) 513-0513; calvinklein.com
(click on "home" to view collection)
Featuring subtle patterns in a spectrum of neutrals, pastels and earth tones, the mega-designer's linens help build a calming, casually elegant bedroom.

THE COMPANY STORE $
(800) 323-8000;
thecompanystore.com
This Wisconsin-based outfit offers a wonderfully comprehensive selection of bedding basics in a wide range of colors, patterns and fabrics.

DONNA KARAN HOME $$–$$$
(888) 737-5743;
donnakaranhome.com
The queen of neutrals' eponymous high-end lines provide subtle colors and textures in luxurious fabrics rich with detail. Her mid-priced DKNY Pure Comfort line is an eco-friendly home collection inspired by the beauty of nature.

DWELLSTUDIO $$
(212) 219-9343; dwellstudio.com
Truly one of a kind, this New York–based design team turns out colorful, modern interpretations of traditional motifs.

FOG LINEN WORK $$
(617) 576-1600; shop-foglinen.com
An offshoot of the Japanese line Fog Linen Work, this shop carries duvet covers, blankets and pillowcases in the brand's soft-to-the-touch linen.

FRETTE $$$
(800) 353-7388; frette.com
Featuring understated design and impeccable materials, the super-luxurious linens from this storied European house are pricey and worth it.

GARNET HILL $
(800) 870-3513; garnethill.com
This well-known catalog brand is an excellent resource for sheets, coverlets and shams. Traditional takes predominate, but there are some more modern styles as well.

JOHN ROBSHAW TEXTILES $$
(212) 594-6006; johnrobshaw.com
The globe-trotting designer's printed bedding is one of our absolute favorites. The hand-blocked and hand-printed patterns mix and match beautifully, and the nursery styles are unusually sophisticated.

LEONTINE LINENS $$$ x
(504) 899-7833; leontinelinens.com
Known for standout monograms and fine embellishments, these luxurious handmade linens can be customized to your exact specifications.

MATOUK $$–$$$
(855) 795-7600; matouk.com
Family-run since 1929, this old-school American brand now collaborates with modern talents like Lulu DK, but still offers traditional touches like custom colors and monograms.

MATTEO $–$$
(213) 617-2813; matteohome.com
Simple in design but made from luxurious natural materials, this L.A.-made bedding has a modern rustic (but not country) chic.

OLATZ $$$
(212) 255-8627; olatz.com
A favorite of high-end designers, Olatz Schnabel's super-indulgent linen-and-cotton sheets boast bold color combinations and elaborate hand-embroidered details.

PARACHUTE $$

(855) 888-5977;

parachutehome.com

We love that this brand's Egyptian and Turkish cotton bedding is certified chemical- and synthetic-free—as well as the fact that it partners with a U.N. organization to donate malaria bed nets.

RALPH LAUREN HOME $$$

(888) 475-7674;

ralphlauren.com/home

Nobody does it like Ralph—his sumptuous, tailored bedding has the same timelessness as his clothing, and everything here coordinates effortlessly.

RAWGANIQUE $$

(877) 729-4367; rawganique.com

A favorite for luxury eco-friendly linens, the organic hemp and organic French linen sheets are durable and very sumptuous.

SCHWEITZER LINEN $$

(800) 554-6367;

schweitzerlinen.com

For the truly discriminating palate, this New York–based collection offers custom everything alongside a comprehensive collection of well-made basics.

SOCIETY $$$

societylimonta.com

This Italian company approaches bedding like fashion, experimenting with textile processes and mix-and-match color palettes to create "couture" for the home.

ENTERTAINING

BARNEYS NEW YORK $$–$$$

(888) 222-7639; barneys.com

This favorite source for luxury goods carries gorgeous Fornasetti platters, elegant servingware and standout pieces by hard-to-find brands like Venini.

BERGDORF GOODMAN $$$

(888) 774-2424;

bergdorfgoodman.com

This Fifth Avenue institution revels in tabletop luxury, offering Kelly Wearstler's sculptural accessories and beautiful wares by Juliska, Moser and William Yeoward, alongside carefully chosen antique objects, including gorgeous silver.

FOOD52 $–$$

food52.com/shop

Home to all manner of food forums and recipes from the ever-growing Food52 community, the site's equally extensive shop offering includes high-quality kitchen- and servingware, as well as great gifts.

GLOBAL TABLE $–$$

(212) 431-5839; globaltable.com

Packed with vibrant, unusual items from around the world (all of them simple and graceful, mostly modern in design). This tiny outfit in New York's SoHo is filled with vases, tableware and trays you won't see elsewhere.

GUMP'S $$

(800) 284-8677; gumps.com

This San Francisco emporium specializes in sophisticated, thoroughly grown-up good design—and the selection is mind-bogglingly comprehensive.

JAMALI GARDEN $

(201) 869-1333; jamaligarden.com

This unexpectedly amazing party resource offers strings of lights and floral designers' tools, as well as votive candles by the dozen.

MOTTAHEDEH $$–$$$

(800) 443-8225; mottahedeh.com

These reproductions of ultra-traditional antique porcelain china are classic, strikingly gorgeous and surprisingly cool.

PEARL RIVER $

(800) 878-2446; pearlriver.com

This is the go-to place for all things Asian and crazily inexpensive—ceramic soup bowls and sake sets, chopsticks and paper lanterns in every style and shade.

RALPH LAUREN HOME $$$

(888) 475-7674;

ralphlauren.com/home

Everything you need to live the Ralph life: a little safari, a little country, all gleaming with old-money swank. The silver-trimmed barware is especially handsome.

SUR LA TABLE $$

(800) 243-0852; surlatable.com

Look for serving pieces and utensils with a slightly rustic, European country feel.

TABLEART $$$

(323) 653-8278; tableartonline.com

The well-traveled owner of this high-end L.A. shop marries unexpected, little-known lines from Europe and Asia with marquee brands like Royal Copenhagen and Meissen.

TABULA TUA $$–$$$

(773) 525-0816; tabulatua.com

The inventory at this Chicago emporium is truly comprehensive (everyday plates, fine china, serving pieces, vases) and the roster of labels (Juliska, Michael Aram) very impressive.

FABRIC AND WALLPAPER (RETAIL)

CALICO CORNERS $

(800) 213-6366; calicocorners.com

The Gap of textile retailers, this national chain with tons of locations and a well-stocked website is a great resource for basic fabrics.

CALICO WALLPAPER $$$

(718) 243-1705;

calicowallpaper.com

Taking inspiration from the marbling traditions of Japan and Turkey—as well as NASA telescope imagery—this wallpaper studio keeps things interesting with eye-catching prints like the Aurora collection.

ESKAYEL $$

(347) 703-8084; eskayel.com

Perfectly faded graphic prints in soft blues, grays and pinks are this environmentally-minded company's signature, as well as nontoxic inks and sustainable materials like grass cloth.

THE BIG BLACK BOOK

FLORENCE BROADHURST $$$
(310) 659-3010; wandrlust.com
We absolutely love the iconic oversize flora and fauna designs by this legendary Australian designer; Woodson & Rummerfield's House of Design in L.A. carries her full line of papers and fabrics.

GRAHAM & BROWN $
(800) 554-0887; grahambrown.com
This well-organized online shop makes it easy to browse the house collections and a wide selection of papers by the likes of Marcel Wanders, Barbara Hulanicki and Julien Macdonald.

LES INDIENNES $$$
(518) 828-2811; lesindiennes.com
Created using naturally dyed cottons and traditional hand-blocking methods, Mary Mulcahy's gorgeously subtle, ethnic prints are a wonderful fit in even the most modern interior.

THE SILK TRADING CO. $–$$
(323) 954-9280; silktrading.com
With its huge array of traditional printed and solid textiles and ready-made curtains—much of it in stock—this spot takes the stress out of decorating.

WALNUT WALLPAPER $$$
(323) 932-9166;
walnutwallpaper.com
Located in Los Angeles but with a nicely comprehensive online gallery, this boutique specializes in unique papers by designers including Erica Wakerly.

FABRIC AND WALLPAPER (RETAIL & TRADE)

DE GOURNAY $$$ x
(212) 564-9750; degournay.com
The incredibly lush, hand-painted papers here align to create epic historical scenes or grand chinoiserie patterns, but even a single panel can remake a room.

FARROW & BALL $$$
(888) 511-1121; farrow-ball.com
The legendary English manufacturer (famous for its highly pigmented paints) crafts its historic wallpapers with time-tested methods and water-based paints, so that each panel's patterns and tones vary ever so subtly.

FLAVOR PAPER $$$
(718) 422-0230; flavorpaper.com
Featuring fire-hydrant toile, Warhol-inspired bananas and even scratch-and-sniff varieties, everything here is exuberant and statement-making—and hand-printed to order, just in case you want your favorite far-out pattern in a different color.

MARIMEKKO $–$$
(888) 308-9817; marimekkous.com
Finland's iconic textile and clothing design house continues to turn out bold, bright naif and classic mod prints that are a beautiful fit in any modern interior or ultra-cool kid's room.

NAMA ROCOCO $$$ x
(413) 652-2312; namarococo.com
We're huge fans of this contemporary line's extravagant, slightly funky wallpapers distinguished by their fusion of ornately old-fashioned and very contemporary design. All papers are sold by the sheet.

STUDIO PRINTWORKS
$$–$$$ x
(212) 633-6727;
studioprintworks.com
Fanciful, bold and graphic, these fabric and wallpaper designs are rooted in traditional motifs yet wholly modern and almost over-the-top.

TWENTY2 $$–$$$ x
(888) 222-3036; twenty2.net
The Connecticut-based studio creates striking abstract printed papers and coolly geometric textiles in an expansive palette of pop colors.

WAVERLY $$$ x
fabric: (877) 292-8375; wallpaper: (800) 375-9675; waverly.com
With an archive featuring 25,000 historic fabric patterns, this classic American brand, which launched in 1923, remains an excellent resource for classic designs.

FABRIC AND WALLPAPER (TRADE)

BRUNSCHWIG & FILS $$$ x
(800) 538-1880; brunschwig.com
This firm—more than a century old—is the place to go for authorized repros of Paule Marrot's cheerful florals and Kirk Brummel's contemporary fabrics and papers.

COLE & SON $$–$$$ x
+44 (0) 208-442-8844;
cole-and-son.com
Considerably bolder than you might expect from an outfit that counts the queen as a client, this British company's offerings run the gamut from exuberant nature prints to mod graphics.

COWTAN & TOUT $$–$$$ x
(212) 647-6900; cowtan.com
Old-fashioned and restrained, with shades of English country, the traditional prints here are sold alongside more colorful updates by Manuel Canovas and the girlishly sweet work of Jane Churchill.

DONGHIA $$–$$$ x
(800) 366-4442; donghia.com
Decorators rely on Donghia for beautifully earthy and textured papers and fabrics—we're particularly fond of its fine silks and durable outdoor textiles.

accessing "to the trade" products

WHAT DOES "TO THE TRADE" MEAN?
"To the trade" refers to fabric, wallpaper and furnishings that are available only at showrooms that sell exclusively to decorators, interior designers and architects.

WHAT DOES IT MEAN TO SELL RETAIL AND "TO THE TRADE"?
Some companies that offer "to the trade" discounts to design professionals also sell directly to consumers—at retail prices.

HOW TO BUY TRADE-ONLY PRODUCTS
Decorators and architects have access to every product under the sun; hire one and you will too. But it's also possible to go it alone. Many regional design centers have on-call staff (sometimes decorators) who can make purchases on your behalf from any of the to-the-trade companies listed in this guide, regardless of whether the company has a showroom on site. But you can even do it from home: If you find a fabric or wallpaper you love online or in a magazine, you can call a design service and ask someone there to buy it for you. Either way, you won't get the professionals' discount: You'll pay retail.

REGIONAL BUYING SERVICES

BOSTON
BOSTON DESIGN CENTER
Designer on Call
(617) 449-5501
bostondesign.com

DANIA BEACH, FL
DESIGN CENTER
OF THE AMERICAS
DCOTA Design Services
(954) 920-7997
dcota.com

DENVER
DENVER DESIGN DISTRICT
Designer Referral Service
(303) 733-2455
denverdesign.com

HOUSTON
DECORATIVE CENTER
HOUSTON
Decorative Center Services
(713) 961-9292
decorativecenter.com

LOS ANGELES
PACIFIC DESIGN CENTER
Pacific Design Services
(310) 657-0800
pacificdesigncenter.com

MINNEAPOLIS
INTERNATIONAL
MARKET SQUARE
Design Connection
(612) 338-6250
imsdesignonline.com

NEW YORK
DECORATION AND
DESIGN BUILDING
Design Professionals
(212) 759-5408
ddbuilding.com

NEW YORK DESIGN
CENTER
Interior Options
(212) 726-9708
nydc.com

SAN FRANCISCO
SAN FRANCISCO DESIGN
CENTER
Access Decor; (415) 565-7115
Buy Design; (415) 626-4944
Just Buy; (415) 626-5730
sfdesigncenter.com

DESIGN SOURCE
(415) 216-7067
designsource-sf.com

SEATTLE
SEATTLE DESIGN
CENTER
Studio Program
(206) 762-1200
seattledesigncenter.com

TROY, MI
MICHIGAN DESIGN CENTER
Featured Designers
(248) 649-4772
michigandesign.com

WASHINGTON, DC
WASHINGTON DESIGN
CENTER
designcenterdc.com

NATIONAL
L.A. DESIGN
CONCEPTS
(562) 439-5626
ladesignconcepts.com
Online buying service providing a website with direct links to more than 300 "to the trade only" manufacturers.

THE BIG BLACK BOOK

DURALEE $$x
(800) 275-3872; duralee.com
Great for all of the basics, this is also a good spot to find fun prints just waiting to be discovered and used to transform a fuddy-duddy hand-me-down.

GP & J BAKER $$$x
(800) 453-3563; gpjbaker.com
Find hundreds of historic and classic English patterns featuring subtle colorations, beautiful small prints and florals. Sprinkled throughout the traditional looks are cut velvets and wovens with a more modern sensibility.

HABLE CONSTRUCTION $$x
(212) 228-0814;
hableconstruction.com
Two girls from Texas own this Brooklyn-based company known for happy, naive-but-not-childish fabrics that strike the perfect medium between fun and sophisticated. A wide selection of the company's ready-made products—including totes, pillows and picture frames—are available online; fabrics are to the trade only.

HOLLAND & SHERRY $$–$$$x
(212) 355-6241; hollandsherry.com
There's no sorting through hundreds of patterns to get to the good stuff at this well-known rep: Everything is top-notch. Find tons of modern-classic looks from Elizabeth Dow, Winfield and Muriel Brandolini—all tasteful and completely un-granny-ish.

JOHN ROSSELLI & ASSOCIATES $$–$$$x
(212) 593-2060;
johnrosselliassociates.com
Those in the know trust this New York–based dealer for sublime textiles and wall coverings by Robert Kime, Peter Dunham, Carolina Irving and more.

KRAVET $$–$$$x
(800) 645-9068; kravet.com
The range of fabrics here is pretty dazzling, but it's the basics—simple colors, beautiful textures and timeless styles—that really move us. Look for designer lines by luminaries including Barbara Barry, Windsor Smith and Alexa Hampton.

LEE JOFA $$–$$$x
(800) 453-3563; leejofa.com
While we love all its luxe printed fabrics and wallpapers, our particular favorite at this established house is the gorgeous array of archival prints.

NEISHA CROSLAND $$–$$$x
(800) 803-2850;
neishacrosland.com
Prints by this London-based designer combine organic motifs with a glam sensibility; her cool circle and oval geometrics are special standouts.

OSBORNE & LITTLE $$–$$$x
(212) 751-3333; osborneandlittle.com
A leader in the industry since the 1960s, this London-based company has reissued its debut collection of papers, which range from opulent to proper. Don't miss designer Nina Campbell's historically inspired prints and Designers Guild's colorful patterns.

PHILLIP JEFFRIES LTD. $$$x
(973) 575-5414; phillipjeffries.com
A company all but synonymous with natural textured wall coverings stocks a rainbow selection of hundreds of grass-cloth papers.

PIERRE FREY $$–$$$x
(212) 421-0534; pierrefrey.com
This luxury house is so quint-essentially French—we love its elegant traditional fabrics and wallpapers, particularly the quirky toiles.

QUADRILLE $$–$$$x
(212) 753-2995;
quadrillefabrics.com
This is the source for the China Seas collection—hand-screened prints that hover between groovily geometric and beach-house boho—and the work of Alan Campbell, whose pop-y graphic designs make a dramatic statement.

RAOUL TEXTILES $$$x
(310) 657-4931; raoultextiles.com
The color-rich, exotic and occasionally eccentric prints rival those found at an authentic Indian marketplace. The sky's the limit in terms of customization—for a nominal fee, you can have your print of choice custom-colored.

SCALAMANDRÉ $$–$$$x
(800) 932-4361; scalamandre.com
A favorite for accurate reproductions of historical papers and textiles, as well as a signature line of luxe, antique-inspired contemporary designs.

SCHUMACHER $$$x
(800) 523-1200; fschumacher.com
This storied American company's designs skew to the classic, but we're also fans of its riskier contemporary design collaborations.

STUDIO FOUR NYC $$
(212) 475-4414; studiofournyc.com
This textile design studio boasts an eclectic inventory, including bright watercolors by Caitlin McGauley and textured florals from Ferrick Mason. Have your own designs in mind? Make an appointment with the in-house weaver to bring them to life.

SUPPLY SHOWROOM $$–$$$
(512) 770-6211;
supplyshowroom.com
Housed in a chic 1930s bungalow, this Austin home goods shop curates a thoughtful mix of wallpapers from small-batch studios such as Flat Vernacular and Relativity Textiles—each more eye-pleasing than the next.

TRAVERS $$$x
(212) 758-7925
Just the thing for a summer home, Travers fabrics are totally luxurious, with a timelessly preppy, almost tropical sensibility.

FLOORING

CARLISLE WIDE PLANK FLOORS $–$$$ x
(877) 627-4118;
wideplankflooring.com
The family business mills wide-plank, heart-pine flooring harvested from a 30,000-acre Alabama plantation, and offers reclaimed products that can all be traced to their structure of origin.

EXQUISITE SURFACES $$–$$$ x
(212) 355-7990; xsurfaces.com
Owner Paula Nataf and her treasure-hunters comb the world for finds, including antique French limestone and French oak, and the company's artisans handcraft beautiful reproductions.

MOHAWK $–$$$ x
(800) 266-4295;
mohawkflooring.com
Among the massive crop of flooring solutions from this behemoth, their line of laminates stands out for its sophisticated parquet and herringbone designs.

PARIS CERAMICS $$$ x
(888) 845-3487;
parisceramicsusa.com
Besides vending centuries-old and newly quarried limestone, the in-house design department here can conjure up mosaics, trompe l'oeil patterns and intricate carvings.

SHAW $ x
(800) 441-7429; shawfloors.com
A reliable source for literally thousands of basic, quality wall-to-wall and area options.

FURNITURE

1STDIBS.COM $$–$$$
Decorators rely on this dream resource filled with high-quality antiques and new items culled from some of the finest shops and showrooms in the US, France and England, all vetted by owner Michael Bruno's discriminating eye.

AMERICAN LEATHER $$–$$$ x
(800) 456-9599; americanleather.com
Known for forward-thinking leather pieces, the company also has more classic shapes (including sleeper sofas with solid wood bases replacing the usual metal bars).

BAKER $$$ x
(800) 592-2537; bakerfurniture.com
This classic American company offers an impressive breadth of shapes and styles, all elegant and handsomely tailored; we're particularly fond of the collections by Laura Kirar, Thomas Pheasant and Jacques Garcia.

BALLARD DESIGNS $$
(800) 536-7551; ballarddesigns.com
An always reliable resource for timeless styles: overstuffed couches, elegant lighting, needlepoint pillows—even adorable monogrammed party supplies.

BDDW $$$ x
(212) 625-1230; bddw.com
Score tomorrow's heirlooms today at this large New York showroom, where dramatically rugged and angular handcrafted minimalist wood pieces are built to last.

BERNHARDT $–$$ x
(828) 313-0795; bernhardt.com
This manufacturer's collection completely erases shopping anxiety: It's so well designed, you can buy all of it.

BOCONCEPT $–$$ x
(888) 616-3620; boconcept.com
The Danish retailer offers clean, contemporary Scandinavian design, including a wide range of appealingly simple beds, couches and dressers.

CB2 $
(800) 606-6252; cb2.com
We love the easy, unfussy modernism here—and the fact that everything is so incredibly priced.

CENTURY $$$ x
(800) 852-5552;
centuryfurniture.com
We love all the classic styles here, from Charlotte Moss, to Richard Frinier, to Candice Olson.

CISCO BROS. $$–$$$ x
(323) 778-8612; ciscobrothers.com
The unfussy classic styles hide a green secret: Everything here is built using sustainable wood and water-based glues, and manufactured with environmentally friendly processes.

DREXEL HERITAGE $$–$$$ x
(800) 444-3682; drexelheritage.com
The established American furniture maker offers a wide range of styles and collections, as well as a personalizable line with multiple finishes and hardware options.

ELITE LEATHER $$–$$$ x
eliteleather.com
A new English-inspired line by Nathan Turner (a former *domino* contributing editor) and designer Lulu DK's subtly glamorous collection bring some edge to this mostly old-school brand.

ETHAN ALLEN $–$$
(888) 324-3571; ethanallen.com
Though it excels at more traditional pieces (including wood canopy beds in dramatic ebony stains), we also like some of the brand's newer, more modern offerings, like leather sofas.

GEORGE SMITH $$$ x
(212) 226-4747; georgesmith.com
Beautifully made, timelessly chic—this is the place to find the upholstered pieces like English-style sofas and ottomans you'll really spend your life with.

GRANGE $$–$$$ x
(800) 472-6431; grange.fr
Hope the grandkids appreciate trad style: These classic European repros are so meticulously made—from the selection of the materials to the application of finishes—they'll be around for generations.

THE BIG BLACK BOOK

HICKORY CHAIR $$–$$$ x
(800) 225-0265; hickorychair.com
Founded in 1911, this company has built its name with well-crafted, highly traditional pieces destined to be heirlooms. Big-name designer collections include Alexa Hampton and Mariette Himes Gomez.

HORCHOW $$
(877) 944-9888; horchow.com
Loaded with carvings and painted insets inspired by Morocco, China and beyond, this establishment's opulent offerings only look as if they cost a fortune.

HUDSON BOSTON $$–$$$
(617) 292-0900; hudsonboston.com
This beautifully curated shop stocks a wide range of furniture (including some vintage treasures), as well as rugs, lighting and smaller accessories, most with a worn-in, preppy New England vibe.

KNOLL $$–$$$
(800) 343-5665; knoll.com
Housed in the permanent collections of museums around the world, this manufacturer's modern tables—the sensuous Saarinen, the sculptural Platner, Noguchi's lighthearted "Cyclone"—are sexy design icons.

MATTER $$–$$$
(212) 343-2600; mattermatters.com
Matter offers iconic designs alongside a host of interesting objects, many of them reflecting the store's environmentally and socially conscious stance.

MECOX GARDENS $$$ x
(212) 2249-5301; mecox.com
This mini-chain has seven locations, but the attitude of all the furniure, lighting, and accessories is distinctly Hamptons-inspired. The outdoor furniture is a standout.

MITCHELL GOLD + BOB WILLIAMS $$
(800) 489-4195; mgbwhome.com
If you thought this beloved company was only about sofas, think again: The constantly updated lighting and accessories collections are every bit as fresh.

MODSHOP $$
(844) 825-7612; modshop1.com
Filled with pieces big (sofas, dining tables and headboards) and small (vases, lighting and pillows), all of it comfortable and relaxed in styles from mid-century modern to Hollywood Regency.

NATUZZI $$–$$$ x
(212) 346-9760; natuzzi.us
The epitome of Italian modern design, its signature leather pieces are low, oversize and inviting. The more casual options, created with real life in mind, are perfect for a media room and cozy enough for kids.

OLY $$–$$$
(844) 354-2925; olystudio.com
This Berkeley, CA-based company is well loved for its updated riffs on classic French styles and its unique ability to mix antique and contemporary silhouettes.

RALPH LAUREN HOME $$$
(888) 475-7674; ralphlaurenhome.com
All-American classics dominate the iconic designer's gorgeous home collection, which is as thought-out and timelessly chic as the looks he sends down the runway.

ROOM & BOARD $–$$
(800) 301-9720; roomandboard.com
This popular American retailer offers easy, modern basics for every room in the house, plus outdoor and office styles. Standouts include desks and occasional chairs.

THOMASVILLE $$ x
(800) 225-0265; thomasville.com
More than 100 years after its founding, this company is adding choices that reference home and fashion trends but still maintain its traditional, unpretentious roots.

VITRA $$–$$$
(212) 463-5750; vitra.com
Since 1950, this company has manufactured furniture for an incredible range of progressive designers, including Charles and Ray Eames, George Nelson, Frank Gehry, Hella Jongerius and Verner Panton.

WILLIAMS-SONOMA HOME $$
(877) 812-6235; wshome.com
A reliable source for sophisticated, clean and tailored modern looks.

WISTERIA $$
(800) 320-9757; wisteria.com
The goods here run the gamut from sofas to votive holders, much of it slightly quirky, and imbued with a globe-trotting, flea-market vibe.

FURNITURE (RETAIL & TRADE)

LEE INDUSTRIES $$ x
(800) 892-7150; leeindustries.com
All of this eco manufacturer's classic upholstery offerings (slipper chairs, settees, sofas) now adhere to the company's Natural Lee standard, which means soy-based cushions, reclaimed-plastic backs and water-based finishes.

FURNITURE FOR KIDS

GIGGLE $–$$
(800) 495-8577; giggle.com
This boutique (and its excellent website) is always up on the latest in modern, child-friendly design. We especially like the cribs.

SERENA & LILY $$–$$$
(866) 597-2742; serenaandlily.com
Available at kids' boutiques nationwide, this contemporary line has a decidedly traditional bent, offering everything for the well-dressed nursery— we especially love the luxe bedding.

KITCHEN AND BATH CABINETRY

BOFFI $$$ x
(212) 431-8282; boffi.com
For more than 70 years, this company has issued cutting-edge, high-modern designs by leading architects. Slick, minimalist and beyond functional, the custom cabinetry here comes in a range of statement colors.

ECHELON CABINETRY $ x
(800) 522-0183;
echeloncabinetry.com
This giant also makes sturdy, mostly traditional-style cabinets.

KRAFTMAID CABINETRY $$ x
(888) 562-7744; kraftmaid.com
One of the first companies to offer affordable semicustom cabinetry.

POGGENPOHL $$$ x
(212) 228-3334; poggenpohl.com
With eye-popping shades and sleek silhouettes, the world's oldest kitchen-cabinet brand seduces like an Italian sports car. Innovations such as motorized drawers and eco-friendly water-based lacquers mean they perform equally well.

ST. CHARLES OF NEW YORK $$$ x
(212) 838-2812; stcharlesofny.com
This sleek, subtly retro all-metal cabinetry comes with a pedigree: It was used by Ludwig Mies van der Rohe at his iconic Farnsworth House and by Frank Lloyd Wright at Falling Water.

KITCHEN AND BATH FIXTURES/ HARDWARE (RETAIL)

DURAVIT $$–$$$ x
(888) 387-2848; duravit.us
Sleekness that doesn't leave you cold. Top styles: "Vero," "2nd Floor" and any of the Philippe Starck soakers.

ELKAY $$–$$$ x
(800) 476-4106; elkay.com
For the high-volume kitchen, the deep stainless-steel sinks with tight squared-off corners and flat sides accommodate pasta pots or a pile of dishes with aplomb.

FRANKE $$$
(800) 626-5771; franke.com/us
Designers adore these sturdy and attractive Swiss-engineered stainless sinks.

GROHE $$ x
(800) 444-7643; grohe.com/us
Europe's largest faucet manufacturer specializes in clean-lined, forward-thinking aesthetics and technological innovation.

HANSGROHE $$–$$$ x
(800) 334-0455; hansgrohe-usa.com
Solidly built European fittings, showerheads and more, ranging from traditional to hyper-minimalist. Top style: the whimsical, high-modern "Axor" line.

KALLISTA $$$ x
(888) 452-5547; kallista.com
A-listers Michael S Smith, Barbara Barry and Laura Kirar contribute stunning, mostly traditional bathware for this high-end manufacturer.

KOHLER $$–$$$ x
(800) 456-4537; us.kohler.com
Family-owned since 1873, this great American concern has everything—all of it incredibly well-made.

NEWPORT BRASS $$ x
(949) 417-5207; newportbrass.com
Conscientious decorators rely on the epic inventory at this affordable kitchen and bath depot. Top styles: #920 and #1600 series.

P.E. GUERIN, INC. $$$ x
(212) 243-5270; peguerin.com
The handiwork of this venerable family business—going strong since 1857—can be seen in historic homes around the US. If money's no object, indulge in the painstakingly crafted hardware.

RESTORATION HARDWARE $$
(800) 762-1005;
restorationhardware.com
Solid customer service and reasonable prices make shopping Resto's selection very satisfying. Top styles: "Spritz" and "Lugarno" faucets; "Hutton" washstand.

ROHL $$$ x
(800) 777-9762; rohlhome.com
Artisanal craftsmanship (e.g., faucets that riff on Edwardian and Georgian architecture), plus the sublime "Modern" line, make this brand feel older than its 33 years.

SIMON'S HARDWARE & BATH $–$$$ x
(888) 274-6667;
simons-hardware.com
This popular Manhattan showroom contains an impressive range of hardware and fixtures, from tiny minimalist hooks to grand old-fashioned tubs.

SUNRISE SPECIALTY $–$$ x
(510) 729-7277;
sunrisespecialty.com
This 44-year-old company carefully crafts authentic reproductions of Victorian-era bathware, including a huge range of cast-iron tubs and faucets, hand showers and tubfills.

URBAN ARCHAEOLOGY $–$$ x
(212) 371-4646;
urbanarchaeology.com
The storied New York destination offers a well-edited selection of stylish lighting, hardware, washstands and freestanding tubs.

WATERWORKS $$$ x
(800) 899-6757; waterworks.com
An established player in the pricey-but-worth-it category. Top styles: "Belle Epoque" and "Palladio" washstands; "Aero," "Easton" and "Julia" faucets; "Etoile" and "Opus" showerheads; and any of the exquisite tubs.

WHITECHAPEL LTD. $
(800) 468-5534;
whitechapel-ltd.com
A mind-boggling assortment of kitchen hardware fills this impressively organized website, from reproduction cabinet pulls to modern hinges to graceful latches.

THE BIG BLACK BOOK

KITCHEN AND BATH FIXTURES/ HARDWARE (TRADE & RETAIL)

E.R. BUTLER & CO. $$$ x
(617) 722-0230; erbutler.com
This high-end American manufacturer lovingly handcrafts a wide range of traditional and custom hardware and produces designs by such luminaries as Ted Muehling. Call to find distributors and showrooms.

THE NANZ COMPANY $$$ x
(212) 367-7000; nanz.com
All of the finely crafted high-end hinges, knobs and pulls here are truly beautiful. Though you won't get the trade discount, you can research products online and call the number above to be directed to a showroom salesperson who will place your order.

KITCHEN AND BATH FIXTURES/ HARDWARE (TRADE)

DORNBRACHT $$$ x
(800) 774-1181; dornbracht.com
The rigorously sleek, architectural hardware for kitchen and bath from this German manufacturer never forsakes functionality. Top style: the super-sultry "Tara" line. Note: Your contractor can buy this company's products for you.

KITCHEN AND BATH TILES

ANN SACKS $$–$$$ x
(800) 278-8453; annsacks.com
One of the biggest names in tile has everything from basic penny rounds to collections by designers Michael S Smith and Angela Adams.

COUNTRY FLOORS $–$$$ x
(212) 627-8300; countryfloors.com
Renowned for its European aesthetic and tiles based on 17th-, 18th- and 19th-century designs, this NYC-based company also showcases beautiful natural-stone and handmade terra-cotta options.

DALTILE $ x
(214) 398-1411; daltile.com
Inexpensive ceramic field tiles in a huge assortment of saturated hues are conveniently available at most home-improvement stores.

HEATH CERAMICS $$–$$$ x
(415) 361-5552 x12; heathceramics.com
Since 1948, this West Coast establishment has turned out the distinctive hand-glazed, gently modern work of groundbreaking artisan Edith Heath.

LIGHTING

APPARATUS $$$
(646) 527-9732; apparatusstudio.com
Sculptural pendant lights—sometimes in fanciful shapes, like the Cloud series—are the hallmark of this Manhattan duo, who also work in brass, marble and even horsehair.

CHRISTOPHER SPITZMILLER $$$
(212) 563-3030; christopherspitzmiller.com
Spitzmiller handcrafts modern lamps with classic influences (such as the gourd shape) in an array of colors and silhouettes.

CIRCA LIGHTING $–$$
(877) 762-2323; circalighting.com
With a tremendous stock of floor and table lamps, sconces and pendant lights—skewed toward the traditional, though nothing's too antique-y—it's no wonder this spot is so beloved by decorators.

ONE FORTY THREE $
(702) 566-8298; shop.onefortythree.com
It's hard to believe that each of the lamps on this site is individually made by a husband-wife team—for a steal, no less.

REJUVENATION $$
(888) 401-1900; rejuvenation.com
Besides a strong collection of antique fixtures and reproductions, the company has a take-back program to ensure its products don't end up in landfills.

SCHOOLHOUSE ELECTRIC AND SUPPLY CO. $
(800) 630-7113; schoolhouseelectric.com
Past and present merge in this up-and-comer's wide range of historically accurate luminaires, all of which can be hardwired to order for eco-friendly compact fluorescent lightbulbs.

THE URBAN ELECTRIC CO. $$$ x
(843) 723-8140; urbanelectricco.com
This Charleston-based concern collaborates closely with top designers (among them *domino* favorite Tom Scheerer) on updated but still timeless options.

YLIGHTING $
(866) 428-9289; ylighting.com
A mega-emporium with a massive assortment of modern options in every category.

PLANTS & OUTDOOR LIVING

THE SILL $$
thesill.com
A one-stop-(online) shop for all things botanical, from ferns potted in brightly colored vessels to succulent starter kits, this user-friendly site also offers tips and how-tos for aspiring green thumbs.

STEEL LIFE $$$
shopsteellife.com
This store's small but considered collection includes mid-century-style vessels in powder-coated steel and plant stands in walnut. For something extra-unique, you can also go the custom-made route.

TERRAIN $–$$
(877) 583-7724; shopterrain.com
A comprehensive source for gardening and outdoor living, Terrain stocks everything you might need for the patio, greenhouse, balcony and beyond— and gets that lightly weathered look just right.

··

RUGS (RETAIL)

··

ABC CARPET & HOME $$–$$$
(646) 602-3101; abchome.com
This sprawling superstore is stocked with rare gems like oversize rugs, unusual antiques and ethnic pieces from far-flung locations, alongside new collections like Madeline Weinrib's.

AELFIE $
(844) 235-3437; aelfie.com
New kid Aelfie offers reasonably priced rugs that are designed in Brooklyn and handmade by artisans in India. We're also partial to the candy-colored sheepskins and hand-dyed flatweave rugs for added boho cred.

CHRISTOPHER FARR $$$ x
(310) 967-0064; christopherfarr.com
In addition to Farr's own Josef Albers–inspired pieces, the innovators here carry works by such designers as Ilse Crawford and John Pawson.

DASH & ALBERT $–$$
(877) 586-4771; dashandalbert.com
Shop for amazingly well-priced colorful patterns, plus a big range of striped and floral options.

EMMA GARDNER DESIGN $$$ x
(877) 377-3144
emmagardnerdesign.com
Gardner turns out gorgeously hand-worked wool and silk rugs bearing her trademark eye-popping whimsical prints.

FLOR $
(866) 952-4093; flor.com
Environmentally responsible modular carpet tile that installs faster than wall-to-wall, goes with you when you move and can be replaced by section if it gets stained.

JUDY ROSS $$$
(212) 842-1705; judyrosstextiles.com
Cheerful and graphic, these organic-modern crewelwork designs in bright, saturated colors and earthy neutrals are hand-embroidered by Indian artisans.

KARASTAN $$ x
(800) 234-1120; karastan.com
Known for durable, well-made reproductions of orientals at all price levels, this trusted brand is revamping its image with modern collections and a super-helpful website that defuses oft-intimidating rug searches.

MANSOUR $$$ x
(310) 652-9999; mansour.com
Favored with the Royal Warrant by H.R.H., the Prince of Wales, these colossal showrooms (in London and L.A.) teem with high-high-end rare antiques from all over the world, plus Arts and Crafts, Deco and contemporary styles.

MANSOUR MODERN $$$ x
(310) 652-9999;
mansourmodern.com
The many inventive, ethnic-inspired patterns at this couture shop are especially strong, but the range of designs encompasses everything from graphic looks (Michael S Smith's collection is a standout) to subdued neutrals, all of it striking and well-crafted.

MERIDA MERIDIAN $$$ x
(800) 345-2200; meridastudio.com
An amazing source for natural-fiber floor coverings like sea grass and sisal, jute, abaca and beyond, all beautifully woven and bound in designs and patterns you won't see elsewhere.

ODEGARD CARPETS $$$ x
(212) 545-0205;
stephanieodegard.com
Company founder Stephanie Odegard introduced handmade Tibetan rugs to the US market, and she continues to offer bold, inspired designs, while promoting positive labor practices in Nepal.

OYYO $$–$$$
(+46) 76 891 19 08; oyyo.se
Working with organic cotton and vegetable dyes, this small Swedish studio uses traditional techniques to create their beautifully timeless weavings.

THE RUG COMPANY $$$ x
(800) 644-3963;
therugcompany.com
Paul Smith, Diane von Furstenberg, Vivienne Westwood, Matthew Williamson and other fashion names are among the collaborators working to revolutionize the rug world.

SAFAVIEH $$–$$$ x
(866) 422-9070; safavieh.com
More on the traditional, tailored end of the spectrum, the selection here includes Thomas O'Brien's cleaned-up ethnic looks and Martha Stewart's classically understated and neutral collection featuring faux bois and botanical looks.

RUGS (TRADE)

BEAUVAIS CARPETS $$$ x
(212) 688-2265;
beauvaiscarpets.com
As much an art gallery as a showroom, this spot is dedicated to fine antique rugs and equally authentic-feeling reproductions for the true connoisseur.

ELSON & COMPANY $$$ x
(800) 944-2858; elsoncompany.com
Handwoven by Tibetan weavers, the rugs here are far from boho. This San Francisco company's stock-in-trade is couture rugs by such respected names as Oscar de la Renta and Lulu DK.

KRAVET $$ x
(800) 645-9068; kravet.com
A great program here makes it possible to customize the color and design of any of the company's plush, understated Tibetan rugs.

STARK CARPET $$$
(844) 407-8275; starkcarpet.com
It's all about the selection and quality here, from antiques to repros, Aubussons to soumaks, and brilliant custom options.

VERMILION $$$ x
(212) 535-7614;
vermilionrugs.com
For modernists who crave thick, luxurious, durable floor coverings (and wouldn't be caught dead with an Aubusson), this is it. Choose from stunning options (including chain-link and Greek key), and be prepared to sink into something truly fantastic.

SMALL GOODS FOR THE HOME

HAWKINS NEW YORK $$
(844) 469-3344;
hawkinsnewyork.com
Artisanal know-how meets effortless chic at this homewares shop, where you can pick up the essentials—Moroccan water glasses, linen pillows, oak cutting boards—along with a few key pieces, like their popular Grady Ladder.

JOINERY $–$$
(347) 889-6164; joinerynyc.com
Purveyor of the famed Eagle and Diamond blankets in minimalist patterns, Joinery is your go-to for well-crafted treasures, like a Pioneer chair or festive papier maché mobile.

MOMA STORE $$–$$$
(800) 851-4509; momastore.org
One of the great museum stores, the Museum of Modern Art's shop is packed with modern classics and collectibles, and features an ever-expanding roster of lines (like Japanese mainstay Muji).

NANNIE INEZ $
(512) 428-6639; nannieinez.com
An Austin fixture, this concept shop prides itself on carrying hard-to-find pieces from around the world—at reasonable prices.

RUBY BEETS $$$ x
(631) 899-3275; rubybeets.com
New and vintage stock here includes farmhouse tables, metal baskets, muslin-upholstered George Sherlock sofas and Serge Mouille lamps. Ideal for finishing touches like wood-framed mirrors and simple oil paintings.

SPARTAN $$–$$$
(505) 600-1015; spartan-shop.com
The name says it all: this site is for lovers of design distilled to the most essential, with a focus on natural materials and rich textures.

Z GALLERIE $
(800) 908-6748; zgallerie.com
Find a wild mix of pieces—both playful and stately—from around the globe.

WINDOWS AND DOORS

ANDERSEN WINDOWS $$–$$$ x
(800) 426-4261;
andersenwindows.com
The name is deservedly synonymous with quality; the designs are all built to last, but it's the natural-wood construction and UV light–blocking technology that seal the deal.

JELD-WEN $–$$$ x
(800) 535-3936; jeld-wen.com
This company creates classic designs in whatever material— wood, vinyl or aluminum—suits your particular project. The accordion-like patio-door system offers streamlined connections between indoors and out.

MARVIN WINDOWS AND DOORS $–$$$ x
(888) 537-7828; marvin.com
A well-kept architect's secret, this is a great substitute for custom. Most of its prices are middle of the road, but the quality and looks are very high-end.

PELLA WINDOWS & DOORS $–$$ x
(877) 473-5527; pella.com
Offering many factory-assembled options that arrive ready to install, this is a good resource for DIY. Bonus: Rustic, handmade Rocky Mountain Hardware is included as an option for many doors.

SMITH & NOBLE $$
(888) 214-2134; smithandnoble.com
The go-to source for window treatments demystifies this complicated subject with well-priced offerings and an easy-to-navigate website.

stores that carry everything

ABC CARPET & HOME $$–$$$
(212) 473-3000; abchome.com
One-of-a-kind mega-emporium stocked with treasures old and new (many of them eco-friendly) from the most remote points on the globe. Look for the world's comfiest sofas and a well-vetted bedding selection.

ANTHROPOLOGIE $$
(800) 309-2500; anthropologie.com
This favorite has perfected a gently worn bohemian aesthetic that's reflected in everything from elegant sofas to small decorative accessories.

BED BATH & BEYOND $
(800) 462-3966; bedbathandbeyond.com
A mecca for home essentials, including amazing kitchen basics and exclusive bath accessories and bedding sets by designers like Jonathan Adler.

BLOOMINGDALE'S $$–$$$
(800) 777-0000; bloomingdales.com
The never-fail purveyor is especially reliable when it comes to tableware (Bernardaud, Kate Spade, Vera Wang) and bedding (everybody from Ralph to Donna). Plus, a big selection of furniture.

THE CONRAN SHOP $$–$$$
(866) 755-9079; conranusa.com
The source for nearly every iconic mid-century light fixture, eye-catching contemporary pieces from Philippe Starck and others, plus great housewares and children's goods.

CONTAINER STORE $–$$
(888) 266-8246; containerstore.com
Every basket and bin you need, plus killer closet-organizing tools and a strong selection of kitchen accessories. Bring in your measurements, and the experienced staff will help you design a custom storage solution.

CRATE & BARREL $$
(800) 967-6696; crateandbarrel.com
Handsome and solidly built, the mass retailer's furniture looks anything but. A favorite with decorators.

DESIGN WITHIN REACH $$$
(800) 944-2233; dwr.com
One-stop shopping for virtually every modern design classic.

THE FUTURE PERFECT $$$
(877) 388-7373; thefutureperfect.com
Once a modest shopfront in Brooklyn, this design emporium has expanded to include a whole array of housewares. We love their clever accents, like trompe l'oeil wallpaper and brass paperweights.

H.D. BUTTERCUP $$–$$$
(310) 558-8900; hdbuttercup.com
This unique concept fills the gap between big-box stores and exclusive design centers. More than 50 top furniture manufacturers offer everything from oriental carpets to luxury mattresses, without the usual middlemen.

HOLLYHOCK $$$ x
(310) 777-0100; hollyhockinc.com
Owner Suzanne Rheinstein's 25-year-old shop brings a dose of Upper East Side chic to La Cienega, with beautiful traditional antiques, from old-fashioned hemstitched napkins to Uzbekistani suzanis.

THE HOME DEPOT $
(800) 466-3337; homedepot.com
The renovator's best friend stocks well-priced kitchen and bath fixtures, cabinetry and outdoor essentials.

IKEA $
(800) 434-4532; ikea.com
Though the printed catalog might be easier to navigate than the massive stores, no one does inexpensive, elegantly modern furniture better.

JAYSON HOME $$–$$$
(800) 472-1885; jaysonhome.com
The superstore has a comprehensive stock of classic furniture and accessories, plus excellent vintage finds and a well-stocked garden section.

JOHN DERIAN COMPANY $$
(212) 677-8408; johnderian.com
While the website gives only a taste of this store's offerings, we had to include this because it is one of our favorite decorating and gift shops. All of the designer's découpaged pieces (plates, lamps and more) and an assemblage of French ceramics, Indian linens and upholstered furniture share the same slightly dark, Victorian feel.

JONATHAN ADLER $$
(800) 963-0891; jonathanadler.com
Design entrepreneur Adler turns out fun, pop-y yet glamorous rugs, ceramics, lamps, mirrors, furniture, objects and more.

LOWE'S $
(800) 445-6937; lowes.com
With its superior customer service and extensive options, this nationwide chain makes home improvement much less daunting.

MENU $$–$$$
(+45) 48-40-6100; store.menudesignshop.com
For the minimalist, Menu is a haven for simple, considered design with a Scandinavian feel (many of the designers hail from Europe).

POTTERY BARN $$
(888) 779-5176; potterybarn.com
The casual, kid-friendly pieces found here are like comfort food for your home.

TARGET $
(800) 591-3869; target.com
Big designers from Thomas O'Brien to Marimekko have done banner collections for this retail giant. Stay tuned for the next new designer rollout.

URBAN OUTFITTERS $
(800) 282-2200; urbanoutfitters.com
Cheery furnishings with a retro-luxe, dorm-room bent. Great for younger apartment dwellers.

WEST ELM $
(888) 922-4119; westelm.com
Modern basics, from perfectly proportioned Parsons tables to classic accent chairs.

WORLD MARKET $
(877) 967-5362; worldmarket.com
These souk-like spaces are packed with handmade furniture and smaller items from exotic locales—all of it very affordable.

acknowledgments

a big thank-you

To Sarah Min for wrestling this book out of our
hands and into print—without her, there
would be no *domino: The Book of Decorating*

To Stella Bugbee for her leadership, grace
and unerring design sensibility

To Ruth Altchek and Deb Schwartz, who wildly
exceeded the totally unreasonable demands
placed on them, and with charm and humor to boot

To Danielle Claro, Lia Ronnen and our
editors at Simon & Schuster,
David Rosenthal and Amanda Murray,
who nurtured this project from the beginning.

TO THE BRILLIANT PEOPLE
IN AND AROUND *DOMINO*
WHO CONTRIBUTED TO THIS BOOK

Melanie Acevedo, Rumaan Alan, Lisa Ano, Kristin Auble, Monika Biegler Eyers,
Kate Bolick, Grace Bonney, Chase Booth, Tom Borgese,
Beth Brenner, Elizabeth Brownfield, Missy Bruggeman, Susannah Kraft Butscher,
Alyson Cameron, Andrew Carbone, Jennifer Condon, Paul Costello,
Billy Cotton, Bridget Dearborn, Tom Delavan, Lili Diallo,
Cindy DiPrima, Kate Doherty, Rebecca Donnelly, Kate Donovan,
Lucilla Eschmann, Julia Felsenthal, Kim Ficaro,
Hilary Fitzgibbons, Miguel Flores-Vianna, Kim France,
Lucy Gilmour, Lauren Goodman, Ruth Graham, Alison Griffin,
Lisa Guernsey, Allison Gumbel, Catherine Halley, Mary Alice Haney,
Kirsten Hilgendorf, Shelley Jefferson, Victoria Jones, Jenny Kim,
Max Kim-Bee, Cynthia Kling, Rita Konig, Katie Levine, Isaac Lubow, Yarrow Lutz,
Stacie McCormick, Marian McEvoy, Clio McNicholl,
Tori Mellott, Olga Naiman, Joni Noe, Nick Olsen, Rebecca Omweg,
Stephen Orr, Nicolette Owen, Amy Peck, Chris Penberthy,
Chassie Post, Jen Renzi, Michelle Rubel, Christine Rudolph,
Eugenia Santiesteban, Allison Sarofim, Jeff Schad,
Sophie Schulte-Hillen, Robin Sillau, Emily Slaughter, Ariana Speyer,
Sunny Stafford, Allison Tick, Kate Townsend,
Stephen Treffinger, Nathan Turner, Lesley Unruh, Gretchen Vitamvas,
Brooke Williams, Bess Yoham, Macon York, Zoë Wolff, Alexandra Sanidad Zangrillo

TO OUR BOSSES FOR MAKING *DOMINO* POSSIBLE

S.I. Newhouse Jr., Charles Townsend, Tom Wallace, Rick Levine

TO OUR FAMILIES FOR MAKING EVERYTHING POSSIBLE

Jacob, Lily and Nathaniel Weisberg
Paul, Harrison and Carolina Costello
David, Sofia and Stefan Steinberger

xoxo, Deborah, Sara and Dara

more big thanks

TO THE HOMEOWNERS AND DESIGNERS WHO OPENED THEIR
DOORS—AND WHO INSPIRE OUR WORK

Jonathan Adler	Austin Harrelson	Serena Rees
Virginia Apple	Johnson Hartig	Suzanne Rheinstein
Kimberly Ayres	Carolina Herrera Jr.	Markham Roberts
Michael Bargo	Allegra Hicks	Kelly Rutherford
Sara Bengur	India Hicks	Schuyler Samperton
Barrie & Matt Benson	Ames Ingham	Michelle & Derek Sanders
Nate Berkus	Carolina Irving	Ahmad Sardar-Afkhami
Barbara Bestor	Katie Lee Joel	Gil Schafer
Elizabeth Blitzer	Jenni Kayne	Tom Scheerer
Sheila Bridges	Liz Lange	Carina Schott
Anita Calero	Celerie Kemble	Suze Yalof Schwartz
Nina Campbell	Delphine Krakoff	Suzanne & Christopher Sharp
Haylynn Cohen	Marisa Leichtling	Sarah Shetter
Eric Cohler	Christian Liaigre	Stephen Shubel
Cristi Conaway	Katie Lydon	Kari Sigerson
Natascha Couvreur ·	Lily Maddock	Sharon Simonaire
Ilse Crawford	Lisa Mahar	Ione Skye
Gray Davis	David Mann	Windsor Smith
James Leland Day	Jenna Lyons Mazeau & Vincent Mazeau	Ruthie Sommers
Cloud Devine & Laura Resen	Annsley McAleer	Estee Stanley
Peter Dunham	Mary McDonald	Matthew Sudock
Ashley Edwards	Mary McGee	Alice Temperley
Stephen Elrod	Will Meyer	The Apartment
Tripp Evans	Charlotte Moss	Laurie Thiel
Krista Ewart	Adrienne Neff	Antony Todd
Erin Fetherston	David Netto	Benjamin Trigano
Vesta Fort	Thomas O'Brien	Camilla Trigano
Fawn Galli	Frouwkje & Stéphane Pagani	Chloe Warner
Steven Gambrel & Chris Connor	Lisa Perry	Timothy Whealon
Meghan Gerety & Michael Phelan	Mary Jane Pool	Ashley Whittaker
Tori Golub	Laura Vinroot Poole	Vicente Wolf
Albert Hadley	Jessie Randall	Lucy Wrubel
	Miles Redd	Laura Yaggy

fabric & wallpaper credits

cover
DE GOURNAY
"Portobello"
#541141
wallpaper in
Blue Gray
degournay.com

p.82
OSBORNE
& LITTLE
"Sabai" #F974/07
fabric
osborneandlittle.com

p.212
HINSON
& COMPANY
"Trixie" #HP-1003-R
wallpaper in Red/
Black on White
(212) 475-4100

p.6
COLE & SON
"Malabar-W"
#66/1006 wallpaper
in Pale Blue and
White
cole-and-son.com

p.108
MANUEL
CANOVAS
"Treillis" #3021-07
wallpaper in
Citrine
cowtan.com

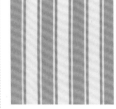

p.238
BRUNSCHWIG
& FILS
"Island
Taffeta Stripe"
#89302.01/440
fabric in Ivy
brunschwig.com

p.10
SCHUMACHER
"Vallier Vine"
#173771 fabric in
Graphite, Matthew
Patrick Smyth
Collection for
Schumacher
fschumacher.com

p.134
LEE JOFA
"Althea"
#879001-LJ
fabric in Beige,
Leafgreen on
Ivory
leejofa.com

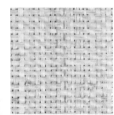

p.250
HINSON & COMPANY
"Coarse Madagascar-
Unbacked"
#HY-0390-AU
wallpaper
(212) 475-4100

p.24
ALAN CAMPBELL
"Saya Gata"
#AC207-45 in Blue
on tinted linen
quadrillefabrics.com

p.162
BOB COLLINS
"Lotus Dynasty"
#KB.V.202 fabric
in Peach and
Turquoise
(800) 282-9971

p.264
GP & J BAKER
#158408C fabric in
#R1375-3 color
gpjbaker.com

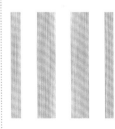

p.50
FARROW & BALL
"Plain Stripe"
#ST 1704 wallpaper
in Grisaille
farrow-ball.com

p.186
TRAVERS
"Grammont"
linen #107133
in Chestnut/
Champagne
(212) 888-7900

photography credits

ABRANOWICZ, WILLIAM
41, 76, 97, 151, 177, 201, 205

ACEVEDO, MELANIE
14-15, 20-21, 37, 66, 67, 69, 71,
73, 75, 78, 80, 94, 97, 99, 128,
140-141, 151, 153, 157, 164-165,
166-167, 179, 192-193, 201, 207,
216-217, 227, 229, 231, 233

ACHILLEOS, ANTONIS
45, 127

ALBIANI, MATT
36, 126, 155

ALLEN, LUCAS
26-27, 39, 69, 71

ARNAUD, MICHEL
103

BELLO, ROLAND
46

BERNHAUT, JUSTIN
43, 95, 101, 123, 155, 203, 229

BLACK, DAVID
79, 157

CAHAN, ERIC
56-57, 101, 178, 205

CALERO, ANITA
180

CARTER, EARL
64, 67

CORONA, LIVIA
103

COSTELLO, PAUL
14-15, 30-31, 40, 41, 52-53, 58-59,
67, 72, 77, 78, 99, 102, 103, 120,
123, 125, 129, 130, 131, 132-133,
142-143, 148, 149, 151, 155, 157,
158, 160-161, 168-169, 174, 177,
179, 181, 182, 184-185, 188-189,
199, 200, 201, 214-215, 224, 227,
228, 229

DEVINE, CLOUD
43

DIRAND, JACQUES
43 (top right, home of Christian
Liaigre), 54-55, 68, 198

DISCHINGER, FRANÇOIS
39

DONNE, TARA
175

ESTERSOHN, PIETER
125

FLORES-VIANNA, MIGUEL
39, 41, 74, 75, 86-87, 101, 121,
154, 156

FREEMAN, DON
45, 65

FRIEDMAN, DOUGLAS
73, 97, 100, 123, 124, 127, 157,
202, 231

GRUEN, JOHN
155

HRANEK, MATTHEW
71, 152, 225, 232

ISAGER, DITTE
129, 199

JAFFE, DEBORAH
18, 19, 69

KIM-BEE, MAX
65, 136-137, 150, 190-191, 203,
204, 207, 208, 210-211, 226

KVALSVIK, ERIK
174

LAGNESE, FRANCESCO
39, 45, 71, 181, 203

McHUGH, JOSHUA
121, 125, 175

MERRELL, JAMES
36, 43, 44, 129, 151

MOORE, ANGELA
28-29

MOSS, LAURA
127

MUNRO, SOPHIE
64, 70

OTSEA, ERIK
103

PENNEY, JASON
198

RESEN, LAURA
84-85, 88-89, 94, 96, 99,
114-115, 153, 225, 227, 229

ROWLEY, ALEXANDRA
122

SAMUELSON, JEREMY
231

SCHLECHTER, ANNIE
42, 46, 48-49, 73, 104,
106-107, 120, 127, 205, 231,
234-235, 236-237

SLERTMAN, MILLA
21

UNRUH, LESLEY
79

UPTON, SIMON
37, 75, 101, 112-113,
138-139, 149, 153, 176, 177,
181, 206, 207, 218-219, 224,
227, 233

VANG, MIKKEL
41, 77, 78, 80-81, 95, 203

WADDELL, JAMES
20-21, 38, 98, 110-111, 177,
179, 230

WALTER, COREY
67, 69

WATSON, SIMON
99, 125

WOLF, ANNA
75, 207

EDITED BY
**Danielle Claro,
Ruth Altchek & Deb Schwartz**

DESIGN DIRECTION
Stella Bugbee

DESIGN BY
James Casey

CHAPTER OPENERS & FURNITURE ILLUSTRATIONS
James Noel Smith

FLOOR-PLAN ILLUSTRATIONS
Matthew Caserta

HANDBOOK ILLUSTRATIONS
Frank Santoro

———————————

PRODUCED BY

Melcher Media, Inc., 124 W. 13th St., New York, NY

Charles Melcher, Publisher
Bonnie Eldon, Associate Publisher
Duncan Bock, Editor in Chief
Lia Ronnen, Executive Editor
Coco Joly & Daniel del Valle, Editorial Assistants
Jessi Rymill, Production Artist
Kurt Andrews, Production Director

———————————

This book was typeset in *domino* Clarendon,
domino News and *domino* Stymie.

domino

Your Guide to a Stylish Home

domino

Your Guide to a Stylish Home

discovering your personal style and creating a space you love

by *domino* editors
Jessica Romm Perez
Shani Silver

Text by Nicole Sforza
Designed by Jennifer S. Muller

Produced by

MELCHER MEDIA

Published by

Simon & Schuster

Simon & Schuster
1230 Avenue of the Americas New York, NY 10020

First Simon & Schuster hardcover edition November 2016

SIMON & SCHUSTER and colophon are registered trademarks of Simon & Schuster, Inc.

For information about special discounts for bulk purchases, please contact
Simon & Schuster Special Sales at 1-866-506-1949 or business@simonandschuster.com

The Simon & Schuster Speakers Bureau can bring authors to your live event.
For more information or to book an event contact the Simon & Schuster Speakers Bureau
at 1-866-248-3049 or visit our website at www.simonspeakers.com.

Produced by
MELCHER MEDIA 124 West 13th Street, New York, NY 10011
www.melcher.com

Printed in China
10 9 8 7 6 5 4 3

Library of Congress Cataloging-in-Publication Data

Title: Domino : your guide to a stylish home / editors of Domino,
Jessica Romm Perez, Shani Silver.
Other titles: Domino (Simon and Schuster, Inc.) | Domino
(Condé Nast Publications)
Description: First Simon & Schuster hardcover edition. | New York:
Simon & Schuster, 2016.
Identifiers: LCCN 2016031819 (print) | LCCN 2016032162 (ebook)
| ISBN 9781501151873 (hardcover) | ISBN 9781501151880 (ebook)
Subjects: LCSH: Interior decoration.
Classification: LCC NK1990 .D66 2016 (print) | LCC NK1990 (ebook)
| DDC 747--dc23
LC record available at https://lccn.loc.gov/2016031819

ISBN 978-1-5011-5187-3
ISBN 978-1-5011-5188-0 (ebook)

Cover art: Timorous Beasties wallpaper pattern "Butterflies"
timorousbeasties.com

to the dedicated readers of *domino*—then, now, and always.

CONTENTS

INTRODUCTION

In our first book, *domino: the book of decorating*, you welcomed us into your space as we defined the essentials that make a home complete. Here, in our second book, we'll find out what makes a home yours.

We couldn't be happier to be home with you again, helping you discover your personal style. We will go beyond basics and show you how style comes to life in a room, and throughout a home. In the pages that follow, we'll walk with you through the design moments that define your personal style, and we'll help you bring them home.

We'll share rooms we love, statement-making ideas to guide and inspire you, side-by-side examples that illuminate ideas, and our favorite home decor finds (and where to shop for them). We'll meet trusted voices in style and interiors who will share their advice on how to create the best space for you. Through it all, you'll find exciting inspiration and design solutions that are relatable, motivating, and above all, brimming with style.

It's good to be home, again. Welcome to *domino*.

Your Editors,

Jessica Romm Perez + Shani Silver

1
OWN YOUR STYLE

Design success comes down to being confident in your choices. So many people decorate for others—they're concerned about outside opinions and wanting to impress. But you don't live in a hotel. You're not decorating for the gala of the century. It's your home, and it should feel like a home— with character and imperfection and all the things that make you happy.

Your home needn't be pristine and poised, as if you're trying to win an award. It should be a place you live your life the way you want. If you can't confidently entertain in your dining room, or relax with a good read in a favorite chair, how can you feel at home? What makes a home great—and great for you—is when it feels like you. And that's our goal here—to help you personalize your surroundings, often with items you already own, so that when you walk through the door, you feel an instant sense of welcome, calm, and home.

A brazen mix of color, pattern, and art expresses the creative nature of the homeowner.

1 get inspired

It's tough to style a space if you don't know what your style is, but there are ways to find your design voice. Zero in on what inspires you. The amount of information out there is overwhelming, but you can use it to your advantage. Scour Pinterest, steal ideas from a favorite restaurant, and start to build inspiration boards. Follow people on Instagram whose style you admire. Check out fashion designers, artists, architects, and gardening gurus.

If you're a hands-on type, great—grab a bulletin board and get to work; use anything from a cool embossed coaster to a fabric swatch in a color you're obsessed with. Tear out magazine pages of rooms that feel right, pin up paint chips, and include pictures of places that speak to you—the woods, the desert, distant destinations—then find images of furnishings that evoke the same feelings. You'll start to see themes developing— colors you're drawn to, pieces that feel right.

Practice gleaning inspiration from your everyday life, too. Look at the places you frequent through a new lens. Maybe you've always admired the light fixture in your favorite coffee shop—ask where it's from. During movie marathons, pay attention to interior scenes and note any items that stand out to you. When you go to someone's house, think about what you like and what you'd change; pinpointing what you don't love helps you identify what you do.

When your home truly starts to resemble you—the clothes you'd wear, the accessories you'd choose—you know you're onto something. It makes sense—your home is an extension of you, an embodiment of your personality. If you're a black, gray, and navy person, with nary a pattern to be seen, maybe that bold print sofa isn't the right fit. If you gravitate toward chunky sweaters, perhaps a slouchy, deep armchair is your thing and you can skip the angular version. So peek into your closet for inspiration.

A wood-paneled wall helps unify a bevy of inspiration and turn it into a point of interest. Mixing clippings with a mobile, necklace, plant, and tapestry sparks imagination and fosters a free-spirited feel.

2 find your aesthetic

Identifying the styles you like is a key component of crafting a home that feels like you.

Maybe you're into modern, clean lines and livable, simple furnishings. If too much stuff stresses you out and you like things with clear function, you may lean more toward minimalism or airy, fresh Scandinavian style. Perhaps you're a flea-market aficionado who spends all day foraging for treasures. Or you're a midcentury fan and the sight of an iconic molded plastic chair or elegant teak bar cart excites you. If you're a go-with-the-flow type who can't be bound by rules—preferring distressed furniture to polished pieces, intricate patterns to blocks of color—then you're more bohemian.

Homebodies and outdoorsy types are often drawn to a rustic style—with comfy sofas, lived-in furniture, weathered wood, and an earthy palette. Traditional types appreciate history, familiarity, and warmth. Some people like to showcase things that others want to hide—piping, bulbs, ducts—and prefer an industrial look.

You don't have to pick one look and stick with it. You can mix things up, pairing a brass sconce with a dhurrie rug. But knowing what excites you helps define your style. Those tough decisions will become few and farther between, because if you've figured out what you like, you'll make decorating decisions from a more relaxed, confident place. And every piece will contribute to making your home a comfortable haven.

3 take action

It's tough to infuse your space with fresh energy when old items bring you down. Furnishings emit a sort of energy, too—so if a chair looks sad and you're just not feeling it, maybe it isn't meant for your space.

Walk around your home with notebook in hand and your go-to style(s) in mind; look at each item and decide if you love it. If you're not into something, let it go; you'll be able to replace it with something you adore. Indecision is stagnation, and making one decision can open the floodgates for others to follow. The more decisions you make, the more confident you'll become.

Group items that make the cut by texture, color, material, and size, so you can see how they work together. And take note of what you need to buy. When it's time to get working, break projects into manageable chunks. Write a to-do list, and be specific: Go to a paint store; test samples; ask friends for painter recommendations; and so on. Maybe you take on one project a weekend, but start small—empty a bookshelf and fill it up with things you love to see when you enter the room.

Commit to creating a home that truly reflects who you are. Push yourself. Typically, the decorating decisions that feel a little bit scary at first are the ones you'll end up cherishing the most.

As you push forward, keep in mind that a personality-packed home:

sparks stories: Meaningful objects—whether an heirloom quilt or a photo blown up from vacation—tell a story about who you are and give people insights into your character. They signal that your home is more about the people within it than the actual furnishings.

evolves over time: People change, tastes change, situations change—and so should your home. Objects are added to vignettes and replaced, photos are swapped out, paint colors evolve.

plays with contrast: Opposing forces give a home a sense of push-and-pull. Black with white, rough with smooth, tall with short, modern with traditional—these are the types of pairings that make a space feel alive.

has rhythm: A home should have an almost perceivable pulse—a certain energy you feel right when you walk inside, a sense of movement that's created from thoughtfully placed patterns, rooms that flow into the next, a color palette that ushers you from room to room.

takes risks: Truly memorable rooms don't always play it safe. A huge painting as a focal point, a moody sculpture, a wooden floor painted an unexpected color all signal that your space is an expression of you with special attributes that no one else can claim as their own. When you can infuse a home with personality and warmth, that's when you've made styling magic.

The best displays aren't just for show—they evoke emotion. Weave in a few of your most intimate personal possessions for maximum impact.

4 let it flow

It's important to note that your home will never truly be "done"—and it never has to.be. It's understandable to want to feel like a project is finished, but your style will evolve, and your home will be an expression of that. When we're so focused on the outcome, we don't enjoy the process (as much). When you see your space as an ongoing project, great things can happen—and stress won't weigh you down. Sometimes when you least expect it, rather than when you're actively looking, a mirror or console that's perfect will come into your life. Be patient and wait to find pieces that inspire you.

Your home isn't simply the items in it—it is more about crafting a space to share with the people you love. It doesn't need to be perfect—it just needs to be perfect for *you*.

Weaving in treasures and artifacts from world travels allows your home to grow with you, turning it into a living, breathing interpretation of your life.

Curvy chairs mimic the lines of a midcentury table, while beadboard walls add textural contrast.

2

SEATING

SEATING
WE LOVE

smart ideas for every
room in the house

office

Swap out a standard desk chair for one with style to spare and
you'll change the whole feel of the room. Plush padding promises
comfort, a solid wood frame guarantees stability, and the small
scale is perfectly proportioned for a space-challenged alcove.

entryway

A rustic wooden bench is welcoming and provides a
place to slip on shoes. Art makes an often neglected
spot feel like a real room.

dining room

Thanks to vibrant green paint, traditional chairs shed their formality and add an element of personal style and boldness. The chairs' spindles echo the vertical lines of the ample windows.

living room

A spacious living room can handle multiple layers of seating, from a comfy couch to deep armchairs to lightweight occasional chairs that can move around with ease. The lipstick-red legs on an Eames wire chair offer a colorful diversion within a neutral scheme.

bedroom

Happiness is a chocolate velvet love seat at the foot of a canopy bed. The settee's small scale adds comfort to the room without overpowering it.

dressing room

Seating should suit the space: In a cool, unexpected nook, a blue stool feels at home among colorful shoes and bags. The hue complements the wallpaper and art, and the texture adds a layered element that completes the corner.

HANDBOOK

understanding upholstery

		why we love it	*take note*
leather		Like a moto jacket, it's tough, cool and luxe, and can handle the occasional spill.	Shinier versions will feel cold on bare skin—have lots of throws on hand.
wool		Durable and soft, plus it's naturally wrinkle- and pill-resistant.	Look for a wool blend for more stain resistance and less chance of felting (where fibers rub together to form felt).
silk		It doesn't get more chic than this. A silk settee? Count us in.	Silk isn't hardy enough for your everyday sofa; it needs professional cleaning if stained.
linen		Crisp and slightly textured, it's an elegant choice that won't fade or pill.	Linen stains and wrinkles easily, and can weaken when exposed to too much sun.
cotton		It can go formal (damask) or casual (canvas). Cotton velvet is sumptuous yet surprisingly durable—the perfect mix.	Dirt and dust will show and so will wrinkles, but blending cotton with other materials makes up for these shortcomings.
synthetics (olefin, acrylic, polyester, rayon, acetate, nylon)		On their own, blended together, or blended with natural fibers, these fabulous options win on many fronts—most are wrinkle-, stain-, and fade-resistant.	Acetate (imitation silk) is still delicate, so, like true silk, it's best for a showpiece not everyday seating.

STYLE
STATEMENTS

snapshots of inspiring ideas

minimalist

the mood: clean, unencumbered, graphic.

styling notes: Finding a sectional big enough for this loft-like space was difficult, so three twin mattresses were framed in plywood instead; the lids along the arms and back flip up to reveal storage. Furthering the low-lying scheme, the coffee table is actually two Ikea TV stands with the legs removed.

classic

the mood: fresh, elegant, cheerful.

styling notes: In a formal room, sunny yellow upholstery feels like a welcome relief, whisking away potential stuffiness and fostering a friendly vibe. The detailing on the chair frames echoes the textured, paneled walls.

eclectic

the mood: unconventional, collected, fun.

styling notes: Solid upholstery and white walls allow the rest of the room to wave its flag (literally). Geometric patterns, from the tiled fireplace to the pillows, are big and bold—small prints would feel too busy in this bustling space.

get the look

↓

midcentury

A lounge-worthy dining set and matching wood floors bring the high ceilings and elaborate 19th-century moldings down to earth. With no upholstery in the room, subtle bursts of color from a cobalt sculpture and orange floor lamp add warmth and energy.

saucer pendant

oval dining table

Ellsworth Kelly
monograph

sheepskin rug

burnished vase

plywood chair

marble arch
candleholder

Turn to page 270 for information on these products.

STYLE
SCHOOL

a few of our favorite chairs

2. the rocking chair

Exciting in both material (lacquered steel slung with leather) and color, this rocker is the brainchild of Belgian husband-and-wife team Hannes Van Severen and Fien Muller. It's a brilliant example of marrying function with flair.

1. the acapulco

Pear-shaped and cushion-free, it brings beach vibes a bit of cool structure. The steel frame is wrapped with comfy vinyl cord that won't get hot in the sun, easily hoses down, and never stays wet.

3. the modern wingback

When you want to shut out the world but still be comfortable, it doesn't get better than a chair with generous proportions and a sense of exclusivity. A wingback looks particularly throne-like at the head and foot of a dining table and pairs well with a large sofa and roaring fire, too. This version, designed by Luca Nichetto, features layered, upholstered panels resting on a solid wood base.

4. the bergère

This stately lounging chair, with an exposed wooden frame, upholstered back, and loose seat cushion, dates to 18th-century France. It blends seamlessly into a French country style, but can also hold its own in an eclectic space, bringing a refined air.

5. the paimio

A stunning example of midcentury prowess, Alvar Aalto's 1932 design is made of a bent birch frame with a thin plywood seat that scrolls at the top and bottom for resiliency. The back reclines slightly for comfort, and two side loops act as chair arms, legs, and floor runners.

6. the bertoia diamond

Designed in 1952, this iconic beauty is a fluid, almost aerodynamic wonder crafted of welded mesh steel that's strong but airy. It manages to be delicate and industrial at the same time.

7. the modern slipper

Introduced in 18th-century Europe, these petite, armless, often low-to-the-ground chairs allowed women wearing layers upon layers of clothing to more easily put on their slippers. Today's tailored, more streamlined silhouettes take over where full-size chairs can't go, such as an awkward corner, a landing, or at the foot of a bed. This plush version pairs a raffia base with linen upholstery.

perfect perches

pouf

frequently spotted...
as a footstool in the living room;
as an extra seat in a packed family
room; or in a kids' room as an
all-purpose activity perch.

specs
These laid-back loungers are
typically 16 to 22 inches in diameter
and about 12 to 17 inches high.

materials
Treat a pouf as an accent piece—
think cool metallics, sleek cowhide,
chunky knits, or the irresistible
softness of Mongolian lamb fur.

ottoman

frequently spotted...
placed in pairs in the living room or at the end of your bed; in the kids' room doing double duty as a desk chair and toy chest—storage versions are clutch.

specs
Roughly the same height as your sofa looks best. Top with a tray and it's a table—just leave a few inches of space all around so you still have room to prop your feet.

materials
Look for hardy materials like leather, indoor/outdoor fabric, or a washable slipcover. And don't go matchy-matchy here—contrast the sofa and use a wild pattern, lots of tufting, piping, or nailhead trim. X-bases add geometry.

bench

frequently spotted...
in the entryway; at the foot of a bed; on one side of a kitchen or dining table to maximize seating and add variety.

specs
Many benches are 18 to 20 inches tall; to ensure two people will fit comfortably, go for at least 48 inches long.

materials
Crushed velvet or silk are fantastic for a piece that doesn't get too much use, and don't overlook outdoor pieces—metal or wood in a fun color can look incredible inside, especially topped with a cushion. If the bench is against the wall, forgo a back (it's airier).

style standoff

symmetry vs. asymmetry

symmetry: Logical, ordered setups suit those craving balance and serenity. Try this if you have a focal point to decorate around, such as a fireplace or built-in bookcases. Keep some things askew, so it doesn't feel contrived. Here, throw pillows share a palette, but their designs differ slightly; same with the art. One floor lamp off to the side prevents the room from feeling too prim.

asymmetry: Unstructured seating feels playful and casual, and instantly puts people at ease. The arrangement allows for more flexibility, giving you freedom to arrange and rearrange on a whim, and to work in one-of-a-kind flea-market finds when inspiration strikes.

style standoff

patterned sofas vs. solid sofas

patterned: Bold prints inject energy, and can happily hide spills and marks. A neutral pattern (this is Brunschwig & Fils' Les Touches) lets you toss in colorful accents and change them at will. Play around with contrast; try a modern print on a traditional sofa, or a sweet floral on a straight-lined couch.

solid: One-note upholstery feels soothing and calm. When paired with a matching rug, you've got a pleasant, muted canvas for introducing pattern elsewhere. A statement wallpaper wall behind the sofa feels fresh.

pattern party

big and small prints

Patterns on opposite sides of the style spectrum (a buttoned-up pinstripe and a free-spirited floral) can play nice as long as they share a similar tone. And everybody has a palette pal—the green floral chairs speak to the fiddle-leaf fig tree, the pink and purple rug to the flowers, and the black-and-white settee to the lamp shade, table base, and dresser.

complementary colors

Orange and blue are across from each other on the color wheel, so the sofa and art intrinsically balance each other. And the value (or vividness) of both colors is similar. Covering a traditional sofa with an electric color feels fresh, as does the all-over pillow parade. Though the pillows are various sizes and patterns, they mesh well because they all feature blue, orange, black, or white.

bonnie's tips

1. Keep it all very natural. I call it "orderly chaos." For example: Instead of putting your collection of cups in one straight line across a shelf, stack them at different heights or put them on top of plate stacks in various colors and textures. It's more interesting to style your home in such a way that is not completely perfect.

2. Use natural light when photographing moments in your house. If necessary, put things near a window to help maximize the daylight.

3. Try to keep the background as neutral as possible, especially if the foreground has a lot going on. Also, be careful to avoid too much clutter when taking a "shelfie" or photographing a vignette. Keep it simple and well-balanced.

4. Make it a true expression of yourself.

5. Don't post randomly. Photograph moments that feel special, and choose the right time to share them. Make sure you are complementing your overall feed, so there's a sense of continuity.

6. Stick to a unified palette when buying special objects. Staying true to the colors that express your personality will not only make for a stronger feed, it will also help define your own personal style.

inspiring style:

bonnie tsang
(on the art of photo sharing)

Originally a graphic designer, Bonnie Tsang took an unusual road to becoming a photographer. While embracing motherhood and with plenty of encouragement from her photographer father, she began documenting her new life with her young child. Her snapshots attracted a large audience. "I started posting pictures of my daughter on Flickr (the social media du jour at the time). Luckily for me photographs of kids happen to be extremely popular and I began to build a real following."

"As a photographer, I love anything that helps me get my ideas out into the world. In the old days, we would just share with our immediate circle of friends, but now—with blogs, Instagram, and Pinterest—there's a huge audience." Photographs might feature anything from a beautiful breakfast she has created, to a still life of her bedside table, to some newly purchased bed linens. "If the lighting is perfect and the messiness is just right, it makes me want to pick up my camera or phone and snap a picture to share with the world."

3 no-fail
seating setups

formal

A squared-off, elegant look, with two chairs facing the sofa, parallel to each
other, and a small table in between, makes for a balanced look that has depth.

something in between

Two chairs facing the sofa but angled toward each other creates a circular,
familial feel with no corners to bump into—great with a round coffee table.

casual

An L-shaped design gives everyone lots of space to stretch out.
Sectionals are perfect for a laid-back look.

playing with height: low-lying seating

Relaxed, inviting, and the epitome of casual-chic, a low-lying arrangement (about 33 or 34 inches high) can make a tight space feel bigger and low ceilings feel taller. The look can be well-traveled and formal or bohemian and fun; either way it'll have a gather-round-and-chat-all-night feel, especially when joined by floor cushions (and a wood-burning fireplace, preferably of the midcentury variety). Use floor-hugging coffee and side tables, so the look feels consistent and it's not awkward to grab a drink or switch on a light; tables should line up with your sofa cushions or be about 2 inches below. Include one or two "regular" height chairs in the mix to accommodate people who might be uncomfortable going low. For a more traditional take on a lower seating option, try an English sofa.

(btw)

In a very large room, you'll want to get creative with seating arrangements to make sure the space doesn't feel empty. Pull furniture off the walls for a cozier feel (walls left bare can take a console with ottomans underneath and a mirror above, or a floor-to-ceiling art treatment). And bring in extra seating to delineate space: Chaises, daybeds, and benches work well because they're easy to see over. Consider carving out a reading nook in a corner with an armchair and an ottoman. Or bring in a small table and two chairs that you can use for writing, playing games, and dinner for two.

seating arrangement suggestions

effortless flow
Keep pathways clear so one has a sense of being ushered into the space. You don't want to step over an ottoman or scoot around a too-big side table to get to the main seating area.

a sense of containment
Use a rug to ground the area and make it feel cozy and inclusive.

sofa sidekicks
Rounded coffee tables are friendly and never look crooked. Square and rectangular tables feel orderly.

room to breathe
The coffee table should be far enough from seating that you don't have to shimmy through, but not too far that you have to strain to grab a drink. About 18 inches away is the sweet spot.

separate zones
In a large room, consider placing sofas or chairs back-to-back (shown left) to carve out two distinct seating areas. Screens, shelves, or large plants can be used to fill space or soften corners.

a chair buffet
Vary your seating options to appeal to the masses. Think deep armchairs for reading, smaller upright chairs for conversing or working, maybe a few comfy floor pillows too. Just pay attention to balance: You don't want a huge hulking sofa opposite two airy Bertoia chairs—the room will feel lopsided.

conversation starters
Intriguing sculpture, artsy books, or photos tucked under a glass-topped table all give guests something to talk about.

an inspiring view
Face a chair to take in the scenery. Use mirrors to reflect pretty items if outside views are limited.

inspiring style:

aurora james
(on statement chairs)

Aurora James, founder and creative director of Brother Vellies, works with artisans from all over the world to create traditional African footwear with her own added flair. Her fashion sense, honed by extensive travel in Africa, has given her an eye for interior design.

When it comes to seating, Aurora loves a chair that makes a statement: "It's my passion! Essentially the chair is the island of the room, and it can make a big impact. It dictates the way you hold yourself: For example, a cozy rocking chair where you can lounge and rock holds a body very differently than a hard wooden stool does. Chairs decide how you are physically interacting with a room—the energy of that space, and how the room's inhabitants are going to communicate."

Aurora's personal favorites are her beloved Milo Baughman chairs. She found them on Craigslist and they stole her heart. "At any one time I'm on the lookout for twenty different things on my wish list, and they always have a way of finding me."

1. Upholstering is a great way to keep things modern and feeling new. Don't be afraid of it. Start with something small, like a stool, that's not a huge commitment financially or emotionally and see how it goes. The process is fun and quite addictive.

2. Look for a vintage chair that has an interesting shape—one that sparks your imagination. Introducing older pieces into a contemporary environment changes the space by adding a layer of history and depth.

3. Nothing has to be perfect. Let your chair be a work-in-progress. One of my pieces, which is upholstered in indigo and old denim, is always being patched and worked on. The flaws have become the chair's story. For me, these are the elements that turn a house into a home.

4. Think long and hard about the colors! It's nice to have something a little surprising and unexpected. Use the chair to make a personal bold statement.

5. Chairs don't always need to have their feet on the ground. I also love my rattan chair that swings from the ceiling.

DIY wall decals, made from cut strips of black gaffer tape, electrify an entry and dictate the room's palette.

3

WALLS

WALLS
WE LOVE

smart ideas for every
room in the house

bathroom

An intricate tile pattern
takes an architecturally
uninspiring bathroom to
the next level. The ornate
Venetian mirror echoes
the curves of the tiles,
while modern sconces and
a sleek faucet ensure the
look doesn't veer too far
into old-world territory.
An open console sink
allows the tile to make an
uninterrupted statement
throughout the room.

bedroom

This enchanting botanical wallpaper is almost transportive, making climbing into bed a true escape. Patterned pillows bring the colors of the wallpaper to the forefront, and a macrame hanging adds a personal touch that makes the room feel lived in. The wallpaper stops short of the ceiling, creating a cozy headboard-upon-headboard effect.

kids' room
Chalkboard paint inspires creativity, guarantees an ever-changing art installation, and even looks good when messy. Furnishings in muted, chalky hues blend effortlessly.

nook

Sometimes you just need to go for it: The powerful wallpaper print, the bold color choice. You're creating a space that makes you happy—rather than following an imagined rule book. Every unique aspect of this nook suggests it was thoughtfully composed, and is loved.

HANDBOOK

paint
your walls

types of paint

Focus on oil-based or water-based. Water-based paint is so saturated and high quality (not to mention mild in odor and fast-drying) it's the most common choice. Oil-based paint is often used for a super-smooth, super high-gloss look on woodwork or doors.

flattering finish

When in doubt, go matte or flat, which doesn't have any shine. Its velvety texture hides minor flaws, absorbs light, touches up easily, and always looks polished. Eggshell, which has a slight sheen and stands up well to moisture, is a good choice for kitchens and bathrooms, but just make sure you're okay with the shine level—some versions may be shinier than your preference. Semi-gloss works well on trim, and allows you to easily swipe smudges from shoes or strollers. Hi-gloss or lacquer can be stunning when you want drama—consider it for a powder room.

to prime or not to prime?

Sometimes a separate primer is truly necessary: When walls are badly stained or damaged (sand any peeling parts first) or when you're painting a light color over a dark color. If your walls are in good shape, opt for a paint-and-primer combination. Swipe walls with a damp cloth first to get rid of surface dust and ensure the paint will cling.

how much to buy?

Figure 1 gallon for every 350 square feet. (Get a general idea by adding up the length of all walls, multiplying by the ceiling height, then dividing that number by 350.) Err on the generous side: You'll want extra paint for touch-ups, and buying a new batch at another time may result in a slightly different color.

mix and match

If you're set on a color from one paint company but love the coverage and consistency of another, ask the paint or hardware store if they'll mix the formula of the first company in the base of the second (many will).

testing

A paint color won't look the same on your walls as it does in the store, at your friend's house, or even in the can. That's because light affects the colors we see—so the same color may look very different throughout the day and may vary based on the light bulbs you choose. Paint a section of wall with a color you're considering. Choose an eye-level spot, and ideally one that can be seen from another room. Peek at the color morning, noon, and night—with the lights on and the lights off—before committing.

weather watch

Rain and humidity may lead to drips and delayed drying times, so choose a dry day.

insurance against mishaps

Create a touch-up kit—pour leftover paint into a jar labeled with the color name and room you used it in.

fun with wallpaper

		why we love it	*take note*
marbled		Organic and mesmerizing, it can feel cool or warm, depending on the colors and pattern.	Striking in the bathroom as a clever twist on traditional marble. Just look for vinyl or non-woven papers, which can handle moisture.
flocked		Velvety, raised designs feel at once playful and glamorous, and hide wall imperfections effortlessly.	Be forewarned: You'll definitely have guests pawing your paper. The textured sections may show dust.
woodgrain		From surprisingly realistic roughcut firewood to cartoon-like planks; adding warmth with wood will forever be cool.	This has the most impact in unexpected places: Try a washed-out woodgrain in a nursery or an indigo version in a powder room.
grasscloth		Tasteful texture might be exactly what's missing from a space.	The material is very delicate, and seams are nearly impossible to conceal; you'll have to live with them as part of the design.
metallic		Fabulous, light-reflective foil can make a small room bigger and a dark room lighter. It's also steam-resistant and easy to clean.	It's fragile, so needs to be installed with care. And since it's thin, it'll show every little lump and bump—only use on clean, pristine walls.

types of wallpaper

pre-pasted
Glue embedded into the paper is activated with a wet sponge.

paste-the-wall
Glue is applied directly to the wall. It's the least mess going up, but trickiest to remove.

peel-and-stick
Like contact paper, the back gets peeled off and up it goes. Designs are limited, though.

where to hang wallpaper

Any room can benefit from wallpaper, whether it's a subtle tactile grasscloth in a hallway (shown right) or an eye-popping, 3D hit for the office (shown opposite). Even the kitchen can be wallpapered without feeling overwhelming. Wallpapering all four walls in a room is a statement for sure, especially if you cover the ceiling for a jewel-box effect. But a focal wall can have just as much impact. When doing one wall, pull out a color from the wallpaper to paint the remaining walls. And save ultra-crazy patterns for behind or next to the sofa, bed, or desk, so you can appreciate the pattern when you walk in without being distracted by it the entire time you're in the room.

(btw)

hire it out

Wallpapering is a specialized skill, with lots of cutting and measurements involved, so we strongly suggest calling a pro. Ask friends and family for recommendations, or tap a local hardware store.

STYLE STATEMENTS

snapshots of inspiring ideas

whimsical

the mood: energizing, fantastical, fun.

styling notes: An animated palm tree print matches the eclecticism of the ephemera resting in front, from vintage glassware and golden pears to a throwback record player and a ceramic pig.

modern

the mood: serene, straight-lined, refreshing.

styling notes: This abstract wallpaper's horizontal stripes stretch out the small powder room; the open vanity and glass shelf keep things airy. Handsome details—a leather mirror, rough-hewn wide-plank floors—are juxtaposed with delicate frosted-glass sconces and fluffy white towels for soothing balance.

bold

the mood: quirky, old-school, opulent.

styling notes: Pink walls (Benjamin Moore's Cinco de Mayo), a technicolor Persian rug, vintage art, and proper fittings give this foyer eclectic but demure charm. Though the 1876 house could have been done up in a more subdued style, the marriage of bohemian and preppy touches makes it unforgettable.

romantic

the mood: picturesque, cheerful, sweet.

styling notes: Deliciously dreamlike de Gournay wallpaper makes it feel like you're being whisked to a faraway land without the flight. With a backdrop this gorgeous, furnishings are kept minimal, so as not to distract from the poetic print.

get the look

---

rustic

White wood-paneled walls, a painted brick backsplash, and cabinets made of reclaimed lumber transform a cabin kitchen into a study in textures and contrast. Marble countertops feel cool, roman shades bring in warmth. Pairing different tones of white keeps the look from feeling sterile.

covered serving dish

traditional rolling pins

oil decanter

glass + leather decanter

Shaker-inspired chair

wooden trencher board

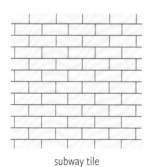

subway tile

copper measuring cups

Turn to page 270 for information on these products.

STYLE SCHOOL

dark walls

There's no reason to be afraid of the dark—at least when it comes to paint. Moody walls instantly ground a room and up its cool quotient. They also mask imperfections, like uneven walls, and create the illusion of infinite space. These five tricks ensure your space skews more daringly dramatic than dreary dungeon.

1. **Blasts of color** act as a welcome respite from the intensity of the hue.

2. **White accents** pop against dark walls. Here, the ceilings, trim, window treatments, and oversize pendant all offer crisp contrast.

3. **Reflective elements** like the porthole-like mirrors, chrome table base, and brass chair legs bounce light around the room.

4. **Traditional details**, such as the carved wooden armoire, pastel oil painting, and mahogany floors, keep the room from feeling stark.

5. **Big art** goes a long way, covering up a large expanse of the dark wall to define the space.

white walls

White paint is often thought of as a throwaway, an almost too-easy default—but it can be the trickiest color of them all. Some whites have sneaky chameleon-like tints; others feel so bright they'll make you squint. Consider:

undertones

When shopping around, look at the fan deck to see if the white leads to an orangey color (then it's warm) or a blue or purplish color (then it's cool). Hold paint chips next to a sheet of white paper to judge their true hue. Complement the tones already in the room. If you have lots of warm colors, try whites with warm undertones (red, yellow, pink, orange). If cool colors abound, consider cool whites (with undertones of blue, green, or purple). If you feel uneasy about going decidedly warm or cool, opt for a balanced white in the middle.

warm whites

These feel comforting and enveloping, complementing neutral tones and pairing nicely with wooden accents and floors (shown right). They also work well with ultra-traditional styles—especially creamy, antique whites that give off a lived-in, been-around-the-block feel.

cool whites

Sometimes cool whites come off as new and crisp—but they can also veer toward cold. Pairing with brass accents adds warmth (shown far right). Cool whites tend to work well in modern spaces and with riotous color. Grayish white is a go-to backdrop for art—many galleries employ gray walls as they make the colors of artwork stand out.

natural light

If your room gets lots of natural light, a warm white may make it feel even warmer, sometimes too warm. Compensating with a cool white will lower the temperature a bit. If you don't have many windows and rely on artificial light, a warm white will cozy up the room.

style standoff

large patterns vs. small patterns

Both large and small patterns act as instant style definers—an in-your-face abstract graphic
screams modern; a wispy floral leans more traditional but can still hold its own in an eclectic space.

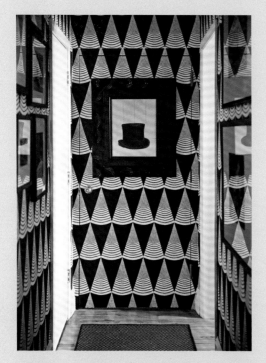

Large patterns steal the show and allow
furnishings to remain minimal. In a wallpapered
hallway, hanging art in the same colorway is a no-fail
way to make a small space feel cohesive; in a bedroom,
wallpapering behind the bed allows you to forgo a
headboard. Large-scale patterns, especially in rich,
dark colors, can make a big room feel more intimate
and a small space feel more important.

Small patterns add depth and texture from afar,
and tell a story up close. They run the gamut from
charming and whimsical to wild and dizzying, so
bring home samples to test out the look. A tiny, airy
print in a pale color can make a space feel bigger; a
dense print in a dark, warm color can make it feel cozy.

pattern effects

A print with movement is the easiest way to invigorate a blank wall. Think zigzags for a shot of energy, florals for a romantic vibe. To add a sense of structure to rooms in need of a focal point, consider a grid that immediately commands attention. Wallpapering all four walls can foster the impression of continuous space.

For an intriguing take on texture, try faux bois or marbleized paper, or paper that mimics stone. A botanical is a smart visual trick in rooms with no views.

In a cavernous space, create intimacy by installing a chair rail and wallpapering below.

The way a wallpaper pattern runs can also help define a space:

horizontal patterns make a room feel wider.

vertical patterns make a room seem taller, especially with ceilings painted white.

diagonal patterns (shown left), called drop patterns, add rhythm and work well if walls and ceilings are uneven—they'll mask imperfections by drawing the eye from corner to corner.

ceilings with character

rustic canopy

Raw wood beams give a serene living room tactile charm and a warm sense of structure. Contrasted against the earthy ceiling stripes, a starburst fixture feels even more otherworldly.

golden glow

A metallic ceiling acts like flickering candlelight in a traditional room, adding warmth, sparkle, and shine (which tricks the eye into thinking the ceiling is taller).

5 ways to treat a ceiling

1. classic
Paint the ceiling white for crisp contrast against colorful walls.

2. enveloping
Match the walls for the effect of being cradled in color.

3. tonal
Go slightly darker or lighter than the walls for a subtle surprise that feels comfortable.

4. bold
Paint the ceiling a completely different color than the walls (think pale pink above, olive all around).

5. cherry on top
Cover the ceiling in a fun color and keep the walls white. Perfect in a space that craves an unexpected moment.

room-to-room views

Always take surrounding spaces into consideration so that there's a sense of flow and continuity. Think of your home as one big palette, rather than separate rooms with distinct colorways.

colors as a bridge
Choose a hue to showcase in all rooms, even if tones vary. A hallway wallpapered in a sunny yellow floral can lead to an office with cream-painted walls, as shown here.

similar shades
If you have dark paint in one room, add white to the can to create a complementary color in an adjacent room. Or look to the paint deck and choose a color on the same card.

furnishings that play along
Use a color from the rug, upholstery, or window treatments in one room as the paint color for another. If you paint two nearby rooms drastically different colors, try rugs that feature each of those colors to help connect the rooms.

common denominators
Keep the color of baseboards, moldings, and door and window frames consistent throughout the home. Repeating accessories from room to room, like white picture frames or one green potted plant, fosters a sense of community.

remedies
for renters

1. Two-tone walls are a smart trick for when you can't adjust the architecture; painting the bottom half high-gloss black helps ground the space, and feels like an unexpected choice for a beach house. Forgo multiple nail holes by clipping art to twine with binder clips, then casually lean some art as well (shown top left).

2. If you're not thrilled about the paint color your landlord chose but don't want to repaint, use wallhangings with abandon—they'll cover up large swaths of wall and add texture and character (shown top right).

3. A curtain can divide a room while adding a layer of softness. White feels fresh and ethereal, like a natural extension of the walls (shown bottom).

window frames

black magic
Painting frames the same glossy black as kitchen cabinetry creates graphic simplicity. Greenery seems almost neon in contrast, and the white ceiling, floor, backsplash, and pendants shed some light on the darkness. Bonus: Pitch-black muntins disappear at night.

monochromatic minimalism
Crisp white surfaces keep a small room from feeling cramped—the eye is immediately drawn to a lush green view just outside.

gutsy contrast
Pulling out a color from the
floor tiles makes window
frames an integral part of
the design, and negates the
need for window treatments.

inspiring style:

barbara bestor

(on color + paint)

Architect Barbara Bestor designs contemporary environments for everyday life by staying true to her manifesto: "Everyone should experience strange beauty every day." "I had a real breakthrough years ago in using color," Barbara explains. "I was building a house for myself and my young girls. I wanted to reflect their interests in my plans. They loved pink and magenta and reds and the clash of colors in that spectrum."

That house, in Echo Park, California, was where Barbara developed not only her signature saturated accent colors but also the dark blue/black paint that she often uses for her exteriors.

Barbara frequently employs a subdued backdrop and uses strong

colors as highlights: bright floor tiles, faucets, cabinet doors, closets, and light fixtures. "Bathroom fixtures are a fun place to use bright colors. If everything else in a room is white, a really cool, brilliantly colored faucet makes it surprising. If you have white or light gray walls, the color can come from furniture and light fixtures. The accent pieces become showstoppers."

Another technique she uses is to "dunk" a room in a solid paint color from top to bottom—including the trim—for an immersive effect. "I guess the big difference is that I use color from an architect's point of view, adding it as a way to replace a material. Perhaps a client can't afford to put in wood floors? A solution might be to do a linoleum floor in bright colors."

barbara's tips

1. Let yourself go crazy with color in the small rooms—like laundry rooms and pantries. These are great places to be bold. Acid green, yellow, or magenta walls with simple white shelves to offset the color will give you a rush of pleasure every time you open the door.

2. Doors are a great way to introduce color into a room. Black and navy or dark gray are nice alternatives to the usual white or wood. Just be careful to paint the door the same color on both sides, so it won't seem half done; and be sure the door color is in harmony with the colors inside the room as well as outside. Use top-quality enamel paint for both the interior and exterior doors. It's worth spending the extra money for rich color that won't fade.

3. A good rule of thumb is that anything that will have fingers touching it should be painted in at least a semi-gloss for easy maintenance. Everything else should be in matte paint. If there are little kids in the house, try a racing stripe of the gloss version of the matte wall paint (from the ground up to about three feet high). It will look great and is easy to keep clean.

4. If your ceiling is in decent shape, paint it with a high-gloss white paint. It essentially acts as an illuminator and fills the room with a magical light.

5. Create interesting features by painting floors or wooden staircases or using colorful floor tiles.

Crisp white art pops against an inky blue wall and speaks to the shape of the console.

4

ART

ART
WE LOVE

smart ideas for every
room in the house

bedroom

Hung corner to corner, a
fringe-laden handwoven
hammock, discovered on a
trip to Tulum, Mexico, spans
the room and billows in the
breeze, eliminating the need
for a headboard.

dining room

A framed grizzly bear photo adds texture, softening the white-painted brick wall and mirroring the richness of the dark ceiling. One big piece rather than a series of smaller ones feels confident and calm.

kids' room

3D art feels appropriate in a spot fit for wild imaginations. Even the Ikea bed flaunts a creative hack thanks to added floral wallpaper that matches the adjacent wall.

kitchen

When a sink doesn't have a view, create one with art.
A grouping of oil paintings gives the room a time-worn
sense of history. Plants and antlers on the wall and
counter push the boundaries of the arrangement.

entryway

A perfectly imperfect floor-to-ceiling gallery wall evokes controlled chaos. One larger artwork anchors the mix of frames—some left empty, others filled with mementos. Sticking to white mats and limiting the frames to gold, white, and black gives the wall a soothing sense of purpose, even with an excess of art.

HANDBOOK

art ideas

consider

old photos
Framed shots of relatives or even yourself as a child feel soulful and special.

graphic posters
When framed simply, pieces from artists like Rothko, Warhol, and Picasso look timeless.

sketches
Even a simple pencil sketch can feel like a treasure.

your own shots
Blow them up to roughly 30 x 40 inches.

black-and-white photography
You can't go wrong. It's sleek, it's graphic, and even inexpensive versions can look high-end.

where to look

flea markets
They are the perfect places to gather unusual pieces.

art galleries
Photographs and prints are typically the cheapest, but you don't have to buy anything. Just notice what you're drawn to—maybe it's seaside scenes or modern city life.

student art shows
A general rule: Stick to abstracts and graphic paintings rather than portraiture.

museum shops
If you like a particular exhibit, snag a poster or print from the show.

places far from home
Vacations are a great way to score meaningful, one-of-a-kind finds. Anything from tapestries by local artisans to photos or sculpture will remind you of your trip for years to come.

(btw)

Not sure where to start? Match the mood. Choose art in a similar style to your room, and all will be well. A casual space will look great with well-worn flea-market frames. A fancy, glam interior? Not so much.

mats
+ frames

mats

Go neutral here; white, cream, or pale gray
showcases art without overpowering it. Fabric
mats (linen/canvas) lend softness and texture
and feel like a natural match for traditional
landscapes.

frames

Custom frames can cost double or even triple
what you paid for your print. Try:

thin black or white
The safest choice, easily lending a minimalist
touch. Works well with posters, photography,
and prints.

sleek silver
Elegant with a crisp white mat and bold,
abstract art.

wood
A wonderful way to add warmth. Use simple
birch frames for a clean, modern vibe.

gilded
Burnished frames complement historical
prints or paintings while giving abstracts (like
the one above by Hugo Guinness) a touch of
glamour. No need to go too ornate here—spare
versions pack enough of a punch.

above a mantel

Leave 3 to 6 inches between mantel and
art. Leaning pieces works well, too.

(btw)

You don't need art on every wall. It's better to create a
few intimate groupings rather than dot the room with
pieces that don't relate.

on a furnitureless wall

Hang art about 58 inches on center
(meaning measure from the floor to the
center of the art); for a gallery wall, treat
all your pieces as one and measure to the
center of the grouping. Hanging at this
height keeps art spaced well in relation
to the other furnishings in the room, and
works whether you're standing or sitting.
Hang too high (as many people do) and
art gets lost.

STYLE STATEMENTS

snapshots of inspiring ideas

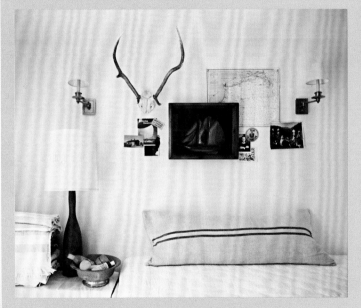

country

the mood: relaxing, muted, quaint.

style notes: An envelope of art around a brass bed feels like a comforting canopy. Central symmetry loosens up on the sides to prevent the grouping from feeling static. Same-color mats that tie to the pillow and blanket unify the room, as do the mostly botanical prints in muted black and gray hues.

collected

the mood: chill, flexible, simple.

styling notes: A collage-like composition. Pieces feel casual and personal—some overlap, others are clustered—for a fluid, art-project appeal. Sconces on either side give the scene a sense of structure.

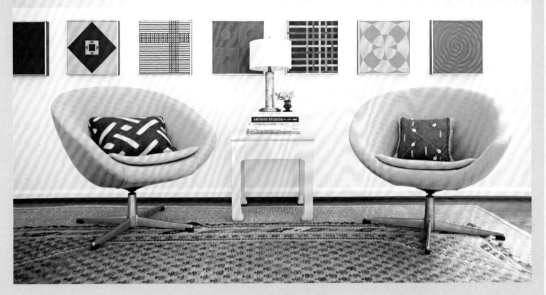

linear

the mood: vibrant, fun, kaleidoscopic.

style notes: Hanging art horizontally underneath an alcove ceiling brings the focus down, creating a cozy, tight-knit nook. Bright-white walls act as a sedate backdrop for the technicolor prints—a series of studies by artist Tom Herbert—while a small lamp breaks the line of art so it's not too perfect. Geometric pillows act as small pieces of art; curvy chairs soften the squares and chunky lacquered side table.

70s

the mood: nostalgic, pure, laid-back.

style notes: Bare wood frames match the rawness of the unpainted door and feel simple and stress-free. No-fail formula: one horizontal, one vertical, and an unusual object (shown here, raccoon tails) to connect the two.

get the look

graphic

A striking, sizable piece of art above the bed makes the need for a traditional headboard feel passé. Hanging the art vertically, as well as topping a leggy side table with a skinny desk lamp, gives the room a sense of height. The art's geometric lines are echoed in the pared down bedding and throw pillow.

bright throw pillow

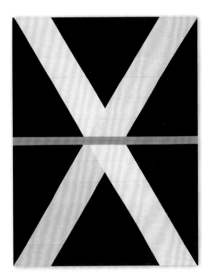

graphic quilt

bold table lamp

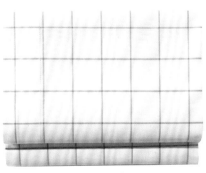

modern stool

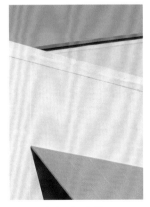

windowpane sheets

abstract painting

Turn to page 270 for information on these products.

STYLE
SCHOOL

how to
hang a
gallery wall

visualize it
Pick a tone you want to set and a loose palette. Some similarity among pieces is good—a shared color, theme, or size. This arrangement leans heavily on black and white, but pops of color keep it fun and tied to the furnishings.

curate it
Gather pieces in similar shapes but throw in a few contrasting objects. An oval or circle will soften all those angles. Plan for varying sizes; large art makes an impact and small art is great for filling in gaps. Go for a mix of frame colors—metal, white, black—so the cluster feels like it was acquired over time. Leaving one piece unframed is a nice touch and feels raw and painterly.

arrange it
Experiment with placement on the floor in front of the wall until the look feels balanced. Place the largest item a bit off-center so the layout feels unpredictable. Vary orientation with vertical and horizontal pieces—too many of one kind will feel stuffy.

hang it
Arranging art above a piece of furniture, like a sofa or console, balances the visual weight below. Plan for about 3 inches between frames—too close and the cluster will feel crowded, too far away and it'll feel disconnected. And use two hooks per piece for stability.

(btw)
Mixing mediums is a good thing. Prints, sketches, photos, paintings, even a child's masterpiece can all cohabitate as long as a shared color palette runs through the arrangement.

living in 3D

Sprinkling in objects, like an instrument or a metal flower, gives what would have been a flat arrangement depth, personality, and substance. Try to keep the item roughly the same size as the art so it blends in. You can even hang art around an existing wall sconce, which will shed light on your new arrangement.

big art

Large pieces command attention, anchor a room, and make an impact that a bunch of small art just can't. And the sheer scale gives a sense of wise intention, even if you're an interior design novice.

color theory

Pairing oversize art with a tiny bouquet in the same palette creates a fun juxtaposition of big and small. The art on the floor completes the scene for a triangular composition that feels casual but considered.

abstract idea

White walls and furnishings set the stage for a symmetrical blast of DIY art—a Pierre Frey fabric stretched over canvas.

natural selection

Two horizontal pieces centered on the wall, rather than the sectional, contrast vertical wall panels and elongate the space. Inspired by the surrounding landscape, the photos (by Melanie Pullen) pull together the colors of the room, while adding depth and mirroring the pair of ottomans in front.

leaning art

No measuring, no nail holes, no commitment. When done right, casually leaned displays feel cool and collected. And—bonus— they can be positioned to hide things like wall outlets and wires and will always stay level. To ensure it doesn't look like you just got too lazy to grab the hammer, cluster a bunch of art of varied heights but similar mood, or work just one piece—either massive or tiny—into a vignette so it feels like it belongs.

on ledges

Varying the space between frames makes this rotating gallery feel spontaneous. Sprinkling in small objects, like rocks found on family beach trips, allows the array to be appreciated up close. Shelves the same color as the walls fade away, keeping the focus on the art.

5 more places to display art

1. on a windowsill
Scenic shots can sweeten a view.

2. above a doorway
A small piece above the molding is a treasure when you look up.

3. on a chair
Dress up an antique that's no longer a comfortable place to sit.

4. on an upright piano
An unexpected way to break up the boxiness.

5. on an artist's easel
A perfect pairing that can fill an empty corner.

on the floor

A floral sketch adds life to the lower half of a room. In a serene space with minimal furnishings, everything appears sculptural.

in a desk

An oil painting tucked into an emerald green nook feels like part of the landscape. Layering objects in front adds dimension.

style skills:
use art to...

subdue a space

create an instant headboard

add soul

A picture of an Italian harbor helps eliminate mental clutter. The frame is similar in texture and color to the hamper, while the white mat matches the chair.

Hang a bold piece of painted linen on the wall to make a floor-bound bed feel purposeful, rather than haphazard.

Blowing up meaningful shots feels appropriate in a bedroom.

mask an uninspiring view

Suspended from the ceiling with fishing line, a vivid print breaks up a blast of beige and distracts from a so-so view when the blinds are pulled up.

lighten the mood

Tucking lighthearted photo strips behind a more serious oil painting (with loose photos casually placed in front) signals this is a home.

unify disparate pieces

A grouping of art extends beyond the sofa to wrap around a side table, mimicking the S-shaped lamp base and creating a whole new vignette.

mirrors
as art

doubles as a window

A well-placed gilded mirror is ornate enough to serve as the dining room's main event, while cleverly reflecting smaller pieces across the way.

bathroom brightener

A 19th-century trumeau mirror moderates the starkness of a modern space with old-school grandeur.

masters of illusion

Hung in columns right up to the 14½-foot ceiling, a grouping of gilded mirrors found in flea markets accentuates a loft's scale and bounces around light.

inspiring style:

graham kostic
(on collecting + displaying)

"Art collections can seem intimidating," says Graham Kostic, creative director of the online video magazine glossedandfound.com, "so I like to keep it theatrical and a little tongue-in-cheek." Graham's passion for collecting started young. "Ever since I was a child I've been completely fascinated by souvenir shopping. On vacations I would always search for the most obscure, authentic items to bring home, where I would display them as collections."

graham's tips

1. Whether you're buying serious, collectible art as an investment, or just collecting flea market treasures, make sure each piece is inspirational, moving, and tells a good story. The joy the piece gives you should warrant the price you pay.

2. Framing something turns it into art. Try framing faded vintage postcards or black-and-white antique photographs to create unique pieces. Do the same with groupings of Polaroid pictures. Once framed and hung together, Polaroids become little mini-art collections of their own.

3. Avoid being precious about displaying art; it is not just about creating a perfect gallery wall. Mix your special things among functional items. Adding art to an open kitchen cabinet or bookshelf can elevate everyday things while giving you the joy of seeing your treasures throughout the day.

4. Creating a grouping of art is a perfect way to offset the potential imperfections of individual pieces. A collection becomes more than the sum of its parts.

5. Stand-alone art should be able to hold its own and be perfect enough to warrant a place on a mantel or coffee table.

Zebra meets chevron in this dynamic tile; two bathmats placed vertically help define double sinks (and echo the floor pattern on a smaller scale).

5

FLOORING

FLOORS
WE LOVE

*smart ideas for every
room in the house*

entryway

Foyers have to handle high impact. These
hand-crafted cement floor tiles have
movement and flow—perfect for ushering
people in and out of a high-traffic spot.
The design mimics the door trim, and the
punchy color, though maybe too much in a
large space, is delightful in small doses.

kitchen

Reclaimed 1920s Moroccan tiles make a simple kitchen
feel like an old soul. The colors of the midcentury chair,
country stool, industrial pendant, Moroccan screen, and
farmhouse table are all represented in the floor, which
helps the various styles to coexist.

dining room

This over-dyed flat weave radiates youthful energy, coaxing the dark floor and serious wood table to join the party.

kids' room

Sophisticated flat weaves
in sweet hues are a
refreshing change from
primary colors. The larger
rug's motif echoes the
ceiling; the smaller rug
defines a play zone and
can be easily tossed in
the wash.

living room

A pale gray mottled rug gives the effect of stone without the chill.

HANDBOOK

flooring materials

		why we love it	*take note*
solid wood		Warm and homey, wood gets better with age, can be refinished several times, and never goes out of style.	Expands in humidity, so not great for damp areas like basements. Pre-finished wood will wear even better but cost a bit more.
engineered wood		Layering a thin veneer of real wood over plywood results in a doppelgänger that's cheaper and less susceptible to humidity.	Sometimes you can feel the difference underfoot. And you'll only be able to refinish it once, if at all.
linoleum		Made of linseed oil and wood products, it's a durable biodegradable choice infused with mineral pigments for bright, fun colors.	Look for versions with a protective coating to resist stains; otherwise, if it's in a well-trafficked area, you'll need to refinish every couple of years.
ceramic tile *(opposite page)*		The mix of clay and minerals results in a powerhouse that resists wear, water, stains, scratches, and dents—especially if glazed.	Textured or matte tiles are less slippery. Grout lines need cleaning; consider dark grout to mask dirt or matching the grout to the tiles so lines disappear.
concrete		An understated, low-maintenance choice that looks amazing and also happens to be hypoallergenic.	Choose a finish to suit your style—matte feels edgy and industrial in a kitchen; polished can be elegant in a dining room.
laminate		Layers of fiberboard with a melamine resin top mimic various materials. Easy to clean, and extremely stain- and scratch-resistant.	Laminate may trick the eye from afar, but up close it won't fool anyone. And standing water will cause damage.

rug
materials

		why we love it	*take note*
wool		Super-soft, wears well, and contains natural oils that keep dirt from adhering to fibers. Plush sheepskins have become requisite bedside companions.	Wool attracts allergens, so you'll need to clean regularly with a HEPA-equipped vacuum. Some wool sheds excessively.
cotton		Casual and soft. Cotton is most often used for flat-weaves like kilims and dhurries. You'll also find cotton-wool blends that are less expensive than pure wool.	Cotton attracts dust and dirt, so it's not great in high-traffic areas. And thin ones won't last a lifetime.
naturals (sisal, jute, coir, hemp, seagrass)		Staples in decor-savvy homes, and for good reason: Woven with plant fibers, they trap dirt (great under kitchen tables!) and are strong, renewable, neutral, and beautifully textural.	They can shed, and the coarse texture isn't particularly foot-friendly—but you can layer with a soft rug on top.
indoor/outdoor		Synthetic materials like polyester and polypropylene mimic natural fibers but are extremely sturdy, fade-proof, and stain-resistant.	You're not going to be reveling in their luxurious feel—these are workhorses.

overdyed rugs

A brilliant blend of modern in-your-face color with a traditional motif, overdyeing typically involves bleaching, dyeing, and washing a rug to get a saturated stunner that has a peek of pattern. With such vibrance underfoot, it's nice to keep furnishings sedate, but that doesn't mean sacrificing texture. The white-painted brick wall, rough-hewn pedestal, and rustic wood floors add dimension.

tile sizes, shapes + patterns

Tiles run the gamut from tiny mosaics to 2 x 4 planks, and then some. Sixteen- and 18-inch squares are popular for floors, but there's a massive size range, and you'll want to consider the effect.

Large tiles can make a room feel bigger, in part because fewer grout lines means less interruption. Small tiles can feel busy and overwhelming in a big space, but in a powder room they work well. Wrapping floors and walls in the same tiny tile (shown right) can blur lines and make the room feel infinite.

To minimize grout lines, choose rectified tiles—their edges are extra precise, resulting in lines that are barely noticeable.

(btw)

The number of grout colors is endless, but caulk (which you'll need for corners, among other things) comes in just a few shades. So if you're picky about grout and caulk colors matching exactly, choose your caulk color first— then match the grout.

The way tiles are arranged has a huge effect on the feel of the space. Laying tiles diagonally can visually expand a room, making it feel wider by drawing the eye to the corners. A straight-on checkerboard feels more strict and structured. A pattern using different sizes of squares and rectangles (called a Versailles pattern) can make a room feel larger. Here, a few of our favorite shapes:

hexagon
Try a floral design, all one color, or a random mix.

subway
Typically done in one color, or various tones of the same color. Metallics and glass tiles offer a nice twist on tradition.

penny rounds
These can swing strikingly modern or charmingly classic.

squares
Try shades of one hue for calm, monochromatic for sleek, an elaborate colorful design for striking.

fish scales
Lovely, and appropriate, in a bathroom.

graphic
An intricate design fosters a global feel underfoot.

rug sizes

It's tempting to choose a rug solely on appearance, but size is crucial. A too-small rug will look like a postage stamp and make the room feel smaller. A rug that's too large, with not enough floor space around it, will feel sloppy (you'll want about 18 to 24 inches of bare floor all around). Standard rug sizes are 4 x 6, 5 x 7, 6 x 9, 8 x 10, and 11 x 14.

A large rug is great for uniting the elements of a room, and a series of smaller rugs can be used to define various seating areas. Either way, a rug shouldn't float like a lonely island in the middle of the room— at least some of your seating options should touch the rug. If you're not sure about size, use this guide: Get a rug 2 feet shorter than the walls of your room. So if your room is 10 x 12 feet, an 8 x 10 should do the trick. Here, some room-by-room tips:

dining room
Rugs here are great for buffering lively dinner conversation; just have them extend 18 inches on all sides of the table so chairs can be pulled out and remain on the rug. This wavy rug softens the linear nature of the room, from the table base's vertical bars to the angular light fixture and gridded art.

bedroom
Rough-hewn wood floors and a giant wool and sisal rug ground the bed in texture. Allowing the rug to peek out about a foot on both sides of the bed ensures a roomy enough landing pad.

hallway
Treat a wide hallway like a destination rather than a journey with rugs and furnishings, such as slim seating, intriguing artwork, and an unexpected place to hang your hat. These three geometric Moroccans play off one another, while feeling distinctly separate. To keep things airy, leave 4 to 6 inches of bare floor between the wall and the rug.

rug shapes

Round rugs are inviting and intimate, providing a refreshing change of pace that instantly enlivens a room and softens its edges. Try them in an entryway, under a round dining table, or in any space that needs to lighten up (an office, a laundry room). Round rugs work nicely as the second rug in a room, to spotlight an area like a reading nook. Just make sure it's big enough so that some furniture can rest on it.

Runners and hallways go hand-in-hand, but also consider them for long, thin kitchens, walk-in closets, and at the sides or foot of the bed. In a bathroom, they can span the length of a double-sink vanity or a gorgeous claw foot tub. Runners are fantastic when they are thick and plush—think of them for luxury rather than just as a way to get from here to there. And since they're often in high-traffic areas, a slip-proof rug pad is a must.

STYLE STATEMENTS

snapshots of inspiring ideas

graphic

the mood: confident, bold, energizing.

styling notes: Open chairs and pale walls let a classic checkerboard floor steal the show. With such a bang underfoot, it's crucial to keep other colors and patterns to a minimum; a blue sideboard and fresh greens are the only bright hits.

beachy

the mood: weathered, casual, cozy.

styling notes: This rug's frame and border give a room with various patterns and organic elements a welcome sense of structure. Selecting a rug the same color as the floor expands the surface area of the room.

industrial

the mood: minimal, unassuming, humble.

styling notes: Though free from bells and whistles, there's something so inviting about an industrial space: Pared down to the essentials, it's not trying to be anything other than what it is. The polished stone floor gets a bit of warmth from simple wood furnishings and stacked rattan poufs.

get the look

scandinavian

A pale wide-plank floor feels fresh, while exposed knots add rustic charm to keep the look from feeling sterile. Scaled back and simple, the room's clean lines evoke a sense of peace and clutter-free serenity. Consistent colors are calming; the floor is the same color as the top of the Swedish trestle table; white Ikea chairs match the walls, window treatments, and candlesticks.

cord pendant

Swedish farmhouse table

Eames chair

beechwood utensils

Nordic dinnerware

folk candlestick tray

Turn to page 270 for information on these products.

STYLE SCHOOL

layering rugs

Like topping a blouse with a blazer, layering rugs is a finishing touch that promises a pulled-together, polished look. A layered look can highlight a specific area; add color, contrast, and texture; and allow you to use a small rug in a big space without it looking like the wrong choice.

sheepskin over stripes
Beachy meets cozy in this opposites-attract match made in heaven.

dhurrie over wool

Similar to how your favorite chambray shirt can tone down an outfit, a blue-fringed number tossed on sophisticated wool makes this office feel less Monday morning, more casual Friday.

kilim over wool

A sunny yellow topper helps a wool rug lighten up, and lines up with the sofa edge to create a precise seating area that still feels playful.

persian over jute

Casual jute tempers the too-traditional feel of a Persian, making it look rebellious rather than rule-abiding.

the white rug: do you dare?

White can be just as practical as darker colors as long as it's in the right room and you follow these guidelines.

do...
Opt for wool or synthetics—they resist stains well. And choose extra stain protection, if available.

Consider fluffy white options like sheepskins and flokatis—their long fibers trap dirt, so it's not as visible on the surface.

Pair with furnishings you really want to showcase—white is a blank canvas that allows others to shine.

Contrast textures—a high-pile rug like a shag is perfect with a sleek leather sofa; a tighter weave may suit velvet upholstery better.

Go for white if you've got a light-haired pet. You won't see fur as much.

don't...
Use white in a room that gets lots of action—entryway, family room, kids' room. Save white rugs for formal living rooms, bedrooms, guest rooms, and offices.

Trample all over your new white rug with shoes—the less grime on these guys, the better. Vacuum regularly to eliminate dirt before it gets ground in.

Get white if you're truly nervous about it. Instead, choose cream with a subtle tone-on-tone pattern. You'll get a similar effect without the stress.

style standoff

dark floors vs. light floors

Dark floors like ebony and walnut are rich and dramatic, providing visual weight below to keep furnishings grounded. And they look fantastic paired with pale walls. But dark floors may show scratches, lint, and dust.

Light floors feel effortless and airy and work with many styles, from bleached-out beachy to glossy stark modern. They can make a dark space feel lighter and a pale space even brighter by reflecting light.

style standoff

patterned rugs vs. solid rugs

Patterned rugs pull all the colors of a room together, making everything from throw pillows and vases to books feel like one big happy family. Try zigzags or stripes to push the boundaries of tight spaces; use a medallion design in rooms that crave an anchor (top with an acrylic coffee table so as not to cover the pattern).

Solid rugs act as a calming foundation, furthering the serenity of a neutral room or chilling out a space that already boasts plenty of prints. Whether you go light or dark depends on the the vibe you want; light rugs visually enlarge a room; dark rugs up the cozy factor.

painted floors

Treating floors like a canvas can take your style up a notch. Look to surrounding art and wallpaper patterns when deciding on a color; whimsical mint green floors (shown right) and pale gray trim feel like a treat. Imagine what this room would have looked like with standard wood floors—not nearly as enchanting.

remedies for renters

1. Vinyl stick-on floor tiles ease the transition from indoors to outdoors. Using an intricate pattern helps tile lines fade away, so the effect is more like a painted floor (shown top left).

2. Placing carpet tiles is an easy way to soften a space and add pattern (shown top right).

3. Top badly stained or scratched floors with a makeshift seating area propped with a throw and floor pillows to make it feel intentional (shown bottom).

inspiring style:

elsie larson

(on having fun with flooring)

Nashville based blogger, designer, and DIY queen Elsie Larson of abeautifulmess.com feels it is important to not ignore the floor. Instead, she encourages using it to make a statement.

"In our current home we took a lot of risks. I wanted to stay away from anything too heavy and serious." As a result, floors throughout her house are, for the most part, painted bright white. The exception? In a bold move, a pretty teal blue high gloss covers her living room floor, inspired by the Surf Lodge Hotel in Montauk, New York. Elsie is a big fan of using inspirational rugs to enhance rooms as well.

elsie's tips

1. Always get the largest rug you can afford. It should cover ¾ of the room. The biggest mistake people make is buying a rug too small for the room. Ideally, the rug should reach beyond all the furniture that you are setting upon it.

2. If you're not in the market for a larger rug and want to work with what you have, just make sure that all of your furniture is touching the rug proportionately.

3. A great and budget-friendly way to cover the floor of a larger room is to layer. Use an inexpensive, neutral jute rug as the base and place smaller, more interesting rugs or cow hides on top of it. This way you can benefit from the look of the smaller pieces without them feeling awkward in a space that's too large for them.

4. Paint a floor with a bold color wash. (For the best results, have your floors painted by professionals.) Use half acrylic paint and half water, finishing with a thick coat of polyurethane on top. This will allow the grain of the wood to stay visible through the color.

5. Be imaginative with tiles. Avoid expensive, specialty tiles by creating your own. Cut down larger-size inexpensive tiles and repurpose them. In our bathroom, we broke up an affordable marble tile into 12 x 4 inch pieces to create a herringbone pattern.

A grid of open shelves with a strict color scheme—white, clear, silver—feels cohesive. Candylike hourglasses inject colors and curves.

6
SHELVES + VIGNETTES

SHELVES +
VIGNETTES
WE LOVE

smart ideas for every
room in the house

living room

Sculptural wood shelves double as
wall art and elevate collections of
bowls, vintage vases, and books. A
floor-hugging shelf spanning the
length of the room lowers the eye
and speaks to loungey seating for a
cozy, stay-awhile vibe.

entryway

An industrial shelf packed
with well-loved film boxes
proves everyday objects can
be stylishly stored in plain
sight. The volume of items
is what saves the scheme;
just one or two boxes might
look random. A red silk
lamp picks up on the colors
and adds just the right
finishing touch.

office

Skeletal shelves blend in rather than scream for attention, allowing wallpaper and art to dominate. A symmetrical setup is smart in an office—it instills order and a sense of professionalism.

hallway

A slim arched alcove feels substantial thanks to accessories that play to its strengths: Stacks of books add height, and art is hung right to the top to extend your gaze as much as possible. A stool below can be easily grabbed when needed.

bathroom

When guests arrive, use vignettes to draw attention away from problem areas. Here, stacks of vintage records and an old-school phonograph block an ugly window and feel dreamy against Fornasetti cloud-print wallpaper.

HANDBOOK

shelf styles

	why we love it	*take note*
floating	Shelves that appear to levitate thanks to hidden brackets are clean and streamlined. They take up minimal space and can be mounted over furniture and in awkward spaces, like the wall under the stairs.	Not the easiest to install, so enlist the help of a friend or professional.
built-in	Making the most of otherwise vacant wall space, built-ins work well lining the wall of a living room or library. We've also seen them elegantly flanking a fireplace, or as a complement to kitchen cabinets.	It will be very hard work to move or eliminate a built-in, so think about location carefully.
fixed-bracket	Brackets attach to the wall, allowing you to place shelves at any height— from the floor up to the ceiling—and move them around with ease.	Go for white brackets or paint them the same color as the wall so they fade away. Metal brackets lend an industrial feel.
freestanding	Stand-alone systems can move from the bedroom to the living room to the kids' room whenever your storage needs change.	Freestanding shelves can delineate space within a room—two-sided versions double the functionality.
corner *(opposite page)*	Always charming, these space-saving options utilize wall junctions and are perfect for displaying a collection.	Opt for modern, clean-cut versions or paint a traditional piece a fresh, vibrant color so the look isn't too sugary sweet.

STYLE
STATEMENTS

snapshots of inspiring ideas

rustic

the mood: earthy, tactile, warm.

styling notes: Thick floating shelves made of reclaimed wood ground a collection of vintage Heath ceramics. Introducing a few reflective elements offers a breather from the matte pieces.

collected

the mood: layered, well-traveled, fun.

styling notes: At first glance, it may seem there's no rhyme or reason to this array, but key decorating principles are at play. The stripes on the shade mirror the striated sideboard and feel nautical, as does the collection of objects: a mermaid, a sailboat, a fish. The pair of lamps bookend the vignette, giving it structure.

classic

the mood: striking, refined, elegant.

styling notes: Dark and light paint create a chiaroscuro effect, with white accessories nestled within a fireplace opening that's painted dusky brown. Sculptural objects loosen up the gridded art display; the candlestick adds height, and, by breaking the line of the frame, acts as a visual connector.

coastal

the mood: energizing, thoughtful, happy.

styling notes: A beachy travel theme connects various elements, from driftwood candlesticks to whale bookends. Limiting the palette to the colors of the seaside—turquoise, brown, sand—ensures the scheme stays afloat.

get the look

serene

A curved niche filled with milky white ceramics feels as beautiful as a window view.
Stacks upon stacks—dishes on books—add subtle texture. Muted pastels allow shapes to demand
attention, from a scalloped platter to a hobnail bowl and curvy candlestick.

Richard Serra
Vertical and Horizontal Reversals

book as art

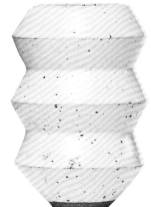

sculptural vase

transparent sculpture

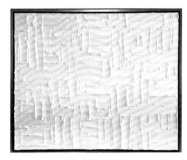

calming art

matte white round vase

beige bowl

glass bowl

Turn to page 270 for information on these products.

STYLE SCHOOL

stellar shelf styling

color for calm
Allow a few main colors to headline the show. Maybe jewel tones with touches of gold (shown opposite), neutrals, black and white, or shades of blue. Establishing a palette makes shelves feel pulled together. What colors should you choose? Look to the furnishings in your room.

horizontal + vertical lines
Stacks of books feel strangely serene; upright books feel poised and proper. Go for a mix of both. Horizontal books can serve as pedestals for accessories and bookends for open-sided shelves. Use sculptures to flank clusters of vertical books. Position titles at or near the shelf's edge.

depth and dimension
Lean some pieces of art, a mirror, or pretty books against the back wall to give the shelf depth and draw you in.

varied landscape
When placing objects, imagine looking at a cityscape, where there's a mix of heights rather than a strict lineup. Short, medium, and tall items keep the eye darting around.

points of light
Use museum-worthy artwork lights, a mini table lamp, or clip-on lights to give certain spots a sense of gravitas.

symmetry, shaken up
Most shelves can be loose and playful but instill some with a sense of order—two vases flanking a stack of books, or a sculpture in the center.

personal ephemera
It's about putting a piece of yourself on display. Lean a baby photo against a row of books, tuck a piece of pottery you made as a child under a glass cloche. Think of each shelf as its own story.

thoughtful contrast
Clustering objects can show off their individuality: a tall vase with a short, chunky pitcher, or a smooth concrete bowl atop a slab of rough-cut wood. Try rustic baskets on sleek industrial shelves, a mod sculpture on traditional shelves.

crowning achievement
The eye is always drawn up, so treat high shelves with intention. Here, trophy-like antlers preside over the festivities.

(btw)
As you style your shelves, take a step back and view them from across the room. Gauge overall balance: Are there too many small objects you can't see individually? Too many large items that make the shelf feel heavy? Play around.

styling
shelving
in a...

kitchen

Wood shelves are welcome in a kitchen, as they warm up a room dominated by functional fixtures. Break up the sea of ceramics and glass with a stack of wooden cutting boards or rustic utensils propped in a crock.

Vary tones, textures, and colors so your kitchen doesn't feel like a store display. (If things do start feeling "commercial," pepper in some non-kitchen items, like a piece of art behind a row of glasses.)

Keep the items you grab most—mugs, bowls, water glasses—within reach. Place less-used wares (ramekins, sake cups) up top.

Pile on the plates—you want shelves to feel loaded and bountiful and still look stocked even with items in the dishwasher.

If you're short on space, attach small hooks to the bottom of a shelf for teacups or mugs.

bathroom

The wall above the toilet is begging for shelves—this would be otherwise wasted space. Paint shelves the same color as the walls so they disappear.

In a small room (especially one with no medicine cabinet), all surfaces have to work hard. The top of the toilet can serve as a shelf for holding small items. Stash extra towels on a shelf under the sink.

Tight spaces need consistency, so use the same material for baskets (in this case, seagrass), and introduce a few other materials as well, like glass or even an unused ceramic sugar bowl, so the look isn't too staged.

Use the baskets for freeing up cabinet space and containing particularly unruly items like hairdryers, curling irons, and brushes.

White accents calm the mind: Think rolled white towels, white candles, a hydrangea tucked into a bottle.

Antique furnishings (like the mirror here) make the bathroom feel like an escape (bed and breakfast, anyone?).

Wood takes the starkness out of a room dominated by hard surfaces. Different tones of wood can coexist, particularly when they share a weathered finish.

office

Built-in shelves tucked into an alcove make the most of usable space. The wash of white fosters a clean backdrop that does not distract.

Uniform storage on each shelf offers a tidy look. Have fun with it—labeling boxes with numbers turns looking for supplies into a scavenger hunt (in a good way). Filling glass jars with bright yellow pencils and old-school pink erasers turns useful items into decor.

Keep some baskets empty, waiting to be filled. Too much stuff will clutter up your mind—a bit of space here and there allows inspiration to strike.

A fresh bloom invigorates a space where natural light is at a minimum.

Wall hooks keep totes and backpacks off the floor.

kids' room

Instill good design sense from a young age. Forgo laminate shelves for gorgeous wood that you'll appreciate, too.

See-through storage for color-sorted toys adds polish and order where you'd typically find chaos.

Organize shelves by type—books on one level, toys on another, mementos grouped together.

One offbeat object can distract from a sea of uniformity. Here, a wooden robot lightens the mood.

Pocket-size plants let kids take pride in growing their own greenery.

inspiring style:

lili diallo

(on minimalism)

Lili Diallo, style consultant and interior brand designer for fashion industry giants, is also the founder of jelovestudio.com, and the online magazine Billie.

Once an avid collector of objects, Lili explains her "less is more" evolution: "Now I am more about the experience. I would rather focus on having only special things, and fewer of them, in my home."

Long gone are the days when Lili was a collector. "Part of my job as a stylist was to find objects. I had an affinity for finding beautiful things, vintage French linens, glass objects, etc., but I became overwhelmed by their uselessness."

These days, for things to have a place in Lili's home, they must serve a purpose. Form and function are most important. A good example is her prized possession, a 1940s Jacques Adnet lamp. Yes, of course it's beautiful, but it also has a use.

Lili still has one weakness as a collector: jewelry. She loves stones and gold and silver. She is particularly drawn to the artistry of Native American jewelry, especially handcrafted, one-of-a-kind Navajo pieces.

lili's tips

1. Every item in your house should ideally be able to stand alone in its brilliance. Clear away things that can only come alive in a group. When there is less, each item becomes more heroic, and its beauty multiplies.

2. Instead of, say, eight objects on a bookshelf, pick just three. Make sure the items are connected and share a common thread, which can be the color or maybe the time period of the piece.

3. Make every effort to edit down all of your belongings. Just keep things that you love and the things you use. Less is more.

4. It is easy to convince people of the beauty of an object. But that very much depends on how you place it in the room. An object becomes a stronger statement when alone, or with a single companion piece.

dressing up the back

paint the back *and* shelves for a shadow-box feel. Or paint the back of each shelf a slightly different shade for an ombré effect.

wallpaper with a pretty floral, a punchy geometric, or with bold stripes.

fabric is a nice alternative to wallpaper.

beadboard feels charming and sweet. Keep it white or paint it deep gray.

wood shims (found at hardware stores) add gorgeous texture.

(btw)

If you're putting a bookcase against a wallpapered wall, pop off the back if you can—why cover up a pattern?

shop your home for 10 shelf + vignette staples

1. books

Books are representations of our passions, our histories, and give others glimpses into our interests. That being said, some books are better for display than others: Relegate your self-help guides to a private spot. Peek under a book jacket and you just might find a gem underneath—something textured and rustic and altogether better than that shiny paper cover.

2. sculptural objects

Large vases, pitchers, and bowls fill up space and have presence from afar. Fill with small stuff to give it visual oomph: Fill a glass ice bucket with wine corks, a bowl with vintage photos, or a jar with river rocks.

3. art

Pieces can be framed, unframed, a child's creation, or something found. Whatever it is, it should be loved.

4. clear items

Acrylic boxes and glass bowls are great for layering without blocking what's behind them.

5. the good stuff

Why relegate all that pretty cut crystal, porcelain, and family silver to the back of the cabinet? Take it out so you can truly appreciate it—you'll be amazed how sleek these pieces look next to modern items.

6. vacation mementos

A stunning postcard or piece of driftwood from the shore will make you happy every time you see it.

7. trays

A must for uniting random objects.

8. collections

Don't think you have one? Three like items make a collection, so look around and see what you find. Think mercury glass, salt and pepper shakers, or figurines.

9. reflective elements

Seek out items that catch light, like a mirrored box, a gilded frame, or a silver bowl.

10. fresh greens

Nothing brings an arrangement more to life than...life. Air plants and succulents are hardy choices that require minimal care.

4 prime places for a vignette

1. bar cart

Edit down your bottles to the spirits you'll most likely serve—and to the prettiest; pour anything with questionable packaging into decanters—they make everything feel special. Always include something unexpected: a cactus, sculpture, stacks of cool books. The best trick for making a bar cart feel stylish: treating the wall behind it. Black paint gives the cart pictured here a moody quality. A leaned piece of art ties to the image on the wall, so the cart feels like an intentional part of the decor.

2. mantel

Balance the heft of a fireplace with a large piece of art, then use that colorway to dictate the rest of the scheme. Here, black and white reign, but a bright yellow vase filled with confectionary pink flowers lightens the mood and ties to the stack of colorful books. Aim for a mix of heights to keep the eye moving; a stack of books is a nice element to balance. Two leaning mirrors loosen up the scheme, while reflecting the ceiling to foster the illusion of height. Filling a nonworking or out-of-season fireplace with a plant gives the space life.

3. dresser

Think layers here. Echo the shape of the dresser with art and work forward, leaning a smaller piece in front and adding elements of various sizes, shapes, and colors. In a bedroom, a subdued color palette is soothing, and personal touches, like a pretty dish for favorite jewelry or a painting done by a friend, make sense. A mix of textures (shiny, matte, rough, smooth) and heights (high, low) creates an intriguing landscape.

(btw)

When you're happy with your vignette, take a photo of it. This way if you move stuff around for dusting (or a curious kid plays around with your perfect positioning), you can easily recreate the look.

4. coffee table

The best view is from above, so style accordingly. For a geometric take, choose items that mimic the shape of the table—boxes, books, and matchboxes fill up a square table and take on the effect of a gallery wall. Stacks are good—they give depth to a large horizontal plane. Include a plant or flowers for color. And don't forget a beautiful box to hide not-so-beautiful remote controls.

style skills:
use shelves to...

camouflage a platform bed

boost bathroom storage

modernize a media center

In a small space, tucking the bed into surrounding bookshelves makes sleeping quarters part of the story, and gives the space a dollhouse quality. Picture ledges display nighttime reading—and take the place of nightstands.

A powder room without a medicine cabinet gets a storage bump thanks to wall-mounted open shelving and a mirror with a frame deep enough to hold essentials like hand soap.

Metal shelving adds structure without the heft. Instead of piling up your cable box and modem, place them on separate shelves to break up the monotony and use strategically placed vases in front of cords. The controlled clutter of books and ephemera takes the focus off the TV—the striking, unexpected wallpaper doesn't hurt, either.

turn plants into wall art

sneak in a desk

serve up martinis

A mini perch for plants elevates greenery to art status. Set pots at different heights for a cute vertical garden.

Space-saving heaven: Midcentury shelves moonlight as office space without cutting into square footage. Since the wood matches other elements, the setup can stay in the living room without stressing you out.

The convenience of a built-in shelf makes a spirited spot for nightcap necessities.

inspiring style:

claire zinnecker
(on shelves + vignettes)

Austin, Texas–based designer Claire Zinnecker describes her pared-down style as "slightly Scandinavian with a splash of Japanese minimalism." She goes for simple, clean lines and white walls, but then layers with color, personality, and quirky details. Working with a blank slate means that the "fun stuff" becomes more noticeable. "I paint my walls white so I can paint my door pink, and it works."

She's also a big DIY-er. "Our homes are our sanctuaries and they should be exactly what we want them to be. That's what's so fun about design and even more fun about DIY design. If I need something, I think of the solution and then I create it, instead of going online and buying it."

"Design for the way you live," Claire suggests. There is no one recipe to follow.

A glass fixture mimics the shape of the table without hindering the view.

7
LIGHTING

LIGHTING
WE LOVE

smart ideas for every
room in the house

bathroom

Brass sconces with attenuated
arms make a statement and can
be angled when needed. Pairing
them with an antique side
table makes the bathroom
feel cohesive.

living room

A streamlined starburst makes a point in an otherwise quiet room. Bookshelf fixtures spotlight a collection of tomes and objects, while imparting an ambient glow.

dining room

A geometric fixture with an exposed bulb helps a charming dining nook feel modern. The open, delicate design allows it to be a focal point without weighing down the room.

kitchen

A lineup of milk-glass orbs breaks up a view of cabinetry and speaks to curvy-topped stools.

HANDBOOK

figuring out fixtures

table lamps
These are the cozy guys of the lighting world—they add character and intimacy, and provide subtle, diffused light to fill in shadows and flatter spaces and faces.

floor lamps
Perfect for illuminating the dark corners of a room, floor lamps work to provide directional and ambient illumination. For a pleasing layered effect, include torchères that shed light upward for ambience and others that shed light down for reading. To bring interest to the lower level of a room, consider a literal version of the term *floor lamp* with a sculptural glowing orb that sits right on the ground.

sconces
Space-saving sconces are multi-functional. You can use a single sconce over a desk, in a nook, or to highlight a piece of art (shown opposite), but in general they look best in pairs—flanking a fireplace, dining room buffet, entryway console, or a bed.

recessed lights
Also called high hats or can lights, these fixtures are embedded in the ceiling to stay out of the way (great for low ceilings). Stick to a small size—about 3 inches in diameter—for the most stylish look.

flush mounts
These hug the ceiling to provide bright, all-over light.

semi-flush mounts
Hanging about a foot down, they typically have more flair than flush mounts but are still high enough to provide head clearance.

pendants
Chandeliers and other fixtures that hang down can light a room (say, an entryway) or spotlight a task (above a kitchen island). Experiment with pendants in place of table lamps; imagine them alongside a sofa or bed.

beautiful bulbs that are just too pretty to hide

edison
The visible filament recalls Thomas Edison's original design. These are low-wattage, so are more for aesthetic appeal than illumination.

silver bowl
Dipped in a metallic finish that softens the light, they're also available with a gold tip.

cut crystal
A gorgeous surprise in a contemporary fixture.

round candelabra
Swap flame bulbs for these and your chandelier will feel instantly more inspired.

STYLE STATEMENTS

snapshots of inspiring ideas

eclectic

the mood: fierce, fearless, handsome.

styling notes: When paired with extreme elements like a glossy black four-poster bed, a cobalt overdyed rug, and graphic wallpaper, a rope chandelier feels less nautical than medieval, giving the room a unique voice.

whimsical

the mood: bright, quaint, nostalgic.

styling notes: Swathed in black, a charming little chandelier gives edge to a room steering toward vintage.

minimalist

the mood: straightforward, calm, beautifully bare.

styling notes: A couldn't-be-simpler wall-mounted fixture makes nightstands unnecessary and folds flat when not in use. The pared down furnishings help strip away stress— just what you want in a bedroom.

industrial

White metal pendants bring utilitarian appeal and much-needed curves to a kitchen's horizontal lines, from the tiled island and backsplash to the rectangular glass table. Wood-paneled walls and mismatched chairs balance the cool of the fixtures and accessories: a pot-scrubber faucet, a stainless-steel counter, and a metal bar for dish towels and utensils.

STYLE SCHOOL

what every room needs

The secret to a well-lit room? Not being able to immediately tell how it's lit. When you walk into a space with perfectly diffused light, it just feels right and comfortable, like you could hang out there all day.

You'll want a mix of:

ambient light: General illumination that covers the whole room.

task light: Bright light for performing jobs (chopping veggies, applying mascara, working at home).

accent light: Spotlights on specific areas, from a cool plant to a bookcase.

a happy medium:
A too-bright room will feel institutional and off-putting; a too-dim room, particularly during the day, will feel dingy. Use lights of different brightness to draw attention to various areas.

different sources:
Overheads mimic the sun in that they brighten large swaths of space—but on their own they create shadows and will tire you out. Supplement with other fixtures to evenly distribute light or your home will feel like a convention center. A mix of sources delivers evenly distributed light and a soothing, flattering glow. Think soft pools of light rather than a beam from just one source.

dimmers galore:
In addition to saving energy, dimmers offer the flexibility to switch from bright light to soft chill-out light at a moment's notice. Installing a dimmer is an easy job for an electrician. Even easier? Buying a clip-on dimmer that attaches to your lamp cord.

natural light:
If one room gets spectacular sun and an adjacent one much less, consider replacing standard interior doors with glass-paned versions to filter light through multiple spots.

separate control:
Put sources on different switches: The worst is flicking one switch and lighting up the entire room like a stage set.

room-by-room lighting guide

living room

A mix of lighting is not only visually appealing, it's functional. Forgo harsh overheads if you can for softer table and floor lamps. Use small lamps to illuminate unexpected spots, like a mantel. Give as many chairs as you can a reading light. Use three-way bulbs to accommodate different moods. And vary the shades rather than repeating one type throughout the room—a drum shade, hexagon, and empire can peacefully coexist and make a space feel collected and intriguing. That being said, you don't want too many shades, or you run the risk of your room looking like a showroom.

dining room

Err on the large side—if a fixture is too small for the space, it will feel like an afterthought rather than a showstopper, which is what this room craves. Go for something that feels like an anomaly—a statement piece with rebel tendencies. Hang the fixture so the bottom is 30 to 34 inches above the table; the width of the fixture should be one-third the length of the table. High ceilings can handle long cylinders or drippy cascading designs; low ceilings prefer a fixture that spreads more horizontally. Supplement with sconces or a small lamp on a buffet for extra warmth—and don't forget candlelight.

bedroom

Position reading lamps or swing-arm sconces so that they shed light on the bed without pointing directly at it. To prevent shadows when reading, you'll want the bottom of the shade to be between your head and the book when you're sitting up in bed—typically this comes to 20 inches above the mattress. Choose a light-colored shade—black looks cool but may not throw enough light for reading. If you don't want to be bound by symmetrical table lamps, you can use two different styles as long as they're of similar heights (stack some books under the shorter one if necessary) and have the same material shade so they shed uniform light.

hallway

Hang pendants low enough so that you can appreciate their beauty, but high enough that they won't feel in the way: Roughly 7 feet from the floor is the sweet spot. Topping a console with a lamp (or sconces, if you're tight on space, hung about 6 feet from the floor) is a welcoming touch. In a hallway, you'll ideally want light every 8 to 10 feet; if you have a long hallway, supplement with sconces.

bathroom

The worst possible light for your bathroom? One overhead fixture, which will throw too much light on your forehead—creating shadows under your eyes, nose, and chin. The ideal situation: a 75-watt overhead with two 60-watt lights flanking the mirror at eye level (about 36 to 40 inches apart), providing an even cross-light (with little glare) that sweeps across your face.

kids' room

Table and floor lamps have toppling potential. Use pretty pendants instead, strategically placed near the bed for reading. Clip-on fixtures are affordable and sweet.

kitchen

You'll want overheads for all-over ambience, plus focused light where you cook. Pendants are best 28 to 34 inches above an island, starting 12 to 15 inches in from either end. Think carefully about materials; rich pendants can make moderately priced kitchens look custom. Consider fitting glass-door cabinets with interior lights for nighttime glimmer.

parmesan cheese
milk
tomatoe paste
oranges
caster sugar
condensed milk

style skills:
use lighting to...

transition between two spaces

create a magical glow

Prominent light fixtures can visually connect adjacent rooms, bringing a sense of balance and order by giving the eye something to focus on. The styles don't have to be the same, but scale and colors should be consistent for maximum impact.

Hanging multiple George Nelson lamps at various heights takes on the effect of hot-air balloons, lending drama to a large space. At nighttime, it's like a starry sky.

inject humor

trick out a tub

In a room that feels somewhat serious (here, an extra-tall screen/headboard is cool but a bit imposing), bringing in a lighthearted lamp could be just the icebreaker a space needs.

An elaborate fixture in the bathroom is pure decadence. For safety, hang it at least eight feet above the tub.

inspiring style:

workstead
(on easy lighting solutions)

Swiss-born Stefanie
Brechbuehler and her
Southern partner, Robert
Highsmith, are interior
designers and the co-creators
of the lighting company
Workstead. Necessity led
them to design their first
lighting fixture—created
for an older brownstone in
Brooklyn. Robert explains,
"There was a lot of woodwork,
and all the electrical boxes
were in strange places. The
dining table needed to be in
the middle of the room, but
the junction box was weirdly
off-center." So the couple
created a unique chandelier
as a way to cope with the
limitations of the room—it
had the utility of an industrial
light fixture but the flexibility
of a sculpture in that it could
be easily moved. The pair, who
have long admired French
lighting designers as well as
historic American lighting
manufacturers, have mixed
their tastes to design exquisite
yet simple lighting solutions.

workstead's tips

1. Always, always have all your light switches on a dimmer, no matter what.

2. A great floor lamp is a perfect solution for a dark corner. If you find a good one, it will bring a quality of warmth and coziness to the room.

3. Avoid clear bulbs. Instead, use soft, frosted bulbs for shaded fixtures as well as pendants, which give off a much prettier light.

4. A cheap and cheerful way to replace canned, recessed lighting is to use little porcelain sockets with oversize, 6-inch, frosted bulbs. (And don't forget to have them on a dimmer!)

5. Rooms should be lit in layers. A person should never walk into a room, flip a switch, and have five lights blasting down from cans. Instead, start with overall ambient ceiling light and then add an accent pendant or a chandelier. Try a floor lamp in the corner, a tiny lamp on a bookshelf, and perhaps an artistic glowing light in a corner. This combination will create an interesting mood in the room.

6. If you're renting, don't forget about plug-in sconces. They're easily installed at eye level and they bring so much to a room.

A tiger print sheet and pillowcase
and a few friendly faces temper the
lines of wood-paneled walls and a
geometric daybed.

8

SOFT STUFF

SOFT
STUFF
WE LOVE

smart ideas for every
room in the house

bedroom

A sheepskin rug rounds
out an angular, minimalist
platform bed and serves as
a source of plush texture.

bathroom

Hung on delicate brass hooks, tasseled towels add texture, color, and pattern to an all-white bath.

living room

Hiding gorgeous super-wide-plank floors under a rug would be a shame. Instead, throw pillows work hard to compensate by pulling colors from the botanical art. Gauzy white curtains framing the doors to the garden create an airy entry.

dining room

Sheepskin rugs tossed over bentwood chairs add cushy comfort while connecting to the Moroccan rug in the adjacent room.

HANDBOOK

throw pillows

shape

square pillows provide the best all-over back support.

rectangular pillows and **cylindrical** bolsters are perfectly suited for a sofa's midpoint. Bolsters work well with leather sofas as they don't slip down the way other shapes do.

circular pillows are sweet, soften the straight lines of seating, and offer an unexpected change of pace.

size

Eighteen-inch pillows look right on most sofas, but try 16-inch options on seating with low backs and 20- or 24-inch versions on large, overstuffed sofas and chairs. When in doubt, err on the large size. In general, it's best to go for a few large pillows rather than a jumble of smaller ones, which have the tendency to look messy.

fill

A foam and polyester combination keeps its shape, but may feel stiff. Down and feathers are lightweight and lush, though they'll need fluffing on occasion. Consider removable covers that can be washed and swapped out easily.

the art of a layered bed

bottom layer: sheets

cotton
The best? Egyptian cotton—it's extremely supple and durable. Don't worry so much about thread count (the type of cotton is more important). Next in line, and less expensive, is pima cotton. You'll find two weaves: percale (matte, crisp, and cool—nice if you get overheated at night) and sateen (thick, lustrous, smooth, and warm). Feel sheets before buying to sense if they're warm or cool to the touch—that's a matter of personal preference.

linen
An all-weather, versatile choice: thick for winter, cool for summer. And the more you wash it, the better it gets.

silk
Elegant and sensuous, silk makes crawling into bed extra exciting. And no, good quality silk sheets don't require dry-cleaning; just wash on gentle using cold water and silk-friendly detergent. Silk may lose some luster over time, but it'll get softer.

middle layer: duvets and covers

down
The soft, fluffy filling is warm and lightweight—a great combination. When shopping around, compare fill power, which is the amount of down per ounce. A fill power of 600 is great, but 500 might be preferable if you get warm at night. Goose and duck down are similar, but goose down's large, lofty clusters make it slightly better at insulating.

down alternative
Man-made fillings, such as rayon or polyester are cheaper, easier to maintain, and ideal for allergy-sufferers. But the stuffing tends to feel heavy, and it's not as adept at regulating temperature.

duvet covers
Cotton is the most common choice. Look for a thread count of at least 300 tpi to ensure down feathers won't poke through.

top layer: throws

These are finishing touches for extra warmth that you can switch out seasonally or whenever you need a change. Place a throw at the foot of the bed folded in thirds, so it can easily straighten when you need to pull it up. Trim or fringe adds another layer of detail.

(btw)

Steer clear of synthetic sheets like polyester, acrylic, and nylon. Though their low price point and wrinkle-resistance may be tempting, a bed just isn't the place to go faux. Synthetic sheets don't feel as soft as other materials, are prone to pilling, and can absorb oil, making stains tough to remove.

10 tactile treats for every home

1. **luxurious white sheets** make other bedroom adornment unnecessary (shown this page).

2. **embroidered tablecloths** give everyday affairs a handcrafted appeal.

3. **tasseled welcome mats** are flirty and functional.

4. **turkish hand towels** offer a refreshing twist from terrycloth.

5. **mohair throws** are lightweight but really warm—the ideal combination for movie nights.

6. **fluffy white towels** bring to mind hotel serenity.

7. **a sheepskin** can transform a cold hard bench into a shaggy-chic delight (shown opposite, top left).

8. **moroccan floor cushions** signal guests to take a load off (shown opposite, top right).

9. **a flatweave rug in the bathroom** is decadent but also smart—it's made to withstand traffic (shown opposite, bottom left).

10. **layered coverlets** turn a bed into a textural haven (shown opposite, bottom right).

STYLE STATEMENTS

snapshots of inspiring ideas

traditional

the mood: refined, rich, vintage.

styling notes: A painterly textile turns a formal headboard into abstract art and acts as a bridge between bright white linens and a rich maroon wall. Subtle details, like nailhead, pom-pom trim, and a preppy striped bed skirt feel like a treat when you realize they're there. A nubby blanket and a pair of velvet ottomans anchor the scene.

graphic

the mood: abstract, fresh, spare.

styling notes: A Marimekko tapestry (secured to the ceiling with ropes threaded through grommets) distracts from tight quarters and recalls a high-seas adventure. The swirly pattern and scalloped pillows soften the boxy space. The black bed skirt makes the bed feel like it's floating, another small-space trick.

modern

the mood: clean, colorful, modern.

styling notes: A tufted headboard gets a hit of pattern and color thanks to a family of throw pillows in lush materials. Even the black-and-white art adds a layer of softness in its own sophisticated way.

get the look

cottage

Matching sheets to wallpaper makes the room feel "done." The headboard's wings carve out a cozy enclosure, and the ample padded back makes reading in bed easy. The bed is casually made—no frills, starch, or strict tuck-action here—so it feels inviting and realistic.

striped throw pillow

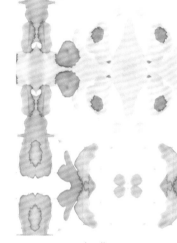

pastel wallpaper

cotton herringbone throw

Pondicherry headboard

linen throwbed

colonial side table

sky blue bedding

Turn to page 270 for information on these products.

STYLE SCHOOL

alternative headboards

fabric

Patterned curtains that complement the bedspread create a sleeping nook that feels regal.

flag

This vintage flag flies high—extending past the bed frame and up to the ceiling to make the room feel taller. Placing the flag behind an industrial bed frame makes it feel less dorm room, more design-forward. And the elegant hanging method—nails hammered directly through—is easy and unexpected.

mirror

A tall mirrored headboard makes a room feel brighter, bigger, taller, and more glamorous. To offset the glass, a sheer canopy is hung from the ceiling.

screen

Tucked behind an upholstered headboard, a screen provides another layer, widening the room and harmonizing with wooden beams, rattan shades, and a hanging wicker chair.

style skills:
use soft stuff to...

warm up a cold bathroom

make a corner cushy

Colorful Turkish rugs take the chill out of a tiled floor, while blasting white surfaces with mesmerizing color and pattern. Ruffly top-down, bottom-up shades offer privacy and let in light from above. "Real" curtains frame the large window, making the space feel like a true retreat.

Layering a thick sheepskin over a thin cowhide turns a sunny section of nursery into a story-time spot. The giant teddy bear softens the corner and acts as a backrest. Sheer curtains gently break at the floor and filter light.

mellow the lines of hard furnishings

create a bed you never want to leave

Sheepskin rugs make everything they land on infinitely cozier (these low-cost versions from Ikea take two side chairs from proper to plush). Toss one on a wooden bench, a rattan chaise, or the back of a wire Bertoia chair. They're even great for softening something already soft; try one in the corner of a sectional to break up the large expanse and watch guests—and dogs and cats and kids—flock to it.

Sheets aren't the place to skimp. Here, layers of sumptuous Matteo bed linens feel like heaven and pool at the floor. Mixing shades of creamy white offers subtle dimension; casually tossed pillows signal laid-back luxury. Backed against a window with billowy white curtains, the bed takes on an ethereal quality.

window treatments

youthful energy

Mixed prints from floor to ceiling give a nursery global glamour rather than childlike charm.

tactile flourish

A macrame curtain is a chic choice for filtering light and looks particularly striking next to a sculptural plant.

graceful + groovy

The subtle beaded print of a linen shade is like a modern version of a '70s classic.

considerations

curtains

length: A good standard is to allow curtains to kiss the floor (half an inch above is fine, as well). Too short and they'll look geeky; too long and they'll collect dust. There are exceptions, though—a casual, informal space might be able to pull off curtains a bit shorter; a formal room could benefit from a romantic pooling on the floor.

width: Buy enough fabric—you'll need fullness for the drape to look right. Figure you'll need 1.5 to twice the width of the window. Hang rods 6 to 8 inches beyond the frame on each side, or wider to make windows appear bigger.

linings: Unless you want curtains to diffuse light or blow in the breeze, it's usually a good idea to get the fabric lined. Linings protect from sun damage, dirt, and condensation. They also add insulation. Decoratively, linings hide seams and stitch holes, keep patterns prominent, and help fabric drape with confidence. Consider blackout liners for bedrooms or nurseries.

shades

inside mounts: The cleanest, most tailored—and most common—application that allows window moldings to be seen and appreciated. They can make a small window look even smaller, though. When measuring, round down to the nearest ⅛ inch so shades have enough space to glide up and down without snagging the frame.

outside mounts: Best for privacy and light control, and for masking less-than-desirable window frames. The rod can be mounted on the window molding or outside of it; the latter makes the window appear bigger.

inspiring style:

frances merrill

(on mixing textiles)

Interior designer Frances Merrill's love of textiles started when she was young. "I remember teaching myself to sew as a child and coming to the realization that the only really interesting part of what I had made was the actual design of the material." She went on to intern for the world-renowned Jim Thompson Thai Silk Company in Bangkok and later studied textile design in Los Angeles.

"I love when things are put together in a new way," says Frances. "By mixing genres of textiles you can personalize a room." Curtains, throw cushions, shams, and upholstery are all great ways to add that second, lived-in layer to a room. "I especially love vintage fabrics because of the muted and faded colors. It's also wonderful to add something that is handmade to the mix."

"As a designer, my favorite textile is a tiny scrap of a Japanese Boro, which is all that is left of a larger piece I once wrapped around my couch cushions. Everyone in my office laughs at me because, without fail, this tiny piece makes it into every client presentation— even when I have a huge box of fabrics I love! I use the Boro to represent all the antique textiles that we will buy for the client."

frances's tips

1. To add some depth to your bedroom, hang an interesting piece of fabric in place of a headboard, or drape some material over an existing headboard.

2. There are no rules for throw pillows, but keep this in mind when layering them: Try something vintage, something soft, something striped; and, of course, something jewel-toned. Experiment! Play with color, pattern, and texture.

3. To make the most of a cheap pillow find from Etsy or eBay, replace the pillow back with velvet or add a shiny satin welt (a covered cord sewn into a seam as trim) for character. A fun striped material works well for the piping.

4. Quilts are another way to add texture and color to a room. They are especially great for a kids' room and can be a way to bring in a vintage element.

5. For drapes, try an inexpensive linen in a solid color—ideally a pretty jewel-tone. Use as much yardage as possible, covering the entire wall. This way, open or closed, the drapes will transform the room. Consider lining the drapes in the same solid color so the room looks really bright and vibrant from the street outside.

Sculptural plants and round accents smooth out the edges of a bathroom heavy on hard surfaces (brick, tile, cement, glass, wood).

9

PLANTS + FLOWERS

PLANTS
+ FLOWERS
WE LOVE

---

smart ideas for every
room in the house

dining room
A lineup of ferns in mismatched
ceramic pots feels right at home
on a rustic table and lightens up
a raw brick wall.

kitchen

Charming topiaries flanking the sink lend soothing symmetry and direct the eye to the textured wood ceiling.

outside

Herbs aplenty: A lush
garden of rosemary, laurel,
coriander, and parsley
surrounds a sundial.

office

A vertical succulent garden creates a stunning backdrop for a vibrant seating area, where a French settee upholstered with Japanese shibori cloth is paired with an African Bamileke table.

HANDBOOK

haute houseplants

	boston fern	string of pearls	split-leaf philodendron
why we love it	Oversize and fantastically frilly, it's a textural treat.	With its fleshy, pealike foliage, this aptly named succulent is botanical jewelry for your home.	Its tropical, large-scale leaves are room-defining—even just one leaf peeking out of a vase will look like art.
take note	Indirect light and high humidity will keep it happy, so hang near a window and switch on a humidifier if you have one. Its heavy, leathery leaves sometimes block moisture intake—so water near the base.	Place in bright light and water every week; in winter you can get away with once a month. Trim any stems that have lost their "pearls" to keep it looking full.	This species prefers to be out of the sun and dry, so only water once a week.
ideal vessel	The plant's ancient roots (figuratively speaking) make it an ideal candidate for a contrasting modern planter. A fun, ceramic urn elevates the whimsical nature of the plant and gives it a bit of polish.	Let it cascade over a sleek, white hanging planter, a crisp backdrop that lets the detailed shape of the plant truly shine.	A simple black cylindrical planter perfectly complements the big modern leaves; place against a white wall so the graphic nature can truly be appreciated.

	snake plant	staghorn fern	succulents
why we love it	Super-straight, sword-shaped leaves add architectural edge— great for filling a corner or adding height to a dresser or sideboard.	Artistic and free-spirited, this wall-mountable air plant doubles as sculpture.	Irresistibly adorable mini sculptures range from spiked and fuzzy to plump and round.
take note	You can neglect it and it'll still be your friend; it lives on minimal light and water. Just don't overwater—the roots can rot.	Mist daily and dunk the base in water weekly. Give it some light and use a humidifier if your space is dry.	Incredibly easy to care for; most like bright light and for soil to completely dry out between waterings.
ideal vessel	Go midcentury here— the sharp angles suit the leaves. It absorbs carbon dioxide and releases oxygen during the night (most plants do so during the day), so place in your bedroom for a breath of fresh air.	Mount onto wood or tuck inside a hanging glass orb to make the unusual species look museum-worthy. Place above a desk or dresser, or hang en masse for extra oomph.	Fill a simple pot with a variety of potted succulents in different shapes and hues. Place on a coffee table so you can take in views from above. Also great as a centerpiece, as their short stature won't block sight lines.

our favorite statement trees

	rubber tree	fiddle-leaf fig tree	kentia palm
why we love it	Its broad, oval leaves are super shiny and leather-like. Plus it's tough to kill and helps purify the air. (Fun fact: The name comes from the sticky sap emitted if injured.)	Designers can't get enough of the large, violin-shaped leaves, which punctuate a room with personality.	Graceful and arching, it can handle low light, underwatering, roughhousing, and general neglect. Totally low-maintenance.
take note	It thrives on indirect light; place next to gauzy curtains.	These trees stretch out and make themselves comfortable, so you might as well pick a roomy spot (indirect light, please) before things get hectic.	Place in a sunny spot, water regularly, and mist monthly to hydrate and remove any dust buildup. Kentia palms can grow up to 10 feet tall, so rooms with high ceilings are best.
ideal vessel	An oval-shaped planter mimics the shape of the leaves; choosing one that's matte will play off their glossiness.	Fiddle-leaf figs and oversize baskets are a perfect match. Their colors and textures are complementary (and photograph well together)!	A hefty, heavy planter (with drainage holes) is key, to avoid tipping and to balance out the delicate fronds. Play up its tropical nature with a fun color, like cobalt blue.

	dragon tree	lemon tree	banana tree
why we love it	Spiky, modern, and graphic, with branches you can angle and twist to your liking, it's an amazing accent for a clean-lined, contemporary space.	The next best thing to a holiday in Capri. It's always either flowering or growing lemons and can be moved outdoors in warm weather.	Exotic and tropical, with supersize floppy leaves, it's perfect for softening corners.
take note	Avoid direct sun—stick to moderate to bright light instead.	Consider a dwarf variety—it won't crowd your living space. Citrus trees need at least eight hours of light a day, so place in a south-facing window. Water regularly and mist in winter.	These need 12 hours of light a day, so place in a sunny spot. Mist regularly, and wipe down leaves now and then to remove dust. They can get big; if space is a concern, consider a dwarf variety.
ideal vessel	A sleek, white planter complements the geometry of the leaves.	An old-school terra-cotta pot will transport you to the old world. Get one with drainage holes, and place stones in the drainage dish for air circulation.	A square container contrasts the round leaves nicely, but go big—you'll need something sizable to handle the roots.

STYLE STATEMENTS

snapshots of inspiring ideas

striking

the mood: lush, riotous, colorful.

styling notes: Thanks to a massive bouquet of lilacs, a handsome black-and-white scheme gets a shot of color without the commitment. Placing the arrangement on a low stool allows it to be appreciated from above.

bohemian

the mood: calm, airy, friendly.

styling notes: The shiny leaves of a fiddle leaf fig spruce up an empty corner and reflect natural light. Dotting the space with small plants—on the windowsill, the coffee table, up high, down low—gives the subdued room a sense of rhythm.

romantic

the mood: bright, playful, optimistic.

styling notes: Why not match flowers to art?
A pretty-in-pink print (*Peonies*, by Kate Schelter) melds
with gorgeous flowers that are actually made of crepe
paper, a beautiful notion by flower artist Livia Cetti.

architectural

the mood: spare, clean, modern.

styling notes: Treat plants like cut flowers by tucking
tropical fronds into vessels—it's an easy way to add color.

fresh

Topping a mantel with an array of fresh flowers in individual vases (some tall, some squat) is a great way to create an ever-changing array. Species that curve and trail break the stark lines of a marble fireplace; a palm tree adds edge. Clusters of flowers throughout the space give each seat a brush with nature.

style standoff

dark flowers vs. white flowers

dark flowers are unexpected and cool. Go for deep hues only—jet black, burgundy, deep brown—or add a few white moments (like heuchera or white lavender) for contrast. Here, purple-flowering oregano, offset by black scabiosa and an extra-tall stem of meadow rue, foster a scene of almost accidental beauty. Pairing a solid and a translucent vase in the same tone adds interest.

white flowers can feel poetic and pure in winter and fresh and fearless in summer. In a white vessel, greenery pops and blooms blend beautifully. We particularly love white roses, hydrangea (cottage charm at its best), and fragrant, dainty paperwhites.

style standoff

wide-neck vessels vs. narrow-neck vessels

wide necks let stems breathe, creating lush, loose displays that allow flower faces to be seen from all angles. If things are flopping all over the place, use floral foam to bring the arrangement back to normalcy. Works best with thick stems and large blooms (pepper in smaller buds to fill in gaps).

narrow necks are the ones to reach for if you're a novice at flower arranging—they corral flowers artfully and make you look like a pro. If there's room, tuck in a few leaves to offset the blooms.

STYLE SCHOOL

bouquet basics

1. start with greens.
Sturdy foliage acts as a structure to keep flowers in place. Think stiff but full and crisscross stems to create a webbing.

2. tuck in flowers.
Choose big "faces" for maximum impact, like peonies, roses, and dahlias. Cut stems to different heights, clustering a few and singling out others. Loosen up the arrangement so it doesn't look too perfect—allow certain blooms to fall forward or back naturally rather than forcing them into submission.

3. fill gaps.
Feathery elements like ferns work well. You can also look to your yard for "filler" flowers— even weeds like Queen Anne's Lace can be beautiful.

kennesha's tips

1. Look at your space, and decide (based on ceiling height, empty places, etc.) which areas need the most attention. You want to create a space that is visually pleasing, one that guides the eye across or into a room.

2. Mix it up. Use indoor plants that have varying colors such as the Chinese evergreen, fern varieties like the Boston fern, bird's nest, staghorn, or dainty maidenhair fern. Try a philodendron to brighten a room. Add some height with a baby palm. Be sure that the plants you choose complement your personal style and will be able to thrive in the environment you've chosen.

3. Think outside the box when placing plants. Plants aren't just for living spaces like the kitchen, family room, or den. Pour a little "plant love" into spaces sometimes forgotten, like powder rooms and offices.

4. The popular fiddle-leaf fig can be a finicky one. If the fiddle isn't your friend, try other varieties of indoor plants like the mass cane or an easier-to-grow genus of ficus. If you're in an area like California or Arizona, you may be successful with a potted olive. That's the stuff dreams are made of! Sometimes if you purchase from them, nursery people will even make house calls to help ensure that your "plant babies" live a long, healthy life in their new home.

5. Let plants help you to style dinners and intimate gatherings. While using plants on the tabletop is great, placement above the table as a chandelier or hanging installation can help to create an amazing atmosphere by adding visual impact. Try using succulents or air plants tucked in small vessels and hung from a metal or wooden structure above the table.

inspiring style:

kennesha buycks

(on plants with personality)

Writer, blogger, inspirational stylist, and creative director of Restoration House, Kennesha Buycks takes inspiration from her Southern roots and her present life in the Pacific Northwest, where she lives with her family. Nature in all its glory—sunsets, mountains, lush vegetation—fuels Kennesha's creativity. Greenery enhances her lifestyle. Kennesha explains: "Adding plants to a room is essential, no matter the color scheme or how large or small the space. Not only do indoor plants bring life and personality to a 'dead' space, certain varieties can also help make the air in your home a little cleaner."

style skills:
use plants +
flowers to...

set a hotel-worthy scene

invigorate a table

decorate a doorway

Adorning a nightstand with a couple of blooms makes bedtime brighter and mornings more doable.

Vibrant flowers clustered by type create a magical color-blocked tableau for a courtyard party.

In an entryway, suspending roses with simple ribbon provides a charming welcome for guests.

create living art

sweeten a shelf

whip up a savory centerpiece

With antler-like fronds, staghorn ferns mounted and arranged into a grid make a poignant statement and feel at once precise and primitive.

A charming cluster of flowers warms up a collection of cool (tending toward chilly) ceramics. Trailing tendrils hang down, uniting the shelves with a bohemian flow.

Transferred from their pots into mismatched teacups, herbs like sage, thyme, rue, and rosemary feel English garden–esque.

inspiring style:

new darlings

(on plants as accessories)

Robert and Christina Martinez, the husband-and-wife team behind the lifestyle blog New Darlings, use house plants as they would any other decorative accessory. "We're so inspired by the whole 1970s' house plant craze," they explain. "We have plants in every corner of our space."

new darlings' tips

1. For those who don't have a green thumb, start with very resilient cacti, air plants, and succulents. These plants are almost impossible to kill and require very little maintenance. Once-a-week watering and a light misting is sufficient. The less attention you give them, the more they thrive.

2. Experiment. Go beyond the typical pot you find at a plant nursery. Driftwood and glass terrariums work well for air plants, and are a perfect way to add a little greenery in the kitchen or on a coffee table. Mix and match ceramics, terra-cotta, glass, and baskets. Using baskets as containers for larger houseplants is a great way to go big without spending huge amounts of money.

3. Keep the taller fig and banana leaf plants in the corner near a window. Larger plants create depth and texture and bring a lot of life into a room.

4. Don't just place plants on a table; think out of the box. Elevation is good for fishhook or lipstick plants. Try setting them up on a mantel, so they cascade down, or place them on a plant swing. Have fun with groupings of pots in macramé hangers to add texture.

5. Factor in trial and error. Plants will tell you where they are the most happy. Move them around the house until they are in the perfect spot.

At a summer dinner party, streamlined place settings allow seasonal flowers in vintage brass vessels to deliver maximum impact.

10
ENTERTAINING

ENTERTAINING WE LOVE

smart ideas for every
room in the house

elegant lunch

Matching the centerpiece to the surroundings feels pulled-together and polished. Feathery fronds speak to green-painted window and door frames, while the hand-carved bowl picks up the tones of burnished copper chairs.

beach picnic

Seaside schemes should blend in to the environment rather than oppose it. Swap loud-patterned blankets for soft cotton sheets, and decant beverages with unsightly labels into glass bottles. Pack food that'll last: Rather than premade sandwiches that'll get soggy, bring a baguette with jams or other toppings that can be spread on-site.

rooftop drinks

Flower boxes and potted plants transform a city terrace into a bucolic escape. Large leaves moonlight as coasters and sprigs of green garnish drinks. A vintage box, repurposed into a pretty, portable bar, keeps cocktail necessities contained.

casual brunch

Break out the tablecloth for intimate affairs, and shake up serving pieces for interest. Rest butter in beautiful bowls; bring out a vintage coffee pot. An asymmetrical splay of luscious blooms is a surefire conversation-starter.

HANDBOOK

dining table shapes + sizes

	why we love it	*take note*
round	Cozy and intimate, round tables allow everyone equal access to conversations. No sharp edges mean it's kid-friendly; also good for game night since the center is easy to reach.	If the table has a pedestal, apply pressure when shopping around to check sturdiness—wide pedestals are typically better.
rectangular *(opposite page)*	The most popular choice, this shape packs in lots of people, especially with a bench on one or both sides.	Guests can chat with those near them, but communicating with those at the opposite end of the table might require the whole party to engage in a group discussion.
square	Balanced and symmetrical, and a shoo-in for square dining rooms. A four-person table leads to relaxed conversation, as everyone has their own side and is equidistant from one another.	More than four people and you could end up with a chasm in the center that's tough to navigate.

6 picturesque place settings

Make sitting down to the meal part of the experience with tablescapes that break from routine and instantly set the mood.

blues

black + white

Turn to page 270 for information on these products.

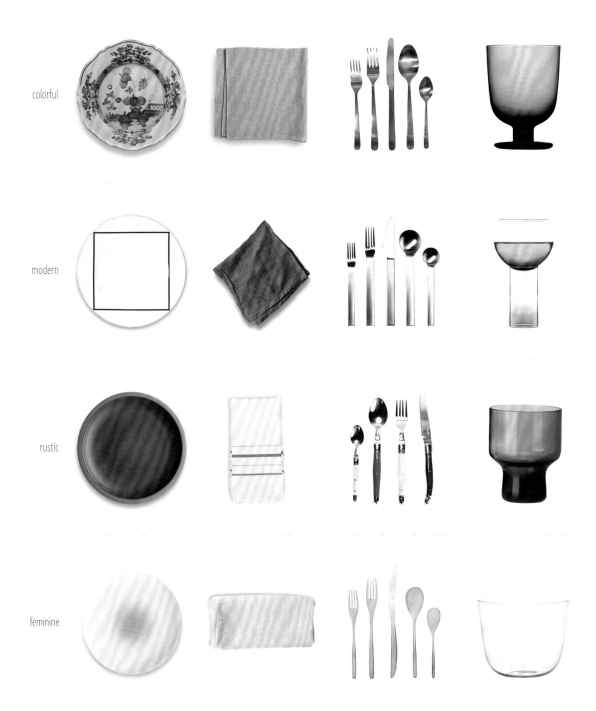

colorful

modern

rustic

feminine

setting up a spirited bar

No need for a cart on wheels. A stationary surface like a console, sideboard, or side table will work just as well. Whichever you choose, prop it with:

a few bar essentials: six bottles, at least to start; go for gin, rum, tequila, bourbon, vodka, vermouth.

decanter: you can't go wrong with crystal and a show-stopping stopper.

corkscrew, bottle opener, ice bucket, and tongs: an excellent opportunity to add thoughtful detail. Try mother of pearl or inlaid bone for subtle glamour.

tray: a must for protecting the surface from spills.

shaker: 28 ounces is the perfect size for two drinks.

3 steps to a quick cocktail party

1. serve one signature drink Surefire winners: a classic old-fashioned, sparking wine with a fruit garnish, pimm's cup, gimlet with fresh mint.

2. offer easy-access snacks Some of our favorites: cheese and crackers, spiced nuts, picholine olives, cornichons, and crunchy crudités with a slightly spicy dipping sauce.

3. perfect your playlist Tailor tunes to match your ideal party mood: jazz, relaxed indie, a medley of Motown.

STYLE
STATEMENTS

snapshots of inspiring ideas

rustic

the mood: outdoorsy, tactile, natural.

styling notes: Layers of texture—a raw wood table topped with a faux bois charger, stoneware plates, and amber glass—create a setting that feels special. The linen tea towel used as a runner unifies the disparate collection of items.

festive

the mood: warm, intimate, welcoming.

styling notes: The trimmings for a merry table can come entirely from your own backyard. Here, airy nandina berry branches and a sweet mound of red brunia in a gold bud vase speak to the striped French napkins, which are topped with greenery tied with jute. Pinecones scattered about feel at home on a weathered table. The centerpiece is a piece of driftwood topped with pine sprigs wrapped in battery-powered string lights.

striking

the mood: unique, stark, daring.

styling notes: Naturally shed pheasant feathers that match the china is a special pairing. The trompe l'oeil resin vases recall the bird's forested terrain, while polka-dotted guinea hen feathers in low cups and on each napkin subdue the starkness and play with scale.

colorful

the mood: animated, upbeat, full of life.

styling notes: This table feels like a painting; a modern vase offering big, boisterous blooms creates an intriguing preppy counterpoint. The vertically striped napkins rival the horizontal striped vase, and the swirly plates smooth out the scene. Peppering the table with a few flowers in shorter vessels creates a varied view.

casual

Mosaic tables, oversize floor pillows, and a flatweave rug all signal a loungy alfresco affair. The setup feels spontaneous, but the design is considered: Geometric patterns and unexpected color combos—dusty rose and pale blue to soften black and charcoal—elevate the look to boho-glamour status.

STYLE SCHOOL

anatomy of a cheese plate

enough for everyone
Buy 3 to 4 ounces of cheese per person, and gather five varieties—more than that will overwhelm the palate.

a trio of types
For a full range of textures and flavors, cover all three milk types—goat, cow, sheep—and experiment with different categories:

> aged (comte, cheddar)
> soft (camembert, triple creme brie)
> firm (manchego, gouda)
> blue (stilton, gorgonzola)

room temperature is best
Take cheese out of the fridge an hour before guests arrive; cold mutes the flavor.

the right knives
Use a butter knife for soft cheese and a triangular knife for hard cheese, like parmesan. Most goat and blue cheeses crumble under the knife; use a cheese wire.

carb control
Skip anything herbed or garlicky—it'll overwhelm the cheese.

perfect pairings
Choose at least one from each section:

something sweet:
in-season fruit; dried pears, cherries, or apricots; fig jam, raspberry preserves, apple chutney, raw honey.

something savory:
cornichons, olives, pickled green beans, roasted red peppers, caponata, spicy mustard.

something meaty:
hard salami, paper-thin prosciutto, sweet sausage bites. If you're not sure what to buy, look to your cheeses—for a French brie, consider saucisson.

something nutty:
Marcona almonds, shelled pistachios, walnuts.

the art of plating
Display cheese clockwise, from mild to most pungent. Be loose with your placement—sprinkle accoutrements throughout so no one has to reach too far. Labeling cheese with toothpick signs is a cute touch.

style skills:
use centerpieces to...

play with place settings

recreate a masterpiece

cultivate a botanical landscape

A crab apple cutting on each napkin mimics the sculptural central arrangement—where fruit brightens the gnarled driftwood—making the table feel like a considered tableau. The plates, with a touch of red, tie in as well.

Check out your fruit bowl for centerpiece inspiration. A simple plating of pears can take on the mesmerizing quality of a Cezanne still life.

Queen Anne's lace, allium, and thistles stand tall on thin, easy-to-see-through stalks that won't hinder conversation. Mismatched earthenware in muted purples, greens, and blues lends richness and depth.

10 out-of-the box serving ideas

1. Rim cocktails with chili salt.

2. Make takeout feel fancy: Serve food in porcelain bowls or pizza on cake platters.

3. Set up labeled dispensers of specially infused water: grapefruit rosemary, grape pineapple, lemon with fresh mint.

4. Create antipasto kebobs: mozzarella balls, stuffed olives, roasted peppers, artichoke hearts.

5. Prepare a vertical charcuterie board—a three-tiered platter piled high with salami, sausage, and prosciutto.

6. Toss a raspberry in each glass of Prosecco.

7. Turn dessert into decoration (shown right).

9. Let a giant serving dish steal the show.

8. Display a rainbow tomato tray with nearby sea salt and olive oil so guests can sprinkle and drizzle to their liking.

10. Make an ice mold filled with pomegranate seeds (or fresh fruit or cinnamon sticks or sprigs of herbs) to chill punch without watering it down.

ingredients for an instant cocktail party

A cocktail + two snacks = haute happy hour

Good Morning Indeed
Spicy Bloody Mary + Shrimp Cocktail + Bacon Strips

Italian Getaway
Negroni + Breadsticks + Hunk of Parmesan

Movie Night Made Better
Beer + Pizza Bagels
+ Chocolate-Covered Popcorn

Spanish Spread
White Sangria + Fried Calamari + Spicy Mini Meatballs

A Touch of Ginger
Dark & Stormy + Steamed Pork Dumplings + Scallion Pancakes

'60s Nostalgia
Old-Fashioned + Pigs in a Blanket + Fondue

Bubbly Essentials
Prosecco + French Fries + Dipping Sauces Galore

mood lighting

Stockpile as many white candles as you can—tapers, tea lights, pillars, the works. Stick to unscented candles, and set them on tables or low ledges rather than high shelves—you don't want anyone's hair to catch fire. Fit table and floor lamps with no higher than 25 watt bulbs, and whatever you do, switch off the harsh overheads. For outdoor gatherings, pile on the twinkle lights and grab a pretty lamp or two from inside for an unexpected glow.

timo's tips

1. Place paintings or photographs along a wall, like a gallery. This keeps the eye moving and visually tricks guests into thinking there's more space between them and the wall than actually exists.

2. A long, narrow table works well at dinner parties, (especially in a railroad apartment) and allows for more intimate conversations. Don't put it up against a wall, though—it's important that there's enough space to walk around it.

3. Alternatively, a perfectly square elevated table with high stools is an elegant way to make a room feel less cramped. (This looks great with a solid color tablecloth.)

4. Avoid clutter on a table; stick with what is being served at that moment. Family style spreads can be a mess; instead, keep all the food in the kitchen, served buffet style. For simplicity's sake, use only one course's worth of silverware.

5. Keep your table near an open window. The view can contribute to a more spacious feeling.

6. Use pared-down and simple greenery, like succulents, instead of larger floral arrangements.

7. Enhance your windows with greenery. Place a tall, lean houseplant, such as a banana leaf plant or stately cactus, next to a window to extend the feeling of spaciousness given by the view.

8. Under-lighting is a great way to enhance the height of the ceiling. Tipping a light upward creates shadows that can expand the room.

inspiring style:

timo weiland
(on small space entertaining)

Timo Weiland is the cofounder and creative director of his eponymous fashion brand. "Interiors play a large role in what we do. We are inspired by midcentury modern architecture and the American classic coastal aesthetic—an East Coast meets California style." Timo lives and plays in New York City. "I once had a party for two hundred and fifty people in a thousand-square-foot apartment." he laughs. "Entertaining in a small space has its benefits. It keeps your gatherings intimate and warm, but there is definitely a science to it."

inspiring style:

athena calderone
(on creating a stunning tablescape)

Athena Calderone, interior designer and founder of the lifestyle blog eye-swoon. com, believes her years of travel with her DJ husband and young son exposed her to diverse cultures, worked to inform her eye, and helped shape her passion for design. But ultimately it was homemaking that blossomed into her career path. "I would seek solace in the kitchen and found that experimentation, playing with different flavors and textures, became a really artful, fulfilling experience." When asked about her aesthetic, Athena says, "Simple ideas, thoughtfully executed, are best. Entertaining, making a meal, setting a beautiful table, and creating a mood are perfect ways to express your creativity."

athena's tips

1. Begin by establishing a palette: Use the seasons to inform the tone of the tablescape, as well as the menu. You might use darker, richer colors for winter, and set a light and easy tone for summer. Allow seasonal ingredients from the menu to spill onto the table. If you're preparing a blueberry dish, use clippings from blueberry bushes on the place settings.

2. Play with contrast. If you're using a mix of dark colors and gold on your table, add sprigs of greenery to counterbalance. This combination of glam and grit will give the tablescape depth. For a finishing touch, try using a chalkboard or hand-painted wooden spoons instead of name cards.

3. Instead of floral arrangements, which can get expensive and may feel too structured, rest three single blooms in a wooden bowl, or sprinkle the table with eucalyptus leaves. Add natural, organic layers to the table with fruit, such as pomegranates or lemons still attached to the branch.

4. Invest in a variety of flatware and ceramics; flea market finds are a perfect way to keep the cost down. If you buy what you love, even mismatched vintage glasses can become a one-of- a-kind collection that's unique to you.

5. Having the food prepared before your guests arrive makes entertaining easy. Place it on a sideboard or credenza and be creative with height when you plan the presentation. Use upside-down salad bowls as pedestals or pile up cork placemats to create several levels. Mix wooden platters and cutting boards with ceramic trivets to add another layer of visual interest. Add a tall vase to balance out the table or include small potted herbs, like lemon grass or tarragon, to accentuate the meal.

6. For a great conversation starter, write thoughtful quotes on small pieces of paper, roll them into scrolls, and bundle them up with twine. It's a novel way to break the ice.

shopping resources

★ = editors favorites   v = vintage   k = kid-friendly   b = budget-friendly

Don't forget to check out **domino.com** for home decor finds that will help you bring *domino* style and inspiration into your home. Shop fresh ideas, current trends, and editor favorites.

WALLPAPER + FABRIC

CALICO WALLPAPER ★
718 243 1705
calicowallpaper.com
Taking inspiration from the marbling traditions of Japan and Turkey—as well as NASA telescope imagery—this wallpaper studio keeps things interesting with eye-catching prints like the Aurora collection.

COLE & SON ★
+44 (0) 208 442 8844
cole-and-son.com
Considerably bolder than you might expect from an outfit that counts the queen as a client, this British company's offerings run the gamut from exuberant nature prints to mod graphics.

COWTAN & TOUT
212 647 6900
cowtan.com
Old-fashioned and restrained, with shades of English country, the traditional prints here (including amazing florals) are sold alongside more colorful updates by designers like Manuel Canovas, whose toiles in bright oranges and pinks look anything but dowdy.

DE GOURNAY
212 564 9750
degournay.com
These incredibly lush, hand-painted papers align to create epic historical scenes or grand chinoiserie patterns, but even a single panel can remake a room.

DONGHIA
800 366 4442
donghia.com
Decorators rely on Donghia for beautifully earthy and textured papers and fabrics—we're particularly fond of its fine silks and durable outdoor textiles.

DURALEE
800 275 3872
duralee.com
Great for all of the basics, this is also a good spot to find fun prints just waiting to be discovered and used to transform a humble hand-me-down.

ESKAYEL ★
347 703 8084
eskayel.com
Perfectly faded graphic prints in soft blues, grays, and pinks are this environmentally minded company's signature, as well as nontoxic inks and sustainable materials like grass cloth.

FLAVOR PAPER
718 422 0230
flavorpaper.com
Featuring fire-hydrant toile and Warhol-esque bananas, everything here is lively and statement-making—and hand-printed to order, just in case you want your favorite far-out pattern in a different color. Look for their '60s- and '70s-inspired prints, which are coveted by movie set designers.

HOLLAND & SHERRY
212 355 6241
hollandsherry.com
Everything is top-notch at this respected purveyor, which started out as a tailor in 1836 and carries fabrics and wallcoverings of the highest quality, including hand-painted prints you'll want to frame.

JOHN ROSSELLI AND ASSOCIATES
212 593 2060
johnrosselliassociates.com
Those in the know trust this New York–based dealer for sublime textiles and wall coverings by Chambord Place, Twigs, and more.

JUJU PAPERS
503 764 7610
jujupapers.com
Hand-printed with playful geometrics and nature scenes, the wallpaper at Portland, Oregon based Juju (meaning "to ascribe magical powers to inanimate objects") adds a touch of whimsy to any room.

KRAVET
800 645 9068
kravet.com
The range of fabrics here is pretty dazzling, but it's the basics—simple colors, beautiful textures, and timeless styles—that keep us coming back. One stand-out: the Museum of New Mexico collection, which is adapted from the organization's archives and includes traditional patterns in saturated, earthy hues.

LEE JOFA
800 453 3563
leejofa.com
While we love all its luxe printed fabrics and wallpapers, our particular favorite at this established house is the array of archival prints.

LES INDIENNES
518 828 2811
lesindiennes.com
Created using naturally dyed cottons and traditional hand-blocking methods, Mary Mulcahy's gorgeously subtle ethnic prints are a wonderful fit in even the most minimalist interior.

MARIMEKKO k
888 308 9817
marimekko.com
Finland's iconic textile and clothing design house continues to turn out bold, bright, and classic mod prints that add character and color to any modern interior or ultra-cool kids' room.

OSBORNE & LITTLE **k**
212 751 3333
osborneandlittle.com
A leader in the industry since the 1960s, this London-based company reissued its debut collection of papers, which range from opulent to proper. Don't miss designer Nina Campbell's historically inspired prints or the lush botanicals from Lorca, as well as exclusive designs in bold colors from Matthew Williamson.

PIERRE FREY
212 421 0534
pierrefrey.com
This luxury house is so quintessentially French—we love the elegant traditional fabrics and wallpapers, particularly the quirky toiles.

QUADRILLE
212 753 2995
quadrillefabrics.com
The source for the China Seas collection—hand-screened prints that hover between groovily geometric and beach-house boho—Quadrille also has fun prints like Uzbek, Tropique, and the kid-friendly Peacock Batik that brighten up a room.

RAOUL TEXTILES
310 657 4931
raoultextiles.com
The color-rich, exotic, and occasionally eccentric prints here rival those found at an authentic Indian marketplace. The sky's the limit in terms of customization—for a nominal fee, you can have your print of choice custom-colored.

SCHUMACHER
800 523 1200
fschumacher.com
This storied American company's offering skews to the classic, but we're also fans of its more contemporary designs, like the aptly named Good Vibrations line featuring abstract ferns in cheerful colors.

STUDIO FOUR NYC ★
212 475 4414
studiofournyc.com
This textile design studio boasts an eclectic inventory, including bright watercolors by Caitlin McGauley and textured florals from Ferrick Mason. Have your own designs in mind? Make an appointment with the in-house weaver to bring them to life.

SUPPLY SHOWROOM ★
512 770 6211
supplyshowroom.com
Housed in a chic 1930s bungalow, this Austin home goods shop curates a thoughtful mix of wallpapers from small-batch studios such as Flat Vernacular and Relativity Textiles—each more eye-pleasing than the next.

WALNUT WALLPAPER ★
323 932 9166
walnutwallpaper.com
Located in Los Angeles, Walnut specializes in unique papers by designers both indie and established. The selection of sweet, whimsical prints from Aimee Wilder, Yukari Sweeney, and Abnormals Anonymous is another draw if you're decorating a child's room.

PAINT

BEHR **b**
877 237 6158
behr.com
Known for high-quality stains and varnishes, Behr also excels in outdoor paints and primers.

BENJAMIN MOORE
855 724 6802
benjaminmoore.com
The gold standard for both design buffs and bright-eyed beginners, these paints go on smooth and have excellent coverage.

FARROW & BALL
888 511 1121
us.farrow-ball.com
The legendary English manufacturer is famous for its highly pigmented paints with poetically evocative names, like Borrowed Light and Setting Plaster.

PRATT & LAMBERT
800 289 7728
prattandlambert.com
Crisp colors and bright whites are the stand-outs at this more-than-a-century-old company.

RALPH LAUREN
800 379 7656
ralphlaurenpaint.com
Nobody does it like Ralph, and that includes his paint collection—a master class in stylish finishes and faux techniques like Suede, Antique Leather, and Indigo Denim.

SYDNEY HARBOUR PAINT COMPANY
310 444 2882
shpcompany.com
This small Aussie manufacturer gets its water-based paint recipes from the founder's grandfather. The colors are each hand-mixed using natural pigments for a richer hue.

FURNITURE

1ST DIBS **v** ★
877 721 3427
1stdibs.com
Every one-of-a-kind gem can be found here, a dream resource for decorators thanks to the always refreshed stock of high-quality antiques and vintage pieces culled from some of the finest shops and showrooms in the US, France and England.

ANOTHER COUNTRY
+44 (0) 207 486 3251
anothercountry.com
Inspired by Shaker style, as well as traditional Scandinavian and Japanese woodworking techniques, this English outfit keeps the design spartan and the materials organic, including hardwoods, stoneware, and brass.

BAKER
800 592 2537
bakerfurniture.com
This American company offers an impressive range of shapes and styles, all elegant and handsomely tailored. We're particularly fond of designer and architect Jean-Louis Deniot's furniture collection in soft grays with hints of Art Deco.

BERNHARDT
828 313 0795
bernhardt.com
Founded in 1889, this shop maintains a crisp edit of well-designed pieces balanced with a few organic elements, such as a petrified wood side table.

CENTURY
800 852 5552
centuryfurniture.com
Century is home to an impressive
assortment of classic furnishings,
from Windsor Smith to Patrick
Aubriot, as well as an Artist in
Residence program for up-and-
coming craftspeople who develop
new work (think sculptural, layered
side tables).

CISCO BROTHERS
323 778 8612
ciscobrothers.com
The sleek inventory here keeps a
green profile: Everything is built
using sustainable wood and water-
based glues, and manufactured with
environmentally friendly processes.

DESIGN WITHIN REACH
800 944 2233
dwr.com
One-stop shopping for virtually
every modern design classic.

ETHAN ALLEN
888 324 3571
ethanallen.com
Though it excels at more traditional
pieces (including wood canopy beds
in dramatic ebony stains), we also
like some of the brand's newer, more
modern offerings, like leather sofas.

GEORGE SMITH ★
212 226 4747
georgesmith.com
Beautifully made, timelessly chic—
this is the place to find upholstered
pieces like English-style sofas and
ottomans you'll have for a lifetime.

LEE INDUSTRIES
800 892 7150
leeindustries.com
All of this eco manufacturer's
classic upholstery offerings (slipper
chairs, settees, sofas) adhere to the
company's Natural Lee standard,
which means soy-based cushions,
reclaimed-plastic backs, and water-
based finishes. We love the small-
space-friendly styles, too.

MITCHELL GOLD & BOB
WILLIAMS
800 489 4195
mgbwhome.com
If you thought Gold & Williams
is only about sofas, the constantly
updated lighting and accessories
collections are also worth a look.

MODERN CONSCIENCE ⓥ
206 682 2443
modernconscience.com
A craftsman and a modern furniture
historian make up the duo behind
this Henry Miller–recommended
renovation studio in Seattle. They
also offer spare parts for your Womb
or Egg chair, a restoration kit (DIY-
er gift alert!) and vintage pieces
ready to be scooped up.

MODERNICA ★
323 933 0383
modernica.net
Midcentury fiends rejoice: This Los
Angeles studio churns out some
of the best reproductions around,
from George Nelson bubble lamps
to fiberglass shell chairs. You'll also
score clean-lined love seats, beds,
tables, planters, and shelves.

ROOM & BOARD
800 301 9720
roomandboard.com
This popular American retailer
offers easy, modern basics for every
room in the house, plus outdoor
and office styles. Standouts include
desks and occasional chairs.

SALVAGE ONE ⓥ
312 733 0098
salvageone.com
Expect the unexpected at this
Chicago-based cavernous ware-
house and events space, where you
might stumble upon an 18th-century
limestone mantel or a 1940s-style
brass and Lucite table lamp.

SERENA & LILY ⓚ ★
866 597 2742
serenaandlily.com
This California brand gets the West
Coast's effortless cool just right with
the Bungalow sofa, folding leather
stools, and other pieces for inspired
family spaces. The dedicated
Kidshop is equally well curated,
with everything from hanging
rattan chairs to luxe bedding.

VITRA
212 463 5750
vitra.com
Since 1950, this Swiss company
has manufactured furniture for
an incredible range of progressive
designers, including Charles
and Ray Eames, George Nelson,
Frank Gehry, Hella Jongerius,
and Verner Panton—in addition
to having its very own campus to
keep things current.

FLOORING

ANN SACKS
800 278 8453
annsacks.com
One of the biggest names in tile has
everything from basic penny rounds
to collections by designers like
Clodagh and Vicente Wolf.

CARLISLE WIDE PLANK
877 627 4118
wideplankflooring.com
This family business mills wide-
plank, heart-pine flooring harvested
from a 30,000-acre Alabama
plantation, and offers reclaimed
products that can all be traced to
their structure of origin.

COUNTRY FLOORS
212 627 8300
countryfloors.com
Renowned for its European
aesthetic and tiles based on 17th-,
18th-, and 19th-century designs, this
New York City–based company also
showcases beautiful natural-stone
and handmade terra-cotta options.

RUGS

AELFIE b ★
844 235 3437
aelfie.com
New kid Aelfie offers reasonably priced rugs that are designed in Brooklyn and handmade by artisans in India. We're also partial to the candy-colored sheepskins and hand-dyed flatweave rugs for added boho cred.

BEAUVAIS CARPETS
212 688 2265
beauvaiscarpets.com
As much an art gallery as a showroom, this spot is dedicated to fine antique rugs and equally authentic-feeling reproductions for the true connoisseur.

DASH & ALBERT
877 586 4771
dashandalbert.com
Shop for amazingly well-priced colorful patterns, plus a big range of striped and floral options.

ELSON & COMPANY
800 944 2858
elsoncompany.com
Handwoven by Tibetan weavers, the rugs here are exceptionally crafted. This San Francisco company's stock-in-trade is couture rugs by such respected names as Oscar de la Renta and Fabien Baron.

FLOR b
866 952 4093
flor.com
Welcome to environmentally responsible modular carpet tile that installs faster than wall-to-wall, goes with you when you move, and can be replaced by section if it gets stained.

LOLOI RUGS
972 503 5656
loloirugs.com
Innovative, intricate handcrafted designs at fair prices are what you can expect from this family-owned Dallas brand committed to merging craftsmanship and originality. We love the distressed designs that pair fantastically well with modern furniture.

MADELINE WEINRIB ★
646 602 3780
madelineweinrib.com
Textile artiste Madeline Weinrib changed the rug industry forever when she debuted her line of eye-popping, globally inspired rugs in 1997. Looking at her designs it's clear that Weinrib, also a painter, was able to find that sweet spot between brush and loom to create truly one-of-a-kind masterpieces for the floor.

MANSOUR MODERN
310 652 9999
mansourmodern.com
The many inventive, ethnic-inspired patterns at this couture shop are especially strong, but the range of designs encompasses everything from graphic looks to subdued neutrals, all of it well-made.

MERIDA MERIDIAN
800 345 2200
meridastudio.com
This is an amazing source for natural-fiber floor coverings like sea grass and sisal, jute, abaca, and beyond, all beautifully woven and bound in designs and patterns you won't see elsewhere.

OYYO ★
+46 76 891 19 08
oyyo.se
Working with organic cotton and vegetable dyes, this small Swedish studio uses traditional techniques to create their beautifully timeless weavings.

THE RUG COMPANY
800 644 3963
therugcompany.com
Paul Smith, Vivienne Westwood, Rodarte and other big fashion names are among the star collaborators at this site.

SAFAVIEH k
866 422 9070
safavieh.com
More on the traditional, tailored end of the spectrum, the selection here includes Thomas O'Brien's streamlined ethnic looks, along with a few statement pieces, like an animal-print rug by Jamie Drake in raspberry silk.

SHARKTOOTH v
718 451 2233
sharktoothnyc.com
If you're in the market for an antique rug, Sharktooth has you covered. The small yet eclectic collection also includes hand-dyed and patched textiles in deep indigos and grays.

STARK CARPET
844 407 8275
starkcarpet.com
It's all about the selection and quality here, from antiques to repros, Aubussons to soumaks, and brilliant custom options.

ZAK+FOX v
212 924 0199
zakandfox.com
A quirky and playful aesthetic prevails over this textiles and rugs store, started by Zak Profera and his Shiba Inu "fox" Shinji. Create your own chic clubhouse with a mid-century Tulu-style rug or "pom" print linen drapes.

LIGHTING

APPARATUS ★
646 527 9732
apparatusstudio.com
Sculptural pendant lights—sometimes in fanciful shapes, like the Cloud series—are the hallmark of this Manhattan duo, who also work in brass, marble, and even horsehair.

CHRISTOPHER SPITZMILLER
212 563 3030
christopherspitzmiller.com
Spitzmiller handcrafts modern lamps with classic influences in an array of colors and silhouettes.

CIRCA LIGHTING ★
877 762 2323
circalighting.com
With a tremendous stock of floor and table lamps, sconces and pendant lights—skewed toward the traditional, though nothing's too antique—it's no wonder this spot is so beloved by decorators.

FLOS
888 952 9541
usa.flos.com
This Italian lighting giant has collaborated with design luminaries like Philippe Starck and Patricia Urquiola, and continues to produce elegant, innovative pieces.

LINDSEY ADELMAN
212 473 2501
lindseyadelman.com
Handblown glass and locally machined metal—not to mention nautical rope and chain mail—give this Manhattan-based designer's pieces a ying/yang effect that we love.

LUMENS
877 445 4486

lumens.com

Stock up on every bulb imaginable—whether a chrome top or a European base—at this lighting emporium.

ONE FORTY THREE b ★
702 566 8298

shop.onefortythree.com

It's hard to believe that each of the lamps on this site is individually made by a husband-wife team—for a steal, no less.

PELLE
718 243 1840

pelledesigns.com

This Brooklyn studio is a true design laboratory, where founders Jean and Oliver Pelle developed an LED light that mimics the warmth of an incandescent bulb, among other marvels.

REJUVENATION
888 401 1900

rejuvenation.com

Besides a strong collection of antique fixtures and reproductions, this company has a take-back program to ensure its products don't end up in landfills.

ROLL & HILL
718 387 6132

rollandhill.com

Find the perfect Art Deco–inspired pendant light or modern desk lamp here—a thoughtful boutique championing small-batch production and a handful of independent designers.

SCHOOLHOUSE ELECTRIC AND SUPPLY CO. b ★
800 630 7113

schoolhouseelectric.com

Past and present merge in Schoolhouse Electric's wide range of historically accurate luminaires, all of which can be hardwired to order for eco-friendly compact fluorescent lightbulbs.

THE URBAN ELECTRIC CO.
843 723 8140

urbanelectricco.com

This Charleston-based stockist collaborates closely with top designers (among them *domino* favorites Oro Bianco and Nickey Kehoe) on updated yet still timeless options.

WARBACH
512 522 0564

warbach.com

If you're on the hunt for a custom piece, Austin studio Warbach might be your answer. The design-build studio crafts geometric chandeliers and sconces from salvaged wood and iron for over a dozen local restaurants and residences in the Texan capital.

YLIGHTING b
866 428 9289

ylighting.com

A mega-emporium with a massive assortment of modern options in every category.

ENTERTAINING

BARNEY'S
888 222 7639

barneys.com

This favorite source for luxury goods carries gorgeous Fornasetti platters, elegant servingware, and standout pieces by hard-to-find brands like Venini.

FITZSU
323 655 1908

fitzsu.com

This couple-owned online store is a dream for hostesses and design purists alike, with entertaining essentials such as Giò Ponti flatware, Goa salad servers, and Aino Aalto glassware.

FOOD52 ★
food52.com/shop

Home to all manner of food forums and recipes from the ever-growing Food52 community, the site's equally extensive shop offering includes high-quality kitchen- and serving-ware, as well as great gifts.

GLOBAL TABLE b
212 431 5839

globaltable.com

Packed with vibrant, unusual items from around the world (all of them simple and mostly modern in design), this tiny outfit in New York's SoHo is filled with vases, tableware, and trays you won't see elsewhere.

HEATH CERAMICS ★
415 361 5552 x12

heathceramics.com

Since 1948, this West Coast establishment has turned out the distinctive hand-glazed, understated, modern work of groundbreaking artisan Edith Heath.

KNOT & BOW
718 499 0414

knotandbow.com

This Brooklyn stationery store stocks adorable party supplies. We can't get enough of the beeswax birthday candles and handmade jumbo balloons filled with confetti.

MERI MERI
650 508 2300

merimeri.com

Score sweet supplies that'll bring out the kid in you and your guests, from marbled paper napkins and paper flower cake toppers to tasseled party picks and wooden cutlery with pretty-in-pink handles.

MUD AUSTRALIA
646 590 1964

mudaustralia.com

Known for organic, timeless shapes in a calming palette of neutrals, this porcelain ceramic studio from Down Under makes each piece by hand.

PAPER SOURCE
888 727 3711

papersource.com

This is the place to personalize a party. Customize anything from place cards and cocktail napkins to coasters and favor bags, and find fun touches like fringe garland, chalkboard banners, and party hats appropriate for the older set.

SNOWE ★
888 439 9397

snowehome.com

For basics without the bore, look no further than this line of everyday essentials by Rachel Cohen and Andres Modak, who weren't thrilled by the offerings when setting up their NYC apartment, so they created their own. From white serving bowls made in Portugal to a sinuous Italian-crafted glass carafe, the wares are functional but gorgeous, and the prices (thanks to no middle man) are reasonable.

TABLEART ⭐
323 653 8278

tableartonline.com

The well-traveled owner of this high-end shop marries unexpected, little-known European and Asian lines (we're a fan of Richard Brendon's playful stripe designs) with marquee brands like Alessi and Royal Copenhagen.

WILLIAMS-SONOMA
888 922 4108

williams-sonoma.com

For every meal there is a setting at this reliable source for sophisticated and tailored goods—whether in hard-working melamine or fine French porcelain.

TEXTILES + BEDDING

ANICHINI
800 553 5309

shop.anichini.com

The luxurious textiles here run the gamut from brocade coverlets to intricate embroidered table linens, all cut and sewn by local craftswomen in an 1860 farmhouse in Tunbridge, Vermont. The company's newest offerings include ornate meditation pillows and washed-linen duvet covers.

AREA
212 924 7084

areahome.com

This design studio specializes in sleek, graphic bedding that's playful but always sophisticated.

BOLL & BRANCH ♭
800 678 3234

bollandbranch.com

This innovative brand prides itself on offering a completely transparent supply chain and a much lower price tag; the certified organic cotton bedding is sourced from Fair Trade farms and made in India.

BRAHMS MOUNT
800 545 9347

brahmsmount.com

One of the last remaining textile mills in the US uses antique shuttle looms to craft classic designs with a twist, like silky-smooth fine wool throws done up in ombré. You're sure to adore the rumpled-to-perfection linen towels suitable for both kitchen and bath.

CALVIN KLEIN HOME
866 513 0513

calvinklein.com

Featuring subtle patterns in a spectrum of neutrals, pastels, and earth tones, the mega-designer's linens help build a calming, casually elegant bedroom.

THE COMPANY STORE ♭
800 323 8000

thecompanystore.com

This Wisconsin-based outfit offers a wonderfully comprehensive selection of bedding basics in a wide range of colors, patterns, and fabrics.

FOG LINEN ⭐
617 576 1600

shop-foglinen.com

An offshoot of the Japanese line Fog Linen Work, Fog Linen carries duvet covers, blankets, and pillowcases in the brand's soft-to-the-touch linen.

FRETTE
800 353 7388

frette.com

Featuring understated design and impeccable materials, the super-luxurious linens from this storied European house are pricey but worth it.

HILL HOUSE HOME
855 244 6630

hillhousehome.com

Made in Europe using Supima cotton, this company's bedding gives a modern spin to classic linen styles—and sells crisp white PJs to match, for those wanting the complete look.

JOHN ROBSHAW TEXTILES ḳ
212 594 6006

johnrobshaw.com

The globe-trotting designer's printed bedding is one of our absolute favorites. The hand-blocked and hand-printed patterns mix and match beautifully, and the nursery styles are unusually sophisticated.

LEONTINE LINENS ḳ
504 899 7833

leontinelinens.com

Known for standout monograms and fine embellishments, these luxurious handmade linens can be customized to your exact specifications.

LIBECO
+32 051 484851

libecohomestores.com

With different collections named after romantic locales like Notting Hill and Brick Lane, this Belgian linen line has that slightly scruffy Euro sensibility we love.

MATOUK
855 795 7600

matouk.com

Family-run since 1929, this old-school American brand now collaborates with modern talents but still offers traditional touches like custom colors and monograms.

MATTEO ⭐
213 617 2813

matteohome.com

Simple in design but made from luxurious natural materials, this LA-made bedding has a modern rustic (but not too country) chic.

OLATZ
212 255 8627
olatz.com
A favorite of high-end designers, Olatz Schnabel's super-indulgent linen-and-cotton sheets boast bold color combinations and elaborate hand-embroidered details.

PARACHUTE b ★
855 888 5977
parachutehome.com
We love that this brand's Egyptian and Turkish cotton bedding is certified chemical- and synthetic-free—as well as the fact that it partners with a U.N. organization to donate malaria bed nets.

SOCIETY
societylimonta.com
This Italian company approaches bedding like fashion, experimenting with textile processes and mix-and-match color palettes to create "couture" for the home.

HARDWARE + FIXTURES

BARBER WILSONS & CO. ★
800 727 6317
barberwilsons.com
Traditional kitchen and bathroom faucets of the highest quality distinguish this British institution, the sole supplier for Queen Elizabeth II and such top London hotels as Claridge's, The Savoy, and The Dorchester.

DORNBRACHT
800 774 1181
dornbracht.com
The rigorously sleek, architectural hardware for kitchen and bath from this German manufacturer never forsakes functionality. (Hint: Your contractor can buy this company's products for you.)

DURAVIT
888 387 2848
duravit.us
Duravit excels at creating an ultra-clean look that doesn't leave you cold. Check out the Delos and Scola styles.

E.R. BUTLER & CO. ★
617 722 0230
erbutler.com
This high-end American manufacturer lovingly handcrafts a wide range of traditional and custom hardware and produces designs by such luminaries as Ted Muehling.

GROHE
800 444 7643
grohe.com/us
Europe's largest faucet manufacturer specializes in forward-thinking aesthetics and technological innovation.

KOHLER ★
800 456 4537
us.kohler.com
Family-owned since 1873, this great American outfit has everything—all of it incredibly well-made.

THE NANZ COMPANY
212 367 7000
nanz.com
Each of the finely crafted high-end hinges, knobs, and pulls from this five-person atelier is truly beautiful, and the custom pieces are works of art.

NEWPORT BRASS b
949 417 5207
newportbrass.com
Conscientious decorators rely on the epic inventory at this affordable kitchen and bath depot. Two of our favorites: the East Square and Miro lines.

P.E. GUERIN INC.
212 243 5270
peguerin.com
The handiwork of this venerable family business—going strong since 1857—can be seen in historic homes around the US. If money's no object, indulge in the painstakingly crafted hardware.

RESTORATION HARDWARE
800 762 1005
restorationhardware.com
Solid customer service and reasonable prices make Restoration a trusty spot for finding modern and vintage designs with unique details, like glossy black glass knobs.

ROHL
800 777 9762
rohlhome.com
Artisanal craftsmanship (e.g., faucets that riff on Edwardian and Georgian architecture), plus the sublime "Modern" line make this brand, launched in 1983, feel older than it is.

SIMON'S HARDWARE & BATH
888 274 6667
simons-hardware.com
This popular Manhattan showroom contains an impressive range of hardware and fixtures, from tiny minimalist hooks to grand old-fashioned tubs.

SUNRISE SPECIALTY ★
510 729 7277
sunrisespecialty.com
This decades-old company carefully crafts authentic reproductions of Victorian-era bathware, including a huge range of cast-iron tubs and faucets, hand showers, and tubfills.

SUPERFRONT
+46 8 68 44 18 14
superfront.com
Taking Ikea hack to the next level, this Swedish company makes sleek handles in leather and brass, tops in materials like Carrara marble, and other design-minded details to elevate your Ikea pieces.

URBAN ARCHEOLOGY
212 371 4646
urbanarchaeology.com
The storied New York destination offers a well-edited selection of stylish lighting, hardware, washstands, and freestanding tubs.

WATERWORKS ★
800 899 6757
waterworks.com
An established player in the pricey-but-worth it category, Waterworks carries top styles like the Aero and Enfield lines, as well as the handsome R.W. Atlas collection.

WHITECHAPEL LTD. b
800 468 5534
whitechapel-ltd.com
A mind-boggling assortment of kitchen hardware fills this impressively organized website, from reproduction cabinet pulls to modern hinges to graceful latches.

PLANTS +
OUTDOOR LIVING

ARCHITECTURAL POTTERY
858 385 1960

architecturalpottery.com

Launched in 1950, this company delivers exactly what the name suggests: custom-made planters and garden accessories in clean, sculptural forms with choose-your-own colors and finishes.

JAMALI GARDEN b
201 869 1333

jamaligarden.com

This unexpectedly amazing party resource offers strings of lights and floral designers' tools, as well as votive candles by the dozen for setting the perfect outdoor fête.

LIGHT & LADDER
401 241 9527

lightandladder.com

Ceramic and leather hanging planters, porcelain bud vases, and elegant accessories like the slim-necked watering vessels are some of the highlights at this Brooklyn-based studio.

LOLL DESIGNS
877 740 3387

lolldesigns.com

A leader in designing with recycled plastic, this company carries durable outdoor furniture in geometric shapes and a bright palette.

THE SILL b ★
thesill.com

A one-stop-(online) shop for all things botanical, from ferns potted in brightly colored vessels to succulent starter kits, this user-friendly site also offers tips and how-tos for aspiring green thumbs.

SPROUT HOME ★
718 388 4440

shop.sprouthome.com

Locations in Chicago and Brooklyn give urbanites a much-needed nature fix. Small-space solutions abound, from hanging glass terrariums and macrame plant hangers to mini planters perfect for windowsills.

STEEL LIFE
shopsteellife.com

This store's small but considered collection includes midcentury-style vessels in powder-coated steel and plant stands in walnut. For something extra-unique, you can also go the custom-made route.

TERRAIN ★
877 583 7724

shopterrain.com

A comprehensive source for gardening and outdoor living, Terrain stocks everything you might need for the patio, greenhouse, balcony, and beyond—and gets that lightly weathered look just right.

SMALL HOME
GOODS

A.G. HENDY & CO. HOME
STORE HASTINGS v
+44 (0) 1424 447171

aghendy.com/homestore

The online home to the lovingly restored London townhouse of the same name offers heirloom-quality goods, both new and vintage, chosen by founder and all-around-creative type Alastair Hendy.

THE CITIZENRY
866 356 4284

the-citizenry.com

"Homegoods with a soul and a story" is how The Citizenry describes its wares—and each item is presented in terms of where and how it was made, from graphic baskets handwoven in Uganda to foldable leather lounge chairs crafted in Argentina.

HAWKINS NEW YORK ★
844 469 3344

hawkinsnewyork.com

Artisanal know-how meets effortless chic at this homewares shop, where you can pick up the essentials—Moroccan water glasses, linen pillows, oak cutting boards—along with a few key pieces, like their popular Grady Ladder.

JENNI KAYNE
310 695 1223

jennikayne.com

Easy breezy California living defines this designer's simple, tailored sensibility. Her curated selection of home wares includes cloth dish covers as an alternative to plastic wrap and white ceramic jingle bells by Michele Quan.

JOINERY ★
347 889 6164

joinerynyc.com

Purveyor of the famed Eagle and Diamond blankets in minimalist patterns, Joinery is your go-to for well-crafted treasures, like a Pioneer chair or festive papier-maché mobile.

LABOUR AND WAIT
+44 (0) 207729 6253

labourandwait.co.uk

Enduring classics reign supreme at this London outpost. Frustrated by constantly redesigning clothing for ever-changing trends, founders Rachel Wythe-Moran and Simon Watkins changed courses, curating a line of home wares fit for the ages. Think galvanized buckets with wooden handles and enamel soap dishes.

LEIF k
leifshop.com

Happy-making home accents and style accessories in fun prints and refreshing colors—a polka-dot tray here, a pom-pom basket there—keep us coming back for more.

THE LINE
646 678 4908

theline.com

This on-point style source tailors an equally sharp selection for the home, including books, candles, and other small luxuries that make the most thoughtful housewarming gifts.

LOST & FOUND k
various locations

lostandfoundshop.com

This Hollywood mainstay, which has since branched out to Santa Monica, is an emporium for refined yet unfussy goods, with something for every taste and budget.

MICHAEL TRAPP v
860 672 6098
shopmichaeltrapp.com
If you're in search of something truly rare, look to Michael Trapp, whose antiques collection spans several centuries and includes a veritable cabinet of curiosities.

MOMA STORE k
800 851 4509
momastore.org
Every design-lover's happy place, the MoMA store is the source for modern classics and collectibles that merge clever with functional, including books, lighting, accessories, kitchenware, and office supplies.

MUJI b
muji.com
Everything at this design-minded Japanese retailer is a practical yet fun purchase, whether a craft-paper notebook or a glass teapot.

NALATA NALATA
212 228 1030
nalatanalata.com
You can feel the care that went into choosing each item at this shop, where the husband-wife team focuses on everyday Japanese goods that aim to delight.

NANNIE INEZ ★
512 428 6639
nannieinez.com
An Austin fixture, this concept shop prides itself on carrying hard-to-find pieces from around the world—at reasonable prices.

NICKEY KEHOE ★
323 954 9300
nickeykehoe.com
Todd Nickey and Amy Kehoe, interior designers and arbiters of good taste, lead this Los Angeles studio full of accessories like Japanese ceramic bud vases, powder-coated steel waste bins, African seagrass baskets, and cast-iron bookends.

OROBORO
718 388 4884
oroborostore.com
East and West coast converge at this Brooklyn boutique, which stocks ceramic wall hangings, traditional woven hammocks, quilted throw pillows, and other must-haves for the modern boho.

POKETO k
213 537 0751
poketo.com
Cheerful colors and smart, playful designs make this small-goods purveyor the retail equivalent of a pick-you-up.

SPARTAN ★
505 600 1015
spartan-shop.com
The name says it all: This site is for lovers of design distilled to the most essential, with a focus on natural materials and rich textures.

STEVEN ALAN HOME k
877 978 2526
stevenalan.com/home-store
Hand-thrown mugs, scented soaps, organic cotton towels, and other necessities round out the clothing brand's understated home offerings.

UMBRA b
800 387 5122
umbra.com
From hooks, shelves, and storage to barware and kitchen tools, you'll find them all here in streamlined Modern shapes and at budget-friendly prices

EVERYTHING FOR THE HOME

ABC CARPET & HOME v
212 473 3000
abchome.com
This one-of-a-kind mega-emporium is stocked with treasures old and new (many of them eco-friendly) from the most remote points on the globe. Look for the world's comfiest sofas, a well-vetted bedding selection, and, of course, a rug oasis across the street.

AMARA
866 896 3804
us.amara.com
In addition to carrying high-end brands like Mulberry Home and Tom Dixon, this smartly curated UK site also develops its own line of home furnishings and accessories.

ANTHROPOLOGIE
800 309 2500
anthropologie.com
This favorite has perfected a gently worn bohemian aesthetic that's reflected in everything from elegant sofas to small decorative accessories.

CB2 b
800 606 6252
cb2.com
The modern and budget-conscious little sister of Crate & Barrel, CB2 is great for small-space furniture and fun accents.

THE CONRAN SHOP ★
+44 116 269 1083
conranshop.co.uk
From vintage to modern and everything in between, this design institution, founded by English designer Terence Conran in 1974, is always on point.

CRATE & BARREL
800 967 6696
crateandbarrel.com
Handsome and solidly built, this mass retailer's furniture line keeps things fresh with of-the-moment styles and palettes.

THE FUTURE PERFECT ★
877 388 7373
thefutureperfect.com
Once a modest shopfront in Brooklyn, this design emporium has expanded to include a whole array of housewares. We love their clever accents, like trompe l'oeil wallpaper and brass paperweights.

H.D. BUTTERCUP v
310 558 8900
hdbuttercup.com
More than 50 top furniture manufacturers offer everything from oriental carpets to luxury mattresses here—minus any middleman prices.

HORNE
877 404 6763
shophorne.com
Enduring design underlies every piece at Horne, a favorite of architects and interior designers for its spirited and eclectic selection.

IKEA b
800 434 4532
ikea.com
Though the catalog might be easier to navigate than the massive stores, no one does inexpensive, on-point design like Ikea.

JAYSON HOME v
800 472 1885
jaysonhome.com
This superstore has a comprehensive stock of classic furniture and accessories, plus excellent vintage finds and a well-stocked garden section.

JOHN DERIAN COMPANY v ★
800 677 3207
johnderian.com
Best known for his whimsical
decoupage work, John Derian also
stocks textiles, candles, and small
furniture, along with lifelike marble
fruit, hand-painted wooden books,
and other wonderfully imaginative
gifts.

JONATHAN ADLER k
800 963 0891
jonathanadler.com
Adler turns out a line of fun,
glamorous furniture, lamps,
mirrors, and more in his signature
jewel tones and punchy patterns.

LAYLA GRACE k
626 356 2133
laylagrayce.com
A home store with a dreamy,
feminine aesthetic (think rose
quartz bowls, botanical framed
prints, and silk-linen comforters),
Layla Grace also carries bedding
and furniture for kids.

LEKKER HOME
877 753 5537
lekkerhome.com
An unfussy approach to design
with an emphasis on natural
materials is what defines this
Boston-based retailer, which has
lesser-known brands, such as
English furniture-maker Ercol,
along with the bigger names.

MANUFACTUM
+49 2309 939 095
manufactum.com
You can find everything imaginable
at this stockist (a home goods
giant in Germany), as well as some
marvelously old-fashioned items,
like a folding linen travel bag and
leather doorstopper.

MATTER
212 343 2600
mattermatters.com
Forward-thinking manufacturer
and showroom Matter bills itself as
a platform for design as much as a
shop—and with its impeccable who's
who of designers both established
(Enzo Mari, Zaha Hadid) and
emerging (resident studio designer
Ana Kras), we agree.

MENU ★
+45 48 40 6100
store.menudesignshop.com
For the minimalist, Menu is a haven
for simple, considered design with
a Scandinavian feel (many of the
designers hail from Europe).

MERCI ★
+33 (0)1 80 05 29 67
merci-merci.com
In Paris's historic Haut-Marais
district lies a bazaar that doesn't
want to be one thing, it wants to be
everything: The mix of home goods
are traditional and contemporary,
low-end and high-brow, one-of-a-
kind and mass-produced. From an
edgy slipcovered armchair to an
exposed-bulb clamp light to prewashed linen napkins, the offerings
have an irresistible European
sensibility and are designed to
delight.

MODISH STORE
888 542 0111
modishstore.com
"Clean" design at this online retailer
means streamlined shapes and
sustainable practices, including
a section dedicated to using
reclaimed and recycled materials.

NORMANN COPENHAGEN b
+45 35 55 44 59
normann-copenhagen.com
Accessible Danish design with
prices to match make this a favorite
for scoring on-trend pieces to
instantly update your space.

RUBY BEETS ★
631 899 3275
rubybeets.com
The new and vintage stock at this
Long Island mainstay includes
muslin-upholstered George Sherlock
sofas and Holmegaard glassware—
as well as finishing touches like
handwoven baskets, sculptural
lamps, and photography prints.

WEST ELM
888 922 4119
westelm.com
Head to West Elm for elegant
basics, from perfectly proportioned
Parsons tables to design-forward
storage pieces to well-made picture
frames in modern materials.

WORLD MARKET b
877 967 5362
worldmarket.com
These souk-like spaces are packed
with handmade furniture and
smaller items from exotic locales—
all of it very affordable.

ART

ART STAR b ★
888 488 757
artstar.com
This genius site serves as your very
own e-curator by custom printing,
framing, and authenticating works
by emerging contemporary artists
that are then delivered right to
your doorstep.

CLIC ★
212 966 2766
clic.com
With locations in New York,
St. Barth and the Hamptons, Clic
carries a chic selection of contemporary photography, travel and fashion
books, as well as small home goods,
to match its nomadic roots.

LARSON JUHL
800 438 5031
larsonjuhl.com
From molding to matboard, modern
to vintage-inspired, Larson Juhl is
a trusted expert for framing your
latest finds.

MASCOT STUDIO
212 228 9090
mascotstudio.com
An East Village cornerstone
since 1982, Mascot offers custom
and pre-made frames that exude
character—much like the space,
which owner and artist Peter
McCaffrey decorates with his famed
doggie portraits and other work by
local artists.

PICTURE ROOM ⓑ ★
212 219 2789

goodsforthestudy.mcnally-jacksonstore.com

Around the corner from New York's McNally Jackson Books, this smartly organized space sells "goods to enrich your study practice"—whether that be a handsome brass paperweight or sleek ballpoint.

MINTED ⓚ
888 828 6468

minted.com

An amazing array of customizable options (not to mention a covetable children's art section) makes Minted our go-to for gifts and special occasions—order a line drawing of your home or frame your favorite quote.

PACE PRINTS
paceprints.com

A quick glance at the roster of artists here—Sol LeWitt, Kiki Smith, Ed Ruscha—will have you measuring every inch of empty space on your walls. Plus, Pace's masterful printmaking techniques, such as woodcut and photogravure, make their works even more unique.

PADDLE8 ⓥ
212 343 1142

paddle8.com

Bid on one-of-a-kind pieces, from museum-quality contemporary art to of-the-moment design objects, through this online auction house.

PATRICK PARRISH ⓥ
212 219 9244

patrickparrish.com

Curator, collector, and artist Patrick Parrish has a sixth sense for finding and exhibiting promising new talent at his New York space, as well as sourcing great midcentury pieces.

RIFLE PAPER CO. ⓑ
407 622 7679

riflepaperco.com

Pick up a graphic botanical print, tapestry-stitched notebook, toile gift wrap, and other flights of fancy (temporary gold floral tattoo, anyone?) at this fine paper purveyor.

SOCIAL PRINT STUDIO ⓑ
socialprintstudio.com

Want to turn your photos into a book? How about a large-format print on glossy Kodak paper? This friendly printing service transforms your best shots into works of art.

TAPPAN ★
213 226 6452

tappancollective.com

The place "where today's best emerging artists meet their collectors," Tappan takes pride in carefully selecting each work—without charging you the steep gallery markup. We especially love Claire Oswalt's abstract watercolor collages in soft blues and grays.

WINDOWS + TREATMENTS

CHATEAU DOMINGUE
713 961 3444

chateaudomingue.com

In addition to the low-profile, streamlined metal windows and doors that founder Ruth Gay fell for while traveling through Europe, this company imports reclaimed roof tiles, arches, columns, and gates, along with antique lights and mirrors.

THE SHADE STORE ⓑ
800 754-1455

theshadestore.com

This family-run business assembles made-to-order Roman shades, custom drapes, and other stylish treatments (look for their exclusive designer fabric collaborations) directly in their workshop.

THE SILK TRADING CO. ★
323 954 9280

silktrading.com

Carrying much more than the name suggests, this Los Angeles house features custom window treatments in velvet, mohair, leather, cotton, and more. Ready-made drapes are also available through the Drapery-Out-of-a-Box line, featuring their best-selling designs for less.

SMITH & NOBLE ⓑ
888 214 2134

smithandnoble.com

From a simple café curtain to Parisian pleat drapes, Smith & Noble offers everything you might need—as well as in-home design consultations to get started.

INDEX

PRODUCT CREDITS

p. 6: Eskayel Madagascar Rose; p. 8: Flat Vernacular To & Fro – Madeleine; p. 26 (from top): Schumacher Couleur Force Leather, Schumacher Chester Wool in Pistachio, Waterhouse Jermyn Street Check in Black Oyster, Peter Fasano Delta Linen in Thatch, Studio Four NYC Fayyaz, China Seas Fez Background; p. 32 (clockwise from top): First Rocking Chair valerie-objects.com/Photo: Fien Muller, De La Espada Blanche Bergère, Acapulco Chair innitdesigns.com; p. 33 (clockwise from top left): Ballard Designs Louisa Bergère Chair, Armchair 41 Paimio by Alvar Aalto for Artek, Oomph Raffia Slipper Chair, Knoll Bertoia Diamond Chair; p. 54 (from top): Astek Inc. Submerged Anemone Shell, Pierre Frey Kazoo, Cole & Son Woodgrain Black & White, Schumacher Feather Bloom, Nobilis Brazilia; p. 108 (from top): PID Floors Oak, PID Floors American Walnut, Aronson's Floor Covering, Imports from Marrakesh Eight Point Star, Waterworks Concourse Field Tile Concrete, The Home Depot Winteron Oak Laminate Flooring; p. 110 (from top): Tibetano, Madeline Weinrib Dhurrie Ditto Blue, Aronson's Floor Covering Abaca, Ernest Outdoor Rug; p. 129: notonthehighstreet.com (top left), FLOR/Bruce Quist (top right); p. 234: Tiina the Store Indigo 10" plate, CB2 Indigo Stripe Napkins, Goa Cutlery White Handle – Brushed Stainless Steel by Cutipol for Horne, Iittala Kastehelmi Tumbler (top row), notNeutral Constellation Plate, Alfred Collection Grid Napkin by photographer Ben Kist for MARCH www.marchsf.com, CB2 Matte Black Flatware, Lobmeyr Series "B" Champagne Glass (middle row), Richard Ginori Oriente Italiano Porpora Dinner Plate, Canvas Home Oslo Cutlery Set in Matte Gold, Lempi Glass Lilac by Iittala for Horne (bottom row); p. 235: Continental Flatware Set by Gourmet Settings, Tulip Tall Glass by Fferrone Design for Horne (top

row), Heath Rim Line Dinner Plate/Photo: Jeffery Cross, Heather Taylor Home Sand Napkins 4, Brookfarm General Store 24 Piece Flatware Set – Linen, Nouvel Studio Cura Glass (middle row), Nikko Ceramics Cloud Dinner Plate, Brookfarm General Store Large Washed Linen Napkin – Rose, Sambonet "Bamboo" 5-piece Place Setting, Lobmeyr Glass Pink Cocktail Tumbler (bottom row)

Get the Look: Midcentury

p. 31 (clockwise from top left); Saarinen Dining Table, Knoll; Nelson Bubble Lamp Criss Cross Saucer Pendant designed by George Nelson/Photo: dwell.com; Courtesy of Phaidon Press, www.phaidon.com; Marble Two Arm Candlesticks by Chen Chen and Kai Williams for The Future Perfect/Photo: Lauren Coleman; Eames Molded Plywood Lounge Chair Designed by Charles and Ray Eames for Herman Miller/Photo: Courtesy Herman Miller, Inc., Source: Herman Miller, store.hermanmiller.com; Flower Bottle, Clamlab/Photo: Clair Catillaz; Reese Sheepskin Rug in Off-White, Safavieh

Get the Look: Rustic

p. 61 (clockwise from top left): Heath Ceramics Medium Covered Serving Dish in Aqua/Photo: Jeffery Cross; Lostine Large Rolling Pin/Photo: Jason Varney; Oil Decanter 2 by Gentner Design for Horne; Kaufman Mercantile Black Walnut Trencher Board; WorkOf Todo Bien Chair, www.workof.com Photo: West of Noble/Brookfarm General Store Copper Measuring Cups; Wrap Decanter by Simon Hasan for Horne

Get the Look: Graphic

p. 89 (clockwise from top center): Louise Gray Throw Quilt No. 1/Photo: Lee Stanford Photography; Winkel 127 Table Lamp - One Arm by Wastberg for Horne; Hayley Reagan for ArtStar; L.L. Bean Pima Cotton Percale Sheet, Windowpane; Champ Stool by

Visibility for Matter Made

Get the Look: Scandinavian

p. 121 (clockwise from top left): Schoolhouse Electric & Supply Co. Luna Pendant; Omero 19th Century Swedish Farmhouse Table; Eames Molded Plastic Side Chair with Wire Base Designed by Charles and Ray Eames for Herman Miller/Photo: Courtesy Herman Miller, Inc., Source: Herman Miller, store.hermanmiller.com; Norman Copenhagen Folk Candlestick Tray in Light Blue; Toss Around by Kibisi for Muuto; New Norm Dinnerware Starter Set by Norm Architects for Dwell

Get the Look: Serene

p. 143 (clockwise from top left): ©Steidl; A Question of Eagles Large Zig Zag Vase, jennikayne.com; Rip by John Hogan, Photo: Lauren Coleman; Lindsay Cowles "White on White," Deborah Ehrlich Medium Bowl, Retail location: Barneys.com & select Barneys New York stores; Christiane Perrochon White Beige Large Centerpiece Vase/Photo: Ben Kist for MARCH; Victoria Morris Pottery

Get the Look: Cottage

p. 195 (clockwise from top left): Loom Decor's Walk the Line Throw Pillow in Blueberry; Eskayel "Splash" in Cerulean; Brahms Mount Cotton Herringbone Throw with Hand Twisted Fringe - White/Cornsilk; Wisteria Colonial Column Side Table, www.wisteria.com; Hedgehouse Majorca Throwbed in Charcoal; Serena & Lily Pondicherry Headboard

PHOTO/DESIGNER CREDITS

Illustrations: Kaarina Mackenzie p 10: Nicole Franzen/Christene Barberich; p. 13: Amber Ulmer/Hey Wanderer; p. 15 (clockwise from top left): Molly Winters/Claire Zinnecker, Nathan Kirkman/Graham Kostic & Fran Taglia, James Waddell, Domino/Dekar Designs, Domino/Anne Ziegler, Domino/Nate Berkus Associates, Molly Winters; p. 17: Bows & Arrows Gemma Ingalls; p. 19: Joy Sohn; p. 20: Domino/Julia Leach; p. 22: Derek Swalwell (left), Nicole Franzen/Christene Barberich (right); p. 23: Laure Joliet/Frances Merrill (top), Domino/Ariel Ashe (bottom); p. 24: Domino/Katie Lee; p. 25: Nicole Franzen/Christene Barberich; p. 27: Domino/Ali Cayne; p. 28: Melanie Acevedo (left), Domino (right); p. 29: Nathan Kirkman/Graham Kostic & Fran Taglia; p. 31: James Waddell; p. 34: Robert Peterson of Rustic White Photography/Mandy Kellogg Rye of MKR Design; p. 35: Anna Wolf/Rebecca Omweg (left), Mia Baxter Smail/Maya Nairn (right); p. 36: Domino/Ali Cayne (left), Matt Albiani (right); p. 37: Patrick Cline/Kate Schelter (left), Domino (right); p. 38: Domino (left), Tiffany Haynes (right); p. 39 (from top): Michael Newsted, Bonnie Tsang; p. 40: Paul Costello (left), Michael Wiltbank (right); p. 41: Tessa Neustadt/Amber Lewis; pp. 42–43: Amy Neunsinger/Rebecca De Ravenel; pp. 44–45: Jenny Gage + Tom Betterton/Aurora James; p. 46: Domino/Katie Martinez; p. 48: Domino; p. 49: Domino/Jen Smith; p. 50: Amy Bartlam/Natalie Myer; p. 51–53: Laure Joliet/Frances Merrill; p. 55: Frances Tulk-Hart; p. 56: Laure Joliet/Frances Merrill; p. 57: Ellen Mesu/Ellie Cashman Design "Dark Floral"; p. 58: Nathan Kirkman/Graham Kostic & Fran Taglia (left), Domino/Nate Berkus Associates (right); p. 59: Domino/Andréa Krueger (left), Domino (right); p. 60: Laure Joliet/Jenni Kayne; p. 61 (bottom right): matdesign24/iStock Photo; pp. 62–63: Mia Baxter Smail/

Sarah Wittenbraker; p. 64: Domino/Julia Leach; p. 65: Laure Joliet/Jenni Kayne; p. 66: Domino/Ron Marvin (left), Laure Joliet/Frances Merrill (right); p. 67: Courtesy of Domino; p. 68: Domino/Lauren Leiss; p. 69: Miguel Flores-Vianna; p. 70: Domino/Anna Burke; p. 71 (clockwise from top left): Domino/John and Christine Gachot, Molly Winters, David Black; p. 72: Gaelle Le Boulicaut (left), Manolo Yllera/Amaya De Toledo (right); p. 73: Domino/Heather Taylor; pp. 74–75: Laure Joliet/Barbara Bestor; p. 76: Wing Ta/Kate Arends; p. 78: Domino/Maryam Nassirzadeh (left), Frances Tulk-Hart (right); p. 79: Joy Sohn/Eddie Lee; p. 80: Domino/Lauren Leiss; p. 81: Molly Winters; p. 83: Domino/Kristen Giorgi & Laura Naples; p. 84: Domino/Milly De Cabrol (left), Domino/Julia Leach (right); p. 85: Domino/Ariel Ashe (left), Domino (right); p. 86: Domino (left), Domino/Lauren Leiss (right); p. 87: Domino/Sally King Benedict (top), Domino (bottom); p. 88: Domino/Ariel Ashe; pp. 90–91: Patrick Cline/Kate Schelter; p. 92: Domino; p. 93: Mia Baxter Smail/Maya Nairn (top), Laure Joliet/Jenni Kayne (bottom); p. 94: Max Kim-Bee; p. 95: Domino/Maryam Nassirzadeh (left), Ashley Gieseking/Amie Corley (right); p. 96–97 (from left): Michael Rubenstein/Brittany S. Chevalier, Domino/Jenni Li, Robert Peterson/Brian Patrick Flynn, Amy Neunsinger/Rebecca De Ravenel, Nathan Kirkman/Graham Kostic & Fran Taglia, Laure Joliet/Frances Merrill; p. 98: Domino/Hayley Sarno & Patrick Mele (left), Domino/Nate Berkus Associates (right); p. 99: William Abranowicz; pp. 100–102: Nathan Kirkman/Graham Kostic & Fran Taglia; p. 104: Lucas Allen (left), Amy Neunsinger/Lily Ashwell (right); p. 105: Robert Peterson; p. 106: Domino/Jenny Komenda; p. 107: Melanie Acevedo; p. 109: Domino/Heather Taylor; p. 111: Domino; p. 112: Jack Coble; p. 114: Tessa Neustadt/Ben & Jolene Kraus; p. 115: Domino/Anna Burke (left), Paul

Costello (right); p. 116: Domino/Jen Smith; p. 117: Domino; p. 118: Domino/Sacha Dunn; p. 119: Mikkel Vang (left), Molly Winters (right); p. 120: Domino/Anne Ziegler; p. 122: Domino/Lynn K. Leonidas (left), Domino/Anna Burke (right); p. 123: Domino/Suzanne and Lauren McGrath (top), Max Kim-Bee/Jonathan Greenwood (bottom); p. 124–125: Domino/Maryam Nassirzadeh; p. 126: Melanie Acevedo (left), Domino/Jenni Li (right); p. 126: Domino/Patrick Mele (left), Michael Wiltbank (right); p. 128: Melanie Acevedo/Chassie Post; p. 129 (bottom): Justin Bernhaut; pp. 130–131: Alyssa Rosenheck/Elsie Larson; p. 132: Laura Resen; p. 134: Melanie Acevedo; p. 135: Joy Sohn; p. 136: Christian Oth/Henry & Co. Design; p. 137: Domino/Anne Ziegler (left), Nathan Kirkman/Graham Kostic & Fran Taglia (right); p. 139: Annie Schlechter; p. 140: Nathan Kirkman/Graham Kostic & Fran Taglia (left), Laure Joliet/Jenni Kayne (right); p. 141: Annie Schlechter (left), Domino (right); p. 142: Domino/Anne Ziegler; pp. 144–145: Alyssa Rosenheck/Lori Paranjape; p. 146: Domino/Ali Cayne; p. 147: Shades of Blue Interiors; p. 148: Lindsey Orton Photography/House of Jade Interiors; p. 149: Domino/Austyn Zung; p. 150: Veronique Rautenberg (top), Ditte Isager (bottom); p. 151: Domino; p. 152: Joy Sohn; p. 154: Domino/Jenny J Norris (left), Domino (right); p. 155: Wing Ta/Kate Arends (top), Laure Joliet/Elise Joseph (bottom); pp. 156–157 (from left): Joy Sohn/Joana Avillez, Melanie Acevedo, Justin Bernhaut, Michael Wiltbank, Pia Ulin/Ulla Johnson, Michael Wiltbank; pp. 158–159: Molly Winters; p. 160: Domino/Katie Martinez; p. 162: Justin Bernhaut; p. 163: Werner Straube Photography; p. 164: Molly Winters; p. 165: Domino/Benjamin Vandiver; p. 167: Ashley Capp; p. 168: Nathan Kirkman/Graham Kostic & Fran Taglia (left), Nancy Neil (right); pp. 169–171: Molly Winters; pp. 172–173: Wing Ta/Kate Arends; p. 174: Domino/Ron Marvin (left), Sara Kerens/Brynn

Elliott Watkins (right); p. 175: Domino (left), Sean Litchfield/Chango & Co. (right); p. 176: Domino/Lauren Leiss (left), Pia Ulin/Ulla Johnson (right); p. 177: Armelle Habib; pp. 178–179 (from left): Simon Upton, Douglas Friedman, Nancy Neil, Domino/Jenny Komenda; pp. 180–181: Matthew Williams; p. 182: Domino/Jen Smith; p. 184: Mikkel Vang; p. 185: Laure Joliet/Jenni Kayne; p. 186: Domino/Anne Ziegler; p. 187: Domino/Chay Wike; p. 188–190: Domino; p. 191 (clockwise from top left): Pia Ulin/Ulla Johnson, Joy Sohn/Eddie Lee, Nicole Franzen/Christene Barberich; p. 192: Domino; p. 193: Simon Upton (top), Alyssa Rosenheck/Lori Paranjape (bottom); p. 194: Max Kim-Bee; p. 195: High Impact Photography/iStock Photo (bottom left); p. 196: Joy Sohn (left), Patrick Cline/Kate Schelter (right); p. 197: Paul Costello; p. 198: Alyssa Rosenheck/Lori Paranjape (left), Mia Baxter Smail/Maya Nairn (right); p. 199: Domino/Anne Ziegler; p. 200: Amy Bartlam/Natalie Myers (left), Pia Ulin/Ulla Johnson (top right), Michael Wiltbank (bottom right); p. 201: Domino; pp. 202–203: Laure Joliet/Frances Merrill; p. 204: Eve Wilson; p. 206: Joy Sohn; p. 207: Domino; p. 208: Max Kim-Bee; p. 209: Domino/Katie Martinez; p. 214: Molly Winters (left), Douglas Friedman (right); p. 215: Patrick Cline/Kate Schelter (top), Miguel Flores-Vianna; p.p. 216–217: Gemma Ingalls; p. 218: Mikkel Vang (left), Domino/Ariel Ashe (right); p. 219: Gemma Ingalls, Deborah Jaffe (right); p. 220: April Valencia/Taylor Patterson; p. 221: Ryan Flynn Photography; pp. 222–223 (from left): Domino/Paloma Contreras, Gately Williams, Sarah Elliott/Dekar Design, Francesco Lagnese, Gemma Ingalls; pp. 224–225: Michael Wiltbank; p. 226: Domino/Heather Taylor; p. 228: Jessica Isaac; p. 229: Beth Kirby; p. 230: Michael Wiltbank; p. 231: Gemma Ingalls; p. 233: Alyssa Rosenheck/Elsie Larson; p. 237: Domino; p. 238: Domino (left), Sonya Yruel Photography/Christina Vo of Conscioustyle (right);

p. 239: Annie Schlechter (left), Sarah Elliott/Dekar Design (right); pp. 240–241: Amy Neunsinger; p. 242: Beth Kirby; p. 243 (from left): Annie Schlechter, Domino, Paul Costello; p. 244: Christina Holmes; p. 245 (clockwise from left): Mikkel Vang, Michael Wiltbank; p. 246: Bobby Fisher; p. 247: Michael Wilkbank/Timo Weiland; p. 248: Nicole Franzen (left), Alpha Smoot (right); p. 249: Nicole Franzen (top), Chloe Crespi (middle), Winnie Au (bottom)

ADDITIONAL TEXT CREDITS

Amelia Fleetwood:
p. 39; pp. 44–45; pp. 74–75; pp. 100–101; pp. 130–131; p. 150; pp. 158–159; pp. 180–181; pp. 202–203; p. 221; pp. 224–225; p. 247; pp. 248–249

Alex Redgrave:
pp. 250–260

The authors would like to thank:
Jen Anderson, Kate Berry, Monika Eyers, Stephanie Harth, Anna Kocharian,
Meghan McNeer, Elaina Sullivan, Lily Sullivan, and Michael Wiltbank.

Our team would like to extend our sincere thanks to the photographers and
homeowners featured in this book. We are inspired by your creativity and style
and are so grateful to share your work and spaces here.

This book was produced by

MELCHER
MEDIA

124 West 13th St., New York, NY 10011
www.melcher.com

President and CEO: Charles Melcher
Vice President and COO: Bonnie Eldon
Senior Editor/Producer: Lauren Nathan
Production Manager: Susan Lynch
Digital Producer: Shannon Fanuko
Editorial Assistant: Victoria Spencer

Melcher Media would like to thank:
Chika Azuma, Callie Barlow, Jess Bass, Emma Blackwood, Amelie Chernin, Karl Daum, Hannah B. Flicker,
Barbara Gogan, Kitt Harris, Luke Jarvis, Aaron Kenedi, Luisa Lizoain, Kaarina Mackenzie, John Morgan,
Jennifer S. Muller, Nola Romano, Laura Roumanos, Anthony Salazar, Rachel Schlotfeldt, Adiya Taylor,
Zoe Valella, Suchan Vodoor, Lee Wilcox, Megan Worman, and Katy Yudin.